Framing Monsters

Framing Monsters

Fantasy Film and Social Alienation

Joshua David Bellin

Southern Illinois University Press / Carbondale

Library of Congress Cataloging-in-Publication Data
Bellin, Joshua David.
  Framing monsters : fantasy film and social alienation
/ Joshua David Bellin.
    p. cm.
  Includes bibliographical references and index.
  1. Fantasy films—Social aspects. I. Title.
PN1995.9.F36B45 2005
791.43′615—dc22
ISBN 0-8093-2623-X (alk. paper)
ISBN 0-8093-2624-8 (pbk. : alk. paper)

                                                    2004023653

For Richard

CONTENTS

ILLUSTRATIONS

ACKNOWLEDGMENTS

I can't speak for the reader of it, but for the writer of it, this book was a unique experience: far more the offspring of a lifetime's love affair than the output of a few years' scholarly labor. So rather than acknowledging the usual suspects—release time and funding streams, foundations and institutions (all of which played, at best, a negligible role in the creation of this book)—I take the opportunity to thank those individuals, past and present, near and unmet, who have nurtured, shared, or honored my love of fantasy and fantasy film:

Willis and Ray, for the King and the Seven.

My parents, for enrolling me in my first animation class, and Tippi, for teaching it.

Stefano, Gary, Mr. Clark, Mrs. Rozewski, and all the art and animation teachers who followed, for sharing their wisdom.

Bumpa, for building my first lightbox.

My father, this time for stumbling across a movie theater in a Cleveland mall that just happened to be showing a certain '77 space opera.

Uncle Walt, mostly for *Fantasia*.

Uncle George, mainly for the Force.

Herman Pearl's mom, for rigging up a movie projector every year at her son's birthday party, and for being moved one year to rent *The Seventh Voyage of Sinbad*.

J. R. R. Tolkien, for turning me on to (and darn near into) hobbits and balrogs.

Vladimir Tytla, Greg and Tim Hildebrandt, Wayne D. Barlowe, Frank Frazetta, John Byrne, and others, for painting the mural of my dreams.

L. Frank Baum, C. S. Lewis, Charles L. Dodgson, H. G. Wells, Terry Brooks, Roger Zelazny, Stephen R. Donaldson, and more, for the guided tour of Faerie.

Cire Gnüoy, Trebor Yksteram, and Mot Rehgellag, for afternoons of D & D.

Gary and Larry of Games Unlimited, for my first-ever job, painting D & D figures at five bucks a pop.

The members of Tarzan's Jungle Band—Jungle Larry, Mr. Umbala, Primitive Ken, and Bongo of the Congo—for inspiring (and then sabotaging) my first fantasy novel.

My daughter, Lilly—two years old when the book began—for loving this stuff almost as much as I do.

My son, Jonah—eleven months old when the book was completed—for loving the picture of Gollum on my desktop.

My wife, Christine Saitz, for loving me despite this stuff.

My cousin Vince, for showing me how to do this stuff.

Ryan McBriar, Mary Ann Bayingana, Jason Dolak, Erin Porta, Audra Snow, and all the students in my "Monsters, Magicians, and Machines" class, for forcing me to explain why this stuff matters.

Aldine King, for taping the Oscars every year.

Cynthia Erb and Rob Latham, for curbing my excesses and for confirming my belief in the pertinence of ideological criticism of fantasy film.

Karl Kageff, Carol Burns, John Wilson, Barb Martin, and all the people at Southern Illinois University Press, for bringing my vision to life.

In addition, I would like to thank the Academy of Motion Picture Arts and Sciences, for permission to quote from the 1993 Oscars telecast. Chapter 2 originally appeared as "'I Don't Know How It Works': *The Wizard of Oz* and the Technology of Alienation" and is reprinted from *Arizona Quarterly* 60.4 (2004), by permission of the Regents of the University of Arizona.

And finally: my dearest thanks to Richard, for helping me chart a course to a charmed galaxy still farther away. Star-sailor, alchemist, wizard: I hope you made it there.

Framing Monsters

INTRODUCTION Monsters of Our Making

Monstrosity actualizes the tendency of all persecutors to project the monstrous results of some calamity or public or private misfortune onto some poor unfortunate who, by being infirm or a foreigner, suggests a certain affinity to the monstrous. Instead of bearing certain faintly monstrous characteristics, the victim is hard to recognize as a victim because he is totally monstrous.—René Girard, *The Scapegoat* (1982)

*M*y favorite movie of all time is *King Kong*. (The 1933 *King Kong*, that is; as a devotee of the original, I obstinately refuse to see any merit in the 1976 remake.) Some of my earliest visual memories are of the great gorilla's many indelible moments: sitting astride a tyrannosaur, wrenching its jaws apart (and then comically flopping the shattered jaw to assure himself of victory); roaring and swatting at sailors and islanders as the village gates come crashing down; standing pilloried on the exhibition stage, shaking his chains frenziedly as flashbulbs explode around him; and, in a particularly haunting image, reeling atop the Empire State Building, limply gripping the zeppelin mooring tower, just moments before his fatal fall. As a child, I decorated my room with posters and plastic models of Kong; I sought out any screening of the film, no matter how obscure, like the one the local natural history museum held (presumably because of the prehistoric angle); I drew countless images of Kong and of the "original"—barely distinguishable—giant apes I planned to put on-screen. When the 1976 version came out, I sat, appalled and seething, through the numbing parade of bad jokes and worse makeup; when my first VCR, a present from my parents, arrived in graduate school, there was no doubt what my first video would be. A while ago, at a dinner party, the subject of favorite movies came up; and while everyone else named "adult" titles like *Rear Window* (1954) and *The Seven Samurai* (1956), I named *King Kong*. Proudly.

I state my love of *Kong* at the start of this study because, in no time at all, I will launch a discussion of the film that seems anything but the fond reflections of a fan. I will term *Kong* an expression of the violent racism of Depression-era America; I will describe my favorite film as one that participated in an urgent early-twentieth-century project of defining and defending the prerogatives of the white race, a project that enlisted as one of its most fearful agencies the ritualized slaughter of the supposed black defiler of white womanhood. Nor, I will assert, is *Kong* the only fantasy film that takes part in the processes of ensuring the authority of dominant social groups by demonizing the outcast and disempowered. Quite the contrary, I will argue that *Kong* is the exemplar, if not the prototype, of a long-standing (and ongoing) tradition in fantasy film that identifies marginalized social groups as monstrous threats to the dominant social order. Thus, as this study develops, *Kong*, which served as a benchmark in the fantasy film tradition, will similarly function as a touchstone for the many films I consider: *The Wizard of Oz* (1939), which I will argue expresses Depression-era fears of lower-class revolution; Ray Harryhausen's Sinbad trilogy, which I will read in light of postwar America's vilification of the Middle East; *Jurassic Park* (1993), which I will suggest joins in the late-twentieth-century attack on the women's rights movement; *12 Monkeys* (1996), which I will critique for its role in furthering the image of the homeless mentally ill as dangerous deviants. What I will illustrate through readings of *Kong* and the many films, past and present, that followed in its wake is that this germinal fantasy film's racism, far from being an exception or an aberration, is in fact a particularly dramatic exhibition of alienating social practices that are prevalent in, and that may even be definitive of, the fantasy film tradition as a whole.

At the simplest, then, I announce my love of *Kong* at the beginning of this study to clarify my position toward it and toward the other films I will discuss. To state this position succinctly: I am not out to bad-mouth or belittle films that others love and in so doing to set myself above those who love them. To be sure, I write from a critical standpoint in this study; I seek not, in the manner of illustrated surveys of the genre,[1] to celebrate fantasy films for their many and undeniable delights but to demonstrate that, far from being "timeless" or "pure" entertainment, they play a vital role in circulating and validating pernicious cultural beliefs embedded within specific social settings. Indeed, my argument depends precisely on questioning the putative "purity" of fantasy films—on showing that it is those cultural places that seem most benign or innocuous that must be most closely scrutinized for their part in harboring widespread, malignant social attitudes. But for me, as I suspect for many critics of fantasy film, fandom not only gave birth to but continues to motivate criticism; it is *because* I was (and am) a fan of fantasy films that my inquiry into them is as compelling, personal, and—if short of reverent—committed as it is. For me, that is, the exploration of fantasy film is driven by a question that troubles both the enthusiast and the skeptic in me: how is it that one can so love films that are in significant respects so hateful?

As this study progresses, such intimate questions will recede, replaced by more narrowly critical questions about the form, features, and functions of fantasy film. But since this question is the one that brought me to the study of fantasy film, it seems fitting to use the question as a means of broaching the other issues I will address. Moreover, it seems to me that this question is neither solely personal nor purely arbitrary. Rather, the paradoxical nature of fantasy films, their lovable hatefulness, seems to me pertinent to the other issues I will take on. Thus I begin by considering the love/hate question because I believe that this question will lead not only to answers about any particular film, such as *Kong*, but to insights into the ways in which fantasy films operate, the reasons for their popularity since the earliest days of the cinema, and the properties of these films as a genre.

To begin to unravel the love/hate paradox, it is first important to consider the approach to fantasy film that has been most widely adopted in critical studies to date—an approach according to which the love/hate question would be mystifying, if not wholly stupefying. For most critics of fantasy film, what matters most about these artworks is not their social contexts, features, or functions; if they possess any such characteristics, these are considered wholly subordinate to the works' embodiment of "universal" elements and themes: mythological master-narratives and archetypes, developmental or psychoanalytical dramas, and so on. The 1970s, an era that saw an intense interest in fantasy (and particularly horror) film, proved definitive for the universalizing approach to the genre: "Sociological explanations of [monster films] fail to recognize the historical fact that there has always been a spontaneous human taste for monsters," Lawrence Alloway warned (124), while Walter Evans announced that such films are so "concerned with certain fundamental and identifiable features of human experience" (53) that cultural contexts are "superficial" or "non-essential" to them (62 n. 10). Even Robin Wood's influential "The American Nightmare: Horror in the 70s" (1975), which seemed to hint at the social contexts of fantasy film in its claim that "the true subject of the horror genre is the struggle for recognition of all that our civilization represses or oppresses, its re-emergence dramatized, as in our nightmares, as an object of horror" (75), ultimately reinvigorated the dominant paradigm by minimizing the historical nature of monstrosity: "The Monster is, of course, much more protean [than the normal], changing from period to period as society's basic fears clothe themselves in fashionable or immediately accessible garments—rather as dreams use material from recent memory to express conflicts or desires that may go back to early childhood" (79). In the case of *Kong*, such postulates have spawned a variety of readings: the film is termed a waking dream by Helmut Färber; labeled a retelling of the Perseus/Andromeda myth by Joseph Andriano (45–52) and of the Cupid/Psyche myth by Harry Geduld and Ronald Gottesman (19); judged a parable of adolescent sexuality by Noel Carroll and by Harvey Roy Greenberg (*"King Kong"*); dubbed a modern version of the "wild man" legend by John Seelye; and deemed a classical love triangle by Anthony Ambrogio. By these terms, the love/hate question simply makes no sense; by these terms, love of fantasy films is uncomplicated, precisely what one would expect from artworks that claim such a deep, global, and all-embracing hold on the human soul.

In recent years, to be sure, this model has been subjected to reevaluation; scholars have argued, as Annette Kuhn does in her collection of essays on science fiction film, that there is "a relationship of some sort between [these] texts and the 'real' world" (Introduction to Part III 147).[2] Investigation of these furtive relationships has yielded intriguing theses, including Cyndy Hendershot's twin volumes on sci-fi and horror film during the McCarthy era, Mark Jancovich's comparable study of horror in the 1950s, Eric Greene's explication of the *Planet of the Apes* series in light of the civil rights struggle, and Daniel Leonard Bernardi's consideration of the *Star Trek* juggernaut in respect to current racial politics. Significantly, however, the bulk of such revisionary work has been performed on *sci-fi* film, a genre that is typically thought to diverge from the fantasy mainstream in being overtly linked to real-world contexts. In the meantime, considerable resistance remains to historicizing films that appear to elude or resist the sci-fi label, films such as *The Wizard of Oz*, the "fairy-tale" fantasia of Tim Burton's *Edward Scissorhands* (1990), or Peter Jackson's screen adaptation of J. R. R. Tolkien's epic swords-and-sorcery trilogy, *The Lord of the Rings* (2001–2003). In the case of such films, writes Barry Keith Grant, universalizing approaches continue to be seen as "the most profitable" (Introduction 4). So pervasive is this commonplace that when, in 1995, Brian Attebery delivered the keynote address to the Twelfth International Conference on the Fantastic in the Arts, both the title of his talk—"The Politics (If Any) of Fantasy"—and its tone indicated his sense that he was broaching a subject quite unprecedented, even heretical, to the majority of his listeners: "The politics of fantasy—what a peculiar thing to talk about! It's not hard to see a connection between fantasy and archetypes, or fantasy and ethics, or fantasy as an expression of metaphysics, but what has politics got to do with it?" (1). I will return to the implications that the ostensible contrast between sci-fi and fantasy films has for the definition of the genre; for the moment, it is sufficient to note the longevity and vigor of the paradigm by which films strongly identified with otherworldliness, innocence, or spectacle are denied a historical genesis or function.

Needless to say, this study depends upon challenging that paradigm. In doing so, however, I do not mean to suggest that universalizing approaches to fantasy film possess no validity, or that they may not work together with a historicizing approach to ground an assessment of fantasy film's cultural work. Fantasy films, as I will discuss at greater length shortly, are indeed protean works; there is little to be gained in reducing them exclusively to vehicles of social alienation. Nor, among the possible readings of fantasy film that one might propose, is it surprising that universalizing readings should have gained the ascendancy; indeed, if one accepts the commonsense definition of *fantasy* as that which "could never have been, cannot be, and can never be within the actual, social, cultural, and intellectual milieu of its creation" (Schlobin xxvi), then the proposition that a film about a giant gorilla-god is deeply, necessarily (rather than fortuitously or tangentially) affiliated with the specific cultural issue of 1930s racially motivated violence against African Americans would automatically be ruled out.

I would argue, however, that it is precisely *because* of the counterintuitive nature of such a proposition that it needs to be entertained. For as I hinted at the outset, I believe that the move to unmoor fantasy films from their social contexts—to dismiss (or laud) them as pure, innocent diversions—is fundamental to these films' social power; any social production that can so readily be denied *as* a social production can perform (or in the denial *has* performed) injurious social work. If, therefore, universalizing approaches are allowed to form a protective cocoon around films such as *Kong*, legitimizing popular and commercial opposition to recognizing the films' often corrosive cultural work, I believe that such approaches do a disservice not only to the films but to the culture that bred them and the audiences that view them. By contrast, universalizing approaches that help to explicate the dimensions of the love/hate paradox are deeply productive for this study—as, for instance, when psychoanalytic theory in the hands of feminist scholars assists us in understanding the truly staggering abhorrence of female sexuality that marks some monstrous-woman films such as *Alien* (1979). At the same time, however, it is important to recognize that the particular shape such unreasoning hatred takes—and the particular popularity of the films in which it appears—cannot be explicated solely through universalizing approaches; it is necessary to situate the films in history to appreciate that their strategies for demonizing women, however they may be fueled by psychosexual anxieties, take forms that are unique to their time and place. The same holds for *Kong*: if myths and archetypes of the dragon and the wild man help explain the brute threat of his rampage through New York, the particularities of that threat are fully realized, materialized, only through the cultural practices and codes that 1930s America mobilized in its assault on African American rights, livelihoods, and lives. In making these assertions, I follow the important distinction proffered by Ismene Lada-Richards in her consideration of "mythic" monsters:

> Despite [their] haunting permanence, the beings or natural phenomena that people of all lands and ages have termed *monstra* possess no fixed, secure, inherent attributes which can attract or justify such a denomination. If we were to look for one single element of constancy within the ever-changing borders of "monstrosity," this would almost certainly be the relativity of the "monster" as a humanly constructed concept, that is to say, the simple truth that its prerogatives and its essence are powerfully interlocked with the perennial dialectic of "Otherness" with respect to "Norm." And, as norms are culturally determined, "monsters" too become inevitably culture-specific products. (46)

As Lada-Richards notes, though the human proclivity to fantasize monstrous threats to the norm may indeed be universal, the specific threats that societies fantasize correlate to the specific norms these societies fear may be threatened. In this sense, if it is unsatisfactory to focus on the universal qualities of fantasy films to the exclusion of all else, this is because the mythic resonances or psychosexual energies of a cultural production such as *Kong* do not exist apart from, or even alongside, its culturally coded anxieties concerning interracial union but, quite the contrary, play a part in conducting (and by the same token are conducted by) its historically specific racist discourse. My decision to place the historical character of fantasy films squarely at the center of my analysis, then, represents an attempt to account for the films in their entirety: to view the "universality" of fantasy films not apart from but within the context of their social-historical grounds. And in this respect, my approach represents as well an attempt to credit the more disquieting elements of the films' fascination, the sense in which films of fantasy may be so entrancing as to stifle criticism of their noxious qualities—not least because those qualities may be accepted as the real, the necessary, the right by the majority of the films' viewers.

It is for this reason as well that I am mistrustful of a common move whereby the hateful nature of fantasy film is, if not wholly denied, then displaced or mitigated—a move that acknowledges the socially alienating character of fantasy films yet seeks to salvage their lovable character by preserving a pure space untouched by social forces. According to such a division, what one loves and what is hateful in fantasy films are two separate things: a film's story or style, say, can be set in opposition to its cultural strategies, such that a well-plotted or well-executed film can be admired, even loved, by those who firmly reject its racist discourse and practice. Andriano, for example, proposes such a distinction when he writes that *Kong* "remains a powerful, stirring, even sublime experience, in spite of its racism" (49). As with the complete partition of fantasy film from social reality, however, this distinction between *parts* of a film cannot be sustained absolutely. Indeed, the distinction Andriano draws exemplifies the riskiness of this approach, inasmuch as it ultimately leads back to the utter separation of fantasy film from history; that is, he is able to find *Kong* "sublime" despite its racism because he is able to identify aspects of the film that remain untainted by the historically based racism that presumably operates at a more superficial level or at a different place in the film. Such a distinction between a film's pure cinematic qualities—its narrative or stylistic virtuosity—and its ideologically suspect substance ignores the fundamental tenet of film criticism that a film's substance *is* its story and style; a film's meanings do not survive independently of its narrative or stylistic elements but exist as such through the operation and interrelation of those elements. Indeed, in the case of fantasy film, such a separation of style or story from substance may be even more unsupportable than it is for other types of film; given that incredible narratives and equally incredible stylistic (special) effects have constituted fantasy film's raison d'être from its beginnings, I will argue throughout this study that to isolate narrative or style from the total system of the film is particularly hazardous when dealing with the fantasy genre. If one loves *Kong*, one loves *Kong*; one cannot draw a clean line between abjuring its message and adoring its medium.

What the foregoing suggests, in fact, is that it is futile to attempt any explanation of the love/hate paradox that depends on establishing an opposition between the "fantastic"—a film's putatively pure qualities—and the "real"—the film's embeddedness in social discourse and practice. Rather, I would argue, an analysis of the love/hate question must *start* from the premise that one should *not* separate what one loves in fantasy films from what is hateful. Quite the contrary, one should view the lovable fantasy and the hateful reality as interrelated and mutually sustaining, such that the fantasy of a movie like *Kong* is integral to the racial discourse, and the racial discourse integral to the fantasy. (Even to phrase it in these terms is to suggest a division between the fantasy and the discourse that I find problematic.) The love/hate paradox, according to this line of reasoning, is far from incidental or whimsical. Rather, according to this line of reasoning, fantasy films function precisely to enable the paradox of *loving what one under other circumstances might recognize to be hateful*. Like all commercial, narrative films, but in particularly potent ways due to the apparent unreality of their far-fetched stories and virtuoso effects, fantasy films enable ugly wishes, beliefs, and fears to take their most naked, extreme, but at the same time seemingly pure (and therefore presumably harmless) forms. As Eric Greene phrases this argument:

> One of the characteristics of fiction is the ability to extract contro-versial problems from their social circumstances and reinscribe them onto fictional, even outlandish, contexts. The acceptability of intro-ducing new worlds and even new forms of life in science fiction and fantasy may make these genres especially flexible in this regard. Dif-ficult issues can be located safely distant, even light years away, from the real ground of conflict and thereby rendered less obvious and less psychologically or politically threatening. Science fiction's distance provides deniability for both the filmmakers and the audience. (18)

In her analysis of the racial contexts of *Bride of Frankenstein* (1935), like *Kong* one of the most enduring of classic monster movies, Elizabeth Young advances a simi-lar argument: "In the logic of racial representation, the very explicitness" of the image of the black rapist "seems enabled by the film's extreme distance from mimesis, its adherence to the safely nonrealist fantasy of science fiction" ("Here" 325). Wood, attempting to balance the social and psychological aspects of his analysis, dubs such films "collective nightmares" (78); I would prefer to call them *dominant social fantasies*, alternate yet intimate realities that serve definite and definable functions within the historical/cultural grounds from which they spring. The real of fantasy film, then, represents the culture's real in a particularly em-phatic, if ironic, sense: for a social real according to which certain individuals and groups pose monstrous threats to the norm is, in reality, a fantasy.

But if this is so, one further point must be made. For the real of the domi-nant social imagination does not exist "before" film, to which it then gives birth; the dominant social imagination is itself constituted, in part, through artistic conventions and productions, including those of film. Thus, to say that fantasy films are social constructs is not solely to say that they are constructed *by* their social contexts. It is, at the same time, to say that they are constructive *of* their social contexts: that they both *produce* and *reproduce* social discourse and prac-tice. Such an assertion moves one beyond the static and outmoded notion that art "reflects" cultural systems, passively, to a dynamic view of art and cultural systems reciprocally and actively shaping and determining one another. In this respect, however tempting it might be to argue that the relationship between fantasy films and social reality is an inverse one—to say, that is, that fantasy films "distort" or "misrepresent" social reality—such a position is ultimately no more tenable than the blunt separation of fantasy and reality. Accordingly, the verb I would use to describe the ways in which fantasy films relate to social reality—a verb that has given me the title to this study—is that fantasy films *frame* social reality: they provoke a perspective, provide a context, produce a way of seeing. As such, if these films function as mass-cultural rituals that give image to historically determinate anxieties, wishes, and needs, they simultaneously function by stimulating, endorsing, and broadcasting the very anxieties, wishes, and needs to which they give image. It becomes the purpose of this study, then, to make visible these interrelations between cultural belief and cinematic practice, to uncover the processes by which historically conditioned social fantasy and historically conditioned monstrous antagonists mutually generate and reinforce one another.

The reader who has followed the discussion this far will, I hope, grant the general point that a relationship exists between fantasy film and social reality, and that it is, accordingly, impossible to separate the fantasy one loves from the reality, however hateful, of which one is a part. Yet to move beyond this general point to an analysis of the specific ways in which fantasy films sustain—and seek to manage—the love/hate paradox, it is necessary to subject my initial premise to closer scrutiny. For to insist that fantasy films articulate and validate the social fantasies of their time and place does not necessarily warrant my contention that a *particular* set of discourses and practices—for example, those of racism—is formative for a particular film—for example, *King Kong*. Many arguments could be leveled against such a contention, but two in particular strike me as pertinent. The first would be that since fantasy films do not relate in any obvious way to their social realities, it is possible to find virtually any meaning one likes in them. The second, to some extent dependent on the first, would be that since fantasy films are so semantically open and hence liable to misreading, the critical act involves wading through a host of *possible* interpretations to arrive at the *precise* interpretation intended by the films' creators. The former argument, what one might call the argument for polysemy, is expressed by Noel Carroll:

> *King Kong* . . . abounds with interpretations. These come in many shapes and sizes—Kong as Christ, Kong as Black, Kong as commodity, Kong as rapist, Kong enraptured by *L'amour fou*, Kong as Third World, Kong as dream, Kong as myth, Kong according to Freud, according to Jung, and even according to Lacan. . . . [P]art of the fascination of the [film is] its openness to interpretive play. (215–16)

The latter argument, what one might call the argument for intent, appears in the following remarks by Orville Gardner and George E. Turner:

Many writers have tried to justify the public's love affair with a gigantic, ugly ape by reading into the film a great deal more *significance* than was intended by its creators. . . . Such notions are firmly denied by the persons behind the film. . . . *King Kong* is exactly what it was meant to be: a highly entertaining, shrewdly conceived work of pure cinema. (9)

Rudy Behlmer cites one such denial from a central figure in the film's creation:

[Director Merian C.] Cooper became irate when we discussed those who attached "symbolic" overtones—phallic and otherwise—to various aspects of *Kong*. As far as he was concerned there were no hidden meanings, psychological or cultural implications, profound parallels or anything remotely resembling intellectual "significance" in the film. [According to him,] "*King Kong* was escapist entertainment pure and simple." (13)

By the terms of this argument, if one cannot prove that the makers of the film intended its racial intonations—and I freely admit that I cannot prove such an intention, much less prove that one existed despite the filmmakers' denials—then one must simply desist from all inquiry along these lines.

This latter argument has been amply addressed in discussions of other film genres and thus can be addressed very briefly here. In general, the argument against intentional analysis hinges on the lack of an authorial figure in film: since, excepting the short features of such pioneers as George Méliès (himself an important figure in the popularization of fantasy film), commercial films are collaborative ventures, it is difficult to settle on an individual whose intentions one is to honor. But to the customary arguments against film "auteurism"—arguments ranging from the limitations on directorial control exercised by studio hierarchies to the effects of the complex division of labor on the film product—I would add that antiauteurist arguments are buttressed by the heightened significance of technical personnel in films of fantasy. *Kong* provides an excellent example: since it relied heavily on the specialized knowledge of Willis O'Brien and his technical crew, the effects unit had at least as much say in designing, shooting, and approving the picture as did director Cooper. (*Kong* lore holds, in fact, that Cooper would shoot live-action sequences only after their animated portions had been completed.) To uphold this argument, it might be noted as well that the signal return to the language of "purity" contained in the quotes above makes plain that the intentional argument is but another version of the retreat from history. If, that is, one can ascribe *Kong* to a single, inspired individual, its social relevance becomes subordinated to the quest for authorial commentary and attenuated by the reduction of cultural context to individual will. But such a displacement of history by biography is itself fallacious, as Greene points out:

> Even if artists do not consciously attempt to make "political statements," artists exist in a world of political and social relations. . . .
> We can reasonably expect therefore that, consciously or not, political realities, events, and themes will register in an artist's work. In fact we should be shocked if a country's political conflicts and social biases do *not* find their way into its cultural productions. (13)

Fantasy film, then, provides a particularly potent and cogent argument against enshrining the author and thereby ignoring the complex, dynamic interaction between works of art and their social-cultural history.

The first argument, the argument for the particularly broad range of potential meaning in fantasy film, is somewhat more demanding to address, in part because I have made the seemingly extravagant claim that racial discourse is not simply a factor in the fantasy of *Kong* but is *integral* to it, and in part because the terms of the critique—in particular the word *meaning*—are themselves in need of refinement. Let me emphasize from the first, then, that I find the argument for polysemy entirely valid, provided it too is not used as a means of reducing a critic's range of interpretation or of denying the validity of interpretation altogether. Though I will continue to reject characterizing *Kong* as a pure fantasy, I grant that even when it is seen within history, it can be interpreted in a great variety of ways: as a commentary on women's rights, a satirical take on Hollywood, a broadside against the merchandising of exotic goods and cultures, a cautionary tale of imperial hubris, a veiled biography of the film's grandiose producer/director, Cooper, or even an *attack* on racism through its portrayal of the smitten and stricken Kong. If, moreover, one permits the film's audience even the slightest degree of responsibility for its cultural work, then it is plain that any one interpretation is necessarily conditional.[3] There is, of course, precedent for focusing on dominant social attitudes; as mass-cultural productions consumed by millions, fantasy films might be expected to inscribe such attitudes, and conversely, dominant social attitudes are, by definition, broadly shared throughout the culture. But by the same token, the films' mass appeal makes them open to other audiences, other attitudes, other readings—even (or especially) readings that emphasize the liberatory rather than the repressive character of their social operations.

One might, of course, respond to this reservation by pointing out that it is merely a restatement of the inherent condition of film viewership: Films suggest many meanings; no viewer can account for them all; hence to focus on racist discourse in *Kong* is not to disclaim other meanings but simply not to address them. Such a response, however, allows to pass unnoticed a critical problem in the term *meaning*—allows, that is, one to revert to an idealized notion of meaning as something independent of the historical-cultural processes within which a film is generated (or, to follow the lead of those scholars who stress a film's reception over its production, within which the film is successively viewed). Taken to its extreme, such a notion would mean that a film becomes involved in racist discourse—or ceases to—at the whim of its viewers and interpreters; an inverted mirror image of the argument for authorial intent, which holds that a film means only what its makers put *into* it, this notion similarly permits a film to float outside its cultural matrix, acquiring meaning solely as a factor of what its audiences get *out of* it. As such, the term I would employ in preference to *meaning* is *ideology*: though *Kong* is surely open to many meanings, as a cultural performance it is demonstrably involved in—shaped by and shaping—pervasive cultural assumptions or ideological formations concerning race and race relations. *Kong* can, undeniably and crucially, be read in multiple ways—even nonracist ways. But as an ideological structure, as the totality of its elements affiliated with the culture that generated it, *Kong* incontrovertibly invites and incites the discourses, beliefs, and practices of racism characteristic of that culture.

This leads me, in the form of two central assertions about *Kong* and a corresponding assertion about fantasy film on the whole, to propose a model of fantasy film's cultural work. First, *Kong*—irrespective of its creators' objectives, and in concert with the many facets of its ideological operations—is a film that participates in the processes and practices of 1930s American racism: *Kong* provided viewers for whom images of dark-skinned men as libidinous brutes were historically entrenched and incessantly reinforced—not least by film—ammunition by which these convictions could be renewed, enhanced, redoubled. And second, since no viewer of *Kong* within its American contexts, then or now, is exempt from the culture's racist ideologies, then love of *Kong* cannot be divorced from the processes of racism active within the society that produced it: viewers of this film, in its time and today, are both heirs to its racial fantasies and vehicles for reproducing those fantasies as if they were real. For a principal function of fantasy film as dominant social practice, I will argue, is the genre's role in rendering real—or *as if* real—propositions that in other contexts (say, political, educational, or religious discourse) are normally only hinted at, explained away as jokes, or dismissed as preposterous—such as the proposition "black men are lustful apes" or, subjects other chapters will take up, "the poor seek to supplant the rich," "foreigners are mysterious and treacherous," "unwed mothers are deadly predators," "the mentally ill are violent criminals," and "the physically different must be banished from the norm." That such propositions *are* regularly articulated, in more or less these terms, by the least tolerant segments of society proves that they are not, in reality, fantastic (in the sense of *unthinkable*); that incautious politicians, preachers, and people on the street periodically give vent to sentiments dangerously close to the above indicates that they are not confined to the lunatic fringe. But even more important than these extreme manifestations, the fact that politically liberal, well-educated people like myself can profess to love a movie despite their recognition of the violent racial strategies it performs, the ugly racial emotions it stirs, and the hateful racial energies it receives from them in turn suggests that fantasy films play a more fundamental part in the construction, dissemination, and maintenance of prejudice than is commonly admitted. Precisely because fantasy films can activate audience prejudices while preventing audiences from recognizing or, more precisely, taking responsibility for such prejudices, they are ideal agents of social alienation: their seeming purity permits their pollution.

To refine my earlier definition of the word *frame*, then, what fantasy films do is not simply construct a *certain* way of looking. Rather, they provide a way of looking that is both negative and unfairly so. The process of "framing monsters," in other words, is a process one might broadly define as stigmatizing or scapegoating: a process whereby individuals or groups who lack an adequate means of self-representation or access to political power are made to bear disproportionate responsibility for social anxieties and ills and are therefore seen as justifiably robbed of human rights for the ostensible good of the whole or of the norm. In short, what this study contends is that, by granting the form and force of the imaginable to deeply rooted yet largely unarticulated cultural beliefs, fantasy films serve to focus, quicken, and vindicate energies of contempt, suspicion, rage, and violence against the vulnerable and disempowered. What this study seeks to achieve, accordingly, is to reconnect fantasy films to their social contexts, to read them in light of specific historical-cultural ideologies, and thereby to demonstrate the ways in which these films validate specific discourses and policies of exclusion, inequity, and victimization.

Before turning to the films and issues I plan to open to such an analysis, let me take a moment to address what seem to me two important conceptual issues pertaining to the choice of films themselves. The first of these concerns the scope of my definition of what constitutes a *fantasy* film. Readers who scan the filmography may object that some of the films I discuss belong not to the fantasy genre but to related genres such as science fiction, horror, or fairy tale. To explain my decision to bring such a diverse group of films together under the heading of "fantasy," it is insufficient to plead that it is the only title that *can* accommodate so large a range of films. At issue, rather, is whether fantasy actually serves as a *productive* rubric under which to classify these films—or, to state this another way, whether the existence, appearance, and interrelation of these diverse films does indeed call for a genre (one that I term *fantasy*) under which all should be grouped.

To begin to answer this question, I would first note that the definition of *fantasy* has proved, so to speak, tenaciously elusive; though countless forays into defining the genre have been attempted, and though all agree that fantasy is that which bears some capricious relationship to reality, little agreement exists as to what precisely that relationship is. Thus, among the most influential definitions of the genre that have been offered in the past thirty years, Rosemary Jackson sees fantasy as that which subverts the status quo; Eric Rabkin understands fantasy as that which violates its own internal rules; Tzvetan Todorov views fantasy as that which engenders a momentary hesitation concerning whether an inexplicable event is real or not; Brian Attebery regards fantasy as that which contravenes what the author considers natural law (*Fantasy Tradition*); and Kathryn Hume, in the most expansive of modern definitions, conceives of fantasy as any departure from consensus reality. One reason for the diversity of definitions, as Attebery has pointed out (*Fantasy Tradition* 3), may be that all are circular, dependent on what counts as fantasy for each critic: Rabkin's thesis, for instance, works best with "nonsense" texts, such as Lewis Carroll's *Alice in Wonderland* (1865), while Todorov's may pertain only to the tiny sample of texts he discusses, such as Henry James's *The Turn of the Screw* (1898). Given this perplexity, some critics have argued that fantasy is beyond definition; others, such as Richard Mathews, have suggested that the problem lies with the definition of *genre*, not of *fantasy*: "There are no pure genres, and fantasy is no exception" (5). Whatever the case, fantasy remains a fugitive genre; though few people older than ten have difficulty identifying a work as a fantasy, the genre itself has proved far more amorphous, and its study far more arduous, than such commonsense classifications would imply.

In the case of fantasy *film*, the picture blurs even further. Indeed, it might be better to say that there have been few attempts to bring *that* picture into focus at all. If literary scholars have labored to pinpoint the characteristics of the fantasy genre, film scholars have generally been content to study the cousin genres of horror and science fiction. That this is so may reflect the differing histories of the two media: where literary fantasy claims aeons-old and globally far-flung examples, film fantasy settled quickly into—or arguably developed from—the popular categories of science fiction and horror. And yet, if anything, this history makes the generic issue more rather than less slippery; if there are scant pure examples of film fantasy (or none), then the genre, such as it is, may in fact embrace films from a host of affiliated genres. If, that is, one could demonstrate that the genres closest to fantasy are not in fact distinct from it, then one could claim the fantasy genre as the umbrella of all.

And, indeed, I believe that such an overlap among putatively distinct film genres not only *can* be demonstrated but *must*: that the attempt to separate fantasy from other genres breeds enormous, stymieing, and unproductive difficulties. To support this claim, let me consider the ostensible divide between fantasy and science fiction, the two genres that have been most routinely, not to mention resolutely, differentiated by scholars. For the majority of critics, the distinction between the two rests on the degree of relationship each bears toward the real. Thus, for example, Jack Rawlins contends that

> there are only two kinds of things, two ends of a spectrum perhaps. One end looks at the fictive landscape and encourages us to examine it rationally as literal object; the other looks at the same scene and encourages us to relate to it emotively as a manifestation of our inner selves. I hesitate to offer names for these alternative orientations . . . but if pressed I would say that "science fiction" and "fantasy" are reasonably good labels. (167)

Less circumspect, Barry Keith Grant asserts that while "science fiction . . . works to entertain alternative *possibilities*," the "distinctive aim of fantasy . . . is to present 'alternative *impossibilities*'" ("'Sensuous'" 17). Similarly, Karl Kroeber argues that fantasy, unlike science fiction, bears no relation to the quotidian world: fantasy "intrudes" into a culture where it is "quite unneeded" (5), while science fiction engages in the "realistic, rationalistic, expository forms" characteristic of modern society (10). And Attebery concludes, "Any narrative which includes as a significant part of its make-up some violation of what the author clearly believes to be natural law—that is fantasy. . . . Science fiction," by contrast, "spends much of its time convincing the reader that its seeming impossibilities are in fact explainable if we extrapolate from the world and the science that we know" (*Fantasy Tradition* 2). The fantasy/sci-fi split, in short, hinges on the apparently robust distinction between the socially relevant (represented by science fiction) and the socially redundant (represented by fantasy).

The flimsiness of this supposedly adamantine divide is, however, hinted at in W. R. Irwin's insistence that "no amount of actual or seeming congruity of material should lead to [fantasy and science fiction] being identified as to generic classification" (99). For, in fact, there is such a massive "amount" of "actual or seeming congruity" between the two as to call into question the "generic classification" itself. At the simplest, there are the generic hybrids, films such as *Alien* and its sequels, that transgress the boundaries these critics erect: "In practice,"

Peter Nicholls writes, "fantastic categories overlap considerably. Is *Alien* science fiction, horror or a monster movie? In fact, it is all three" (7). That such hybrids may in fact have supplanted any avowedly purebred sci-fi films is suggested by Brooks Landon's observation that throughout the sci-fi genre there is "a persistent conflict" between "neorealism and out-and-out fantasy" (249). Landon tracks this conflict to the films' technical feats, increasingly the sine qua non of their identity: "Special effects virtually guarantee that SF film will have a strong fantasy component, confronting us with visual experience of things we know cannot be, images that remain miraculous in spite of any cognitive explanation offered in the film" (253). Nor, at that, need one locate the identity between fantasy and science fiction solely in the realm of special effects; one might note as well that *science fiction* is simply not a very useful designation for many films that bear its stamp, films such as *12 Monkeys* in which the nod to science is so perfunctory as to be, effectively, fantastic. C. N. Manlove holds that science fiction always "throws a rope of the conceivable (how remotely so does not matter) from our world" to its own, whereas "fantasy . . . does not" (7). I would argue that at such "remote" reaches, what "does not matter" is whether one terms a work *science fiction* or *fantasy*.

For the crossover works in the other direction as well: if many sci-fi films are intrinsically fantastic, so are many fantasy films intrinsically science-fictional. As George Slusser and Eric Rabkin put it, "science fiction appears . . . (openly or tacitly) as the form in relation to which other forms of fantasy film . . . shape and define themselves" (viii). Thus a film such as *Edward Scissorhands*, though most would term it a fantasy, contains sci-fi elements: most obviously, there are the robotic claws that give the title character his name, but less overtly, there are the unremitting intertextual references to other films of science fiction (and horror) that provide layers of resonance for the film and its audiences. Even so seemingly fantastic a film as *The Wizard of Oz*, as I will argue in the second chapter, is beholden in the most fundamental of ways to the science fiction of its time; if this film seems misplaced as science fiction today, that is simply because we have lost the original context in which Depression-era viewers of the film would have experienced what we now name a pure fantasy. In sum, there are simply too many factors that compromise the attempt to differentiate science fiction from fantasy. Unsurprisingly, then, attempts to sustain the distinction regularly twist the critic into knots, as in Donald Palumbo's tortuous attempt to sort out a motif that occurs in both fantasy and sci-fi films:

> Although the underground journey motif signals and reinforces the death and rebirth theme in both fantasy and science fiction films, it does not operate in quite the same way in both. The confluence of

motif and theme is handled more literally and immediately in fantasy films, where the mystical already has precedence over the rational, but is handled more symbolically and abstractly in science fiction films, where the rational is superficially preeminent even though the audience is still affected by the same processes of magical thinking and by the same onslaught of mythic archetypes. (211)[4]

Too, efforts to keep fantasy and science fiction pristine often lead the critic to stray into the antiquated notion that certain forms of art passively and perfectly reflect the real world, as in William Coyle's claim that

the realist [sci-fi artist] looks outward at a world he never made; he observes a looking-glass and objectively records what is reflected there. The fantasist looks inward to a world that never was, the jungle of his own psyche; he passes through the looking-glass into a subjective world of distortion and illusion. (1)

Even more problematically, this lapse into reflectionist thinking all too commonly undergirds the argument that since fantasy (as opposed to science fiction) bears no relationship to social reality, its significance must lie in its universal qualities. As Attebery phrases this argument:

Science fiction is so much a mirror of the writer's own time and place that SF stories from the turn of the century or the 1950s could be used by historians as documents of vanished world-views, of futures past. Fantasy, on the other hand, posits a barrier between the fictional universe and the reader's own. Because the fantasy world and the axioms that underlie it are radically unlike our own, the reader is forced to seek connections in other than rational, external directions, relating the portrayed reality instead to myth, dream, and other manifestations of psychological or metaphysical principles. (*Strategies* 109–10)[5]

What such ingenious discriminations, polarities, and oppositions fail to entertain is precisely what the thesis of this book contends: that it is the capricious relationship fantasies bear toward their social contexts that lends them their social power. If, then, my choice of fantasy films seems overly inclusive, I believe that such inclusiveness is necessary not only to do justice to the actual dimensions of the genre but to forestall what I consider to be insupportable implications about the fantasy genre's relation to social reality.[6]

At the same time, if such inclusiveness more accurately maps the outlines of the *fantasy* genre, I believe it likewise offers a more robust, capacious understanding of film *genre* itself. If, that is, fantasy and sci-fi genres show signs of inter-breeding and tend to collapse when viewed through any number of individual lenses, this may reflect the fact that genre consists not solely or simply of a film's observable *features* but of the relationship between these textual factors and the realm of cultural work or social *function*. Kuhn believes that "efforts to draw lines of demarcation between science fiction and its neighbouring genres have proved on the whole unsatisfactory" because "more interesting, and probably more important, than what a film genre *is* is the question of what, in cultural terms, it *does*—its 'cultural instrumentality'" (Introduction 1). I would argue that what film genre "is" is not uninteresting but is interesting precisely because what genre is depends in large part—indeed, may be indistinguishable from—what genre does. Genre, according to this prescription, would emerge only through a multidimensional approach such as the one sketched by Steve Neale, an approach that situates film texts in social and historical context:

> What is required is a set of concepts with which the pressure of genre can begin to be located: in terms of the relations of subjectivity involved; in terms of the structures and practices both of the cinematic institution as a whole and of that sector known variously as "Hollywood" or as "the commercial cinema"; and in terms of the determinants and effects of each of these within and across the social formation and its component areas. (qtd. in Kuhn, Introduction 3)

In accordance with Neale's model, it becomes less consequential to the question of generic identity that *12 Monkeys* contains advanced technology and futuristic settings (characteristics normally reserved for science fiction) or that *Species* (1995) contains sudden scares and grotesque makeup (characteristics normally imputed to horror) than that, as with all the films studied herein, these and other textual features, operating in conjunction with industrial pressures, audience subjectivities, and social formations, perform particular cultural work. Thus all the films in this study are fantasy films because of their doubly ambiguous relationship to social reality: by rendering fantastic scenarios incarnate, they lend false propositions ("black men are lustful apes," "unwed mothers are deadly predators," and the like) the lineaments of the credible. Ultimately, then, grouping all of these films as fantasies grounds an argument both for the fantasy genre and for genre itself: it enables a recognition of genre as enacting a common cultural work, and it enables a recognition of the fantasy genre's cultural work as the activity of amplifying specific existing prejudices through specific imaginary elements.

This being the case, I turn to what might seem a second quirk in my choice of films: my habit of employing as the representative of a particular form of alienation not the most obvious case but, quite the contrary, films that have routinely been understood as flights of pure fancy, related to their social contexts only in the sense of representing technical milestones in the history of the cinematic apparatus. *The Wizard of Oz*, for instance, serves as my example of the alienation of the poor; *Jurassic Park* is my principal illustration of the attack on female liberation; Harryhausen's Sinbad trilogy is my test case for the travestying of foreign peoples in film and fact. In each case, more notorious possibilities spring to mind: for the first, James Whale's *Frankenstein* (1931) or any of its modern reincarnations; for the second, *The Brood* (1979) or *The Witches of Eastwick* (1987); for the third, *Men in Black* (1997) or Disney's widely decried *Aladdin* (1992). I chose less straightforwardly alienating films, however, to further two interrelated ends. On the one hand, I wished to illustrate that even the most seemingly fantastic of films can be placed in their specific social contexts and plumbed for their role in the activity of framing monsters. On the other, I hoped to support the claim I just made concerning the *common* cultural work of the fantasy genre— to show that processes of social alienation are characteristic of the fantasy film genre *as a whole* and not merely of the relatively few films this study could accommodate. Just as the wayward, puckish character of some fantasy films is strategic for their ideological operations, the blurriness of the fantasy genre may serve as an impediment to recognizing the genre's corporate project: the all-over-the-map nature of the genre militates against attempts to understand such injurious cultural work synthetically, not as the work of individual exceptions or aberrations but as the work of the whole. As such, my choice of films was motivated by the belief that excavating this work in extreme cases—*extreme* in the sense of *unlikely*—might illustrate my claims for the whole better than my studying more transparent examples. At all times during the writing of this study, I have been aware of the pressure of those other examples crowding the background; I have resisted including them here, but I hope that their presence will be, at least tangentially, evident to the reader as well. (To cite only two examples that have been particularly painful to resist: I have spared only brief moments for the *Star Wars* and *Lord of the Rings* sagas, two of the most powerful examples of fantasy film— and of alienation therein—of recent years, but examples that came to the screen too late and seemed too sprawling to discuss fairly and comprehensively.) As such, if the reader concludes that other, perhaps more suitable, choices could have been found, I trust that this study will have played a part in calling those choices, the strategies they perform, and their place within an enduring tradition to the reader's attention.

This study, in sum, considers the ways in which, throughout their long history, fantasy films have spoken to a shifting, contingent, but nonetheless coher-

1

KILLING THE BEAST *King Kong* in Black and White

The persons who participated actively in the lynchings were primarily responsible, yet those sympathizers who stood by shared in the lawlessness,
and curious onlookers who rushed in merely because something unusual
was happening were not without guilt.—Arthur F. Raper, *The Tragedy of
Lynching* (1933)

*V*iewing one of the most celebrated scenes in *King Kong* (1933), the scene
of Ann Darrow's disrobing by her simian captor, from the vantage of more than
seventy years, it may be hard to perceive the threat embodied there. That such a
threat was perceived at the time, however, cannot be doubted: screened in the
film's initial release in 1933, the year before Joseph Breen took over directorship
of the Hollywood Production Code, but cut from its 1938 theatrical re-release,
the scene was plainly deemed too risqué for public exhibition.[1] Yet at the same
time, the disrobing is remarkable as much for what it suppresses as for what it
insinuates. For one thing, in contrast to the shot/reverse-shot pattern that characterizes many of the encounters between Kong and Darrow—a pattern of alternating, screen-filling close-ups swooping in to Kong's frankly leering face and
Darrow's cringing reaction—this scene is designed as a static medium shot with
Kong in profile, a framing that minimizes the suggestion of rape the former device
unavoidably suggests. For another, the scene is played to foreground Kong's bestial
(as opposed to carnal) appetites: he shows far more interest in Darrow's clothes,
which he sniffs with exaggeratedly waggling nostrils, than in what lies beneath.
And finally, when Kong does behave in ways more typical of a human sexual partner—when he tickles Darrow's side—composer Max Steiner's otherwise melo-
dramatic score breaks into a teasing, gassy trill set to the wriggling of Kong's finger, as if to affirm that this is, after all, a sketch, a "bit," a digression from the
story rather than a development of it.

The truth of the matter, however, is that far from being a digression, the disrobing was integral to the story's conception, Willis O'Brien's sketch of the scene being one of several that made the rounds with director Merian C. Cooper as he pitched the *Kong* project (Haver 19). Moreover, teaser posters for the film, circulated before its title was changed from *Kong* to *King Kong*, featured this same sketch. The significance of the scene is further suggested by the pains that were taken to heighten its believability: save for a very brief shot following Kong's defeat of the tyrannosaur, this is the only sequence in which the viewer perceives the full Kong figure and the actual Fay Wray coming into (apparent) contact. In all other instances, O'Brien and his technical crew fostered the illusion of contact via two devices: either a miniature, animated Darrow writhes in the hand of the miniature, animated Kong, or the full-scale, essentially inanimate hand of Kong grips Wray. (Careful model substitution lends continuity to those scenes that require a transition from the real to the animated Wray: in Kong's lair, for instance, Wray, miniature-projected into a crevice in the cave wall, crawls into a recess from which Kong's fishing hand emerges with a stop-motion substitute.) The technical difficulty of the disrobing scene may help account for its singularity: the scene required that Wray, cradled within the full-scale hand, be miniature-projected behind the stop-motion Kong, whose movements O'Brien coordinated with wires that had stripped Wray's clothing during live-action filming.[2] But one mistakes the significance of this scene if one regards it solely as a tactical or theatrical nightmare (or triumph); this perilous special effects trick, elaborately staged and framed to be—in both senses of the word—incredible, is central to *Kong*'s cultural work, its ability to promote racial alienation while maintaining a posture of innocence.

At root, the disrobing sequence manifests the threat of black male sexual predation that motivates *Kong*, providing the film its principal impetus for formal and cultural existence. Such a claim may at first appear unexceptional, for it has become something of a critical commonplace to mention the racial contents of *Kong*. David Desser, for instance, deems the film "a thinly veiled allegory on race relations" (85); James Snead considers it an "allegory of the slave trade" (17); and Harold Hellenbrand notes that "Kong's blackness and the threat that he posed to white womanhood" connect the film to fantasies of interracial rape (90). Typically, however, critics have been at pains to divorce *Kong*'s racial *contents* from its racial *contexts*. At the extreme, the racial angle in *Kong* has been treated as little more than a poorly kept inside joke; as Anthony Ambrogio winks, "Kong is the biggest black of all" (135). More commonly, critics emphasize the racial angle's ephemeral nature in contrast to the film's universal—and hence presumably more pressing—significance. Thus Walter Evans argues that the "power and appeal" of *Kong* are "much more fundamental than class or political consciousness" (53), which is "non-essential material" (62 n. 10); Joseph Andriano writes that, however "the abduction of the white goddess by the black god reflects the white man's fear (and stereotype) of black male sexual prowess," the film, "on a deeper level," is really about the joining of "an unlikely archetypal complementary pair: Kong and Ann as yang and yin" (47); and Harvey Roy Greenberg, though admitting that *Kong* hints at "the white man's daydream of the black brute . . . feasting on violence and rapine" (*"King Kong"* 344), salvages the film by closing with something like glee: "[Darrow's] taking by Kong is rich in associations with bacchanal and Dionysian revel" (345).[3] In readings of this sort, though *Kong*, through no fault of its own, may touch on certain racist images, such incidental and innocent contact deflects attention from what the film is "really" about. With the exception of a single brief analysis by David Rosen, the film's flirtation with interracial sexual encounter has itself been read as a sort of archetype, abstracted from the dominant ideologies of 1930s America and 1930s Hollywood concerning race, rape, and miscegenation.[4]

The archetypal qualities of *Kong* may indeed contribute to the film's power and appeal. Nonetheless, I would like to challenge the assumption that *Kong's* archetypal depths redeem the film or, more precisely, that they distance the film from the racism of its cultural moment. Such a challenge might begin by noting that the curious irresolution of the critics' terms—*although* the film is racist, it is *nevertheless* not racist—duplicates the vacillation I have observed in the disrobing sequence, where exhibitionism and containment work to titillate yet restrain, to horrify yet deny, to engross yet distance. What this coincidence of the lurid and the chaste suggests, on the one hand, is the fallacy of separating surfaces from depths within a cultural performance such as *Kong*: clearly enough, multiple meanings do not so much coexist in this film as profoundly, indeed inextricably, shape and inform one another. And if so, what this suggests further is that far from nullifying or mitigating its racism, the film's ambivalence or equivocation is both productive and strategic for *Kong* as Depression-era racist fantasy. In my introduction, I advanced the proposition that fantasy films, because of their semantic openness and apparent disconnection from social reality, may permit repugnant social attitudes to operate under the veil of innocence and may thereby lend such attitudes the appearance of the real. *Kong*, I believe, exemplifies this function; as evidenced by how readily critics can justify the film's racism due to extenuating circumstances, *Kong* provides racism an authority deriving from resistance to critical scrutiny. As Mark McGurl puts it, "the deniability factored into [*Kong's*] tactical racism refuses responsibility for its divisiveness; it throws down the gauntlet of what can now be suggested is only the 'liberal' critic's racializing paranoia" (438).[5] The devices by which *Kong* encourages critical delicacy today, that is, are the same vehicles that carried forward its alienating work in its own day; the film enables the "curious onlookers who rushed in merely because something unusual was happening" (Raper 12) to savor the spectacle of African American immolation while remaining insulated from an awareness of having participated in the act. And the continued refusal to name *Kong* a racist film both measures the effectiveness of this insulating function and signals the persistence of the racial climate from which the film was born: *Kong* served, and serves, as a site for the simultaneous dissemination and disavowal of the racist ideologies of its time and of ours.

The purpose of this chapter, then, is to resituate *King Kong* within its historical and cultural matrix, to illustrate that it is coextensive with the racial ideologies and racially motivated violence of its era, violence that employed the specter of miscegenation as its spark and standard. What I will argue is that rather than being connected to issues of race only incidentally, *Kong* is deeply, inextricably, indeed indistinguishably involved in a pervasive and urgent early-twentieth-century cultural project to define and defend whiteness, a project that ritualistically found its fulfillment in the conjuring to life, and condemning to death, of a fantasized scapegoat: the black ravisher of white womanhood. I begin my investigation of the framing of monsters with *King Kong*, then, not only because I believe that it is the greatest fantasy film of all but, more important, because I believe that an essential aspect of its greatness lies in its inseparable tie to that most undying of America's monsters—race—and hence to its particularly volatile enactment of the processes of alienation that will be kindled within its cinematic heirs.

Whiteface, Black Monster

In the United States, the first three decades of the twentieth century—the period of the cinema's development as a technology, art form, and industry—were marked by intensifying struggles to secure a dominant white identity that had been viewed as precarious and besieged since at least the middle of the previous century. As Grace Elizabeth Hale puts it, "By the dawning of the twentieth century in the South and by the 1910s across the nation, racial essentialism dominated white thinking, dividing the world into black and white" (22). The roots of such essentialist thought varied with regional and sectional differences, but in all instances, perceived threats to racial purity underlay the drawing of the battle lines. Beginning in the 1890s, an influx of immigrants, largely from southern and eastern Europe, dramatically changed the ethnic makeup of the nation's cities, families, and workforce. By the first decade of the twentieth century, the sense of an imbalance between "pure" and "alien" Americans had become so severe that those who considered themselves to belong to the former company began to predict, as did Jack London in 1913, that "the dark-pigmented things, the half-castes, the mongrel-bloods" of the inferior races would soon overwhelm the Anglo-Saxon stock (qtd. in Higham 172). Formalizing such fears, nativist and eugenic theories, most memorably articulated in Madison Grant's *The Passing of the Great Race* (1916), held that "the mixture of two races, in the long run, gives us a race reverting to the more ancient, generalized and lower type" (15–16), producing a "population of race bastards" (69). In turn, dire warnings such as Grant's provided a spur to restrictive immigration law, culminating in the National Origins Act of 1924, which set stringent admission quotas on immigrants of "undesirable" breed.

During the 1920s, too, negrophobia vied with xenophobia in the race consciousness of the nation. It was during this time that the Great Migration from the rural South brought hundreds of thousands of African Americans to the urban centers of both South and North (Takaki 340–69); to provide only one measure of the demographic shift this movement effected, whereas in 1890 only one in every seventy people in Manhattan was identified as African American, by 1930 the figure had skyrocketed to one in every nine (Douglas 73). As early as 1835, Alexis de Tocqueville had noted that in the absence of institutional bars to interracial contact, anxiety over racial purity could exaggerate racial separatism: "In the North the white man no longer clearly sees the barrier that separates him from the degraded race, and he keeps the Negro at a distance all the more carefully because he fears lest one day they be confounded together" (343). With the twentieth century ushering in heightened chances for racial mixing, Tocqueville's words took on added gravity. As Matthew Pratt Guterl notes, alarms over the "Negro Problem" served Euro-Americans in the North, as they had served and continued to serve those in the South, as a means by which members of the "white race" came to recognize, promote, and stabilize their identity *as* whites: "The deepening national popular fascination with whiteness and blackness . . . eased class tensions within whiteness [and] masked ethnic differences" (61). Guterl continues: "The intensifying focus on 'the Negro' . . . turned northeastern racial discourse away from its traditional Anglo-Saxonism and toward a unified sense of race-as-color, or as whiteness and blackness" (80). Most obviously, this fascination with racial purity took the form of segregation, ideological and actual: not only were scientific and legal racial classifications adjusted during this period, as Michael Rogin points out, in the interest of "redefining the in-between statuses that threatened Anglo-Saxon purity" (*Blackface* 101), but such philosophical discriminations sustained physical discrimination throughout the land. In one particularly grievous case, a 1919 race riot in Chicago was touched off when a single individual failed to respect a color line drawn not in the sand but in an even more fluid element:

> Hundreds of White and Negro bathers crowded the lakefront beaches at Twenty-sixth and Twenty-ninth Streets. . . . An imaginary line in the water separating the two beaches had been generally observed by the two races. Under the prevailing relations . . . this line served virtually as a challenge to either side to cross it. . . . Eugene Williams, a Negro boy of seventeen, entered the water from the side used by Negroes and drifted across the line[,] supported by a railroad tie. He was observed by the crowd on the beach and promptly became a target for stones. He suddenly released the tie, went down and was drowned. (Boskin 32)

The absurdity of an imaginary line painted in water and the ferocity with which this absent presence was defended indicate how feverishly and furiously the project of racial definition was fought during this period. Fueled by a range of factors—preexisting racial antipathy, physical proximity, economic competition, and the fact that skin color appeared to erect a less porous barrier than the ingenious yet tenuous classifications of ethnicity—this deadly project produced a climate in which racial segregation, discrimination, and hostility were the norm in New York and Philadelphia as much as they were in Atlanta and Memphis.[6]

Throughout the land, meanwhile, an even more extreme manifestation of the turn toward a transcendent (and ascendant) whiteness was evident in the swelling ranks of white supremacist groups such as the Ku Klux Klan, which was officially resurrected in 1915 and which boasted some three to four million members nationwide by its mid-1920s peak (with its capital, at least in terms of membership, being not some backwater bastion of southern racism but the modern metropolis of Chicago).[7] Laura Browder considers the reborn Klan symbolic of the uncertainties of racial identity during this period, as its highly public demonstrations of race consciousness paradoxically transformed whiteness into a spectacle rather than an essential quality: "For the first time, whiteness could be an achieved ethnic identity. The 1920s KKK found a way to theatricalize whiteness . . . which turned whiteness itself into a subject for ethnic performance" (145). Indeed, with their faces and figures concealed beneath gleaming white cloaks, the members of the KKK powerfully bodied forth the anxieties of twentieth-century white identity, the very assertion of which announced the threat of its effacement.

In the racist mind, moreover, no more certain course toward the erasure of white identity existed than that posed by interracial sexual union. Thus Grant, adding black-white miscegenation to his list of hazards to the great race in the 1930s , wrote darkly, "it is by no means certain that the percentage of individuals with Negro blood in their veins is not increasing relatively to the pure Whites in spite of all statements to the contrary" ("Closing" 23). The waffling construction and tortured syntax of this sentence hint at the ruinous consummation Grant and his fellows foresaw in race mingling; it is as if the ambiguity born of miscegenation has not only nullified the distinctions between races but has infiltrated his own prose, making of his words a mongrel thing, neither this nor that. To whites, if social intercourse between the races was a nightmare, then sexual intercourse was the breeding ground of real-life monsters.

Thus, it is unsurprising that the specter of miscegenation was invoked not only to back ominous admonitions but to justify bloody deeds. To early-twentieth-century apologists for lynching, it was the black man's insatiable hunger for white women that made such vigilantism necessary. The racist portrait of the African American male as "a monstrous beast, crazed with lust" for the white woman (qtd. in Young, "Here" 324), had, of course, a long and ignominious pedigree. In the hands of slavers such as Thomas Jefferson, who likened the black man's "preference" for white women to "the preference of the Oran-ootan for the black women" (138), such rhetoric served to disguise the fact that the slave system institutionalized the rape of black women by white men.[8] The lasting value of this hoary cliché is suggested by statistics on the nearly three thousand African Americans lynched between 1889 and 1933; though fewer than one-quarter were directly accused of raping or attempting to rape a white woman, rumors of rape were almost always circulated to vindicate, if not any particular act, then the more general need for lynching as a means of keeping the savage sexuality of the black "buck" in check.[9] According to the Association of Southern Women for the Prevention of Lynching, an organization formed in the wake of a dramatic rise in lynchings from 1929 to 1930, "When men get rid of a Negro for reasons acceptable to them but not to the community[,] they allege that their victim had given offense to a white woman. This excuse is reasonably sure to protect the lynchers from the disapproval of their law abiding neighbors" (7). In yet stronger terms, the association's male counterpart, the Southern Commission on the Study of Lynching, averred, "The very fact that this type of rumor enrages the mass of whites is the reason why unscrupulous white men and women can use it so effectively in efforts to conceal their own misdeeds" (21). There is even evidence that such "misdeeds" extended to the creation of the circumstances that would lend the rumors substance: one Depression-era source reported that white prostitutes were encouraged by southern police to set aside a "Nigger Day," during which time they would take black clients, so that if the community "wanted to charge a black man with rape, to organize a lynching bee, they would have a man who could not deny" sexual involvement with a white woman (qtd. in Terkel 297).

Given how explosively the mere hint of miscegenation—or, if the preceding story is true, its vicious and cynical engineering—sparked the flames of racial violence, it is important to note that accusations of this sort continued to multiply in the years leading up to the release of *King Kong*. Though in absolute numbers, lynching had declined markedly since its peak in the 1890s, the first third of the 1930s still saw well over fifty cases of individuals lynched, of whom over 90 percent were African American. These figures, moreover, may be underestimates; for the disparity between *reported* lynchings and *actual* lynchings may have widened during this period. As Robert Zangrando puts it, "As opposition mounted in the 1920s and 1930s, . . . southern whites found it wise to suppress the news of mob violence. . . . [L]ynchers continued to terrorize and murder black people; but now select committees might be assigned to abduct, torture, and kill victims without public fanfare" (4). And even if the number of lynchings *had* dwindled, the supposed offenses that incited them, the righteous fury that fueled them, and the wanton cruelty that signalized them had not. Even the deliberately dispassionate prose in which the Southern Commission couched its descriptions of lynch cases is revealing of the rabidity of the accusers, the goriness of their sentences, the public and participatory nature of the murders, the complicity of legal authorities in the crimes, and the impunity with which any white person could exact vengeance on a black man accused of violating white womanhood:

> Eight of the Negroes lynched in 1930 were accused of rape. Henry Argo of Chickasha was stabbed to death in his jail cell presumably by the transient farm wage hand whose wife he was accused of raping. At Ocilla, James Irwin, accused of murdering and raping a sixteen-year-old girl, was tortured and mutilated, and then burned. At Sherman, George Hughes, accused of an assault on the wife of a white tenant farmer, was left in the vault of the burning courthouse, then dragged through the streets, and afterwards burned. In a rural community in Union County, South Carolina, Dan Jenkins, accused of rape, was captured, and his body riddled with bullets; the National Guard reached the scene thirty minutes too late. (34)

The year of *Kong's* release, Zangrando reports, "mob violence and summary justice were very much in the news" (103)—in the Alabama lynching of three black prisoners and in the Maryland lynching of a black man by a mob of some two thousand citizens, an act the *New York Times* characterized as "the wildest lynching orgy the state has ever witnessed" (qtd. in Zangrando 103). Hoping to stanch the flow of blood or at least to boost the paltry rates by which the guilty were brought to justice—in 1933, one study estimated that "only about eight-tenths of one per cent of the lynchings in the United States since 1900 have been followed by conviction of the lynchers" (Chadbourne 13)—the NAACP lobbied throughout the 1930s for a federal antilynching bill; but the bill, which President Franklin Delano Roosevelt refused to support for fear of forfeiting the votes he needed for Depression relief programs, was repeatedly defeated by Southern legislators who considered it, in the memorable words of one, "a bill to encourage rape" (qtd. in Newby 140).[10] Nor, for that matter, was extralegal violence the only means by which African Americans were terrorized by white communities. In the infamous Scottsboro case of 1931, for example—a case that Zangrando concludes "had all the earmarks of a legal lynching" (99)—nine African American youths were accused of raping two white women on a train passing through Scottsboro, Alabama, and in a judicial proceeding that lasted a mere two weeks from arrest to conviction, an all-white jury condemned eight of the nine to death. In the months just before *Kong*'s release, the case was in the news again because of a scheduled March 1933 retrial, widely circulated NAACP petitions for financial support of the legal-defense effort, and the recantation of Ruby Bates, one of the women who had originally cried rape. Her appeal that "i wish those negroes are not Burnt on account of me" was but one particularly poignant acknowledgment of the climate of racist violence that prevailed at the time.[11]

As with less dramatic forms of racial conflict, moreover, acts of community-orchestrated and court-sanctioned violence were not confined to the South. As Harvard Sitkoff writes, "Whites lynched Negroes in almost every major city above the Mason-Dixon line in the Progressive era" (15). Closer to the release of *Kong*, the courts and the press took over as the mobs waned. When, for example, Richard Wright sought source material for his novel *Native Son* (1940), his talent for creating fictional stories and speech lay largely unspent; rather, he was able to excerpt virtually verbatim the *Chicago Tribune*'s coverage of a 1938 case in which a black Chicagoan was accused of raping and murdering a white woman:

> "He looks exactly like an ape!" exclaimed a terrified young white girl who watched the black slayer. . . .
>
> Though the Negro killer's body does not seem compactly built, he gives the impression of possessing abnormal physical strength. . . . His lower jaw protrudes obnoxiously, reminding one of a jungle beast.
>
> His arms are long, hanging in a dangling fashion to his knees. It is easy to imagine how this man, in the grip of a brain-numbing sex passion, overpowered little Mary Dalton, raped her, murdered her.

. . . All in all, he seems a beast utterly untouched by the softening influences of modern civilization. (Wright 322–23)

When one compares this fictional description with the journalistic account—which, among other things, terms the killing "the work of a giant ape" (qtd. in Kinnamon 5)—it becomes evident that racist fantasy had so deeply infected interracial fact as to render the vision of Kong himself anything but a wonder to whites and blacks alike.[12]

In short, during the first third of the twentieth century, white Americans were caught up in a fascinating, fatal quest to sanctify and safeguard the prerogatives of whiteness—a quest in which the fantasized figure of the black rapist was at once the most convenient and the most convincing scapegoat. The anxieties that underlay this quest did not ease during the Depression; if anything, with the customary distinctions of wealth and culture seeming ready to topple and with movements toward social equality just beginning to dawn, the putative difference between white and black provided many Americans one of the only means by which privilege could be defined. Thus, as W. E. B. Du Bois wrote in 1934, racial discrimination thrived during this period:

> The difference between North and South in the matter of segregation is largely a difference of degree; of wide degree certainly, but still of degree. . . . We have by legal action steadied the foundation so that in the future, segregation must be by wish and will and not law, but beyond that we have not made the slightest impress on the determination of the overwhelming mass of white Americans not to treat Negroes as men. (745–46)

This same determination shaped New Deal relief policies, which (most egregiously during Roosevelt's first term) discriminated against African Americans in the realms of employment, housing, social welfare, and the like. In identifying such trends, I do not mean to imply either that racist violence was identical to these more subtle forms of discrimination or that such violence can be traced exclusively to the needs of white self-definition. Clearly enough, other, interrelated factors—economic competition, the quest for social control, or more generally the legacy of the nation's racist past—underlay the violence of the period; and just as clearly, the extremes of mob violence were only the most radical, not the most typical, of the many means by which whites sought to uphold their authority and identity. Nonetheless, I do want to argue that such violence was both continuous with and expressive of the larger project by which white individuals and communities defined themselves amidst anxieties about race. Studs Terkel cites the words of one African American man who foresaw in the leveling effects of the Depression the first portents of racial equality: "In the Depression, there were so many whites who were on relief. So the Negro would look, and he wouldn't see any great difference" (437).[13] One way to think of the racial violence of this period is to see it as an attempt to reassert the "great difference" that the Depression threatened to erode, an attempt to ensure that the white "look" was not plundered by some dark intruder who could, as it were, ape white society by overpowering its guardians, trespassing on its quarters, and usurping its treasures.

In this enterprise, it is perhaps needless to say, one of the principal vehicles for promulgating and codifying the white look was the cinema.[14] That the cinema was so deeply invested from its beginnings in the spectacle of racial clarification and classification—and as such, in the history of violence against African Americans—is no doubt related to its emergence as an urban, mass-cultural form. Film, that is, arose within the sites in which the meaning of whiteness was most subject to ambiguity yet in which more extreme forms of racist violence were neither ingrained nor legitimized. Placed in such sites and reliant on the processes of identification by which audiences are drawn to the theater, film thus developed its own (or its culture's) race consciousness, one that capitalized on audience expectations while participating in the audience's self-construction. As with the origins of racial violence, it would of course be reductive to trace the origins or popularity of the cinema to any single source. Nonetheless, it seems clear that in the cinema's function as a public ritual through which a heterogeneous urban populace came to recognize and name itself, race not only played a pivotal role but perhaps provided a vital impetus. The cinema, that is, became both necessary and infectious in part because, with its ability to realize in fantasy what had proved so arduous to draw in fact—namely, an inviolable line between black and white—it helped ground a dominant racial identity that had become increasingly troubled and uncertain.

Therefore, it is understandable why the cinema, like the society within which it was forged, labored to remove any taint of interracial mingling from the screen (and, thanks to the Jim Crow arrangements of everything from production companies to dressing rooms, from the world behind it). In his study of images of African Americans in film, Thomas Cripps notes that early one-reelers were rife with offensive stereotypes aimed at defining blacks as a race apart. At the same time, these films did not shy away from visiting retribution on any who violated racial boundaries: "One catalogue listed a movie depicting 'the catching, tar[r]ing and feathering and burning of a negro for the assault of a white woman" (13–14). More generally, as Susan Gubar demonstrates, racist representations of African Americans in film, including traditions of blackface minstrelsy, can be seen as "public performances of torture inflicted on the black body" (78); the "mimetic violence" of "blacking up" is not only coterminous with but analogous to the "physical violence of lynching" (79).[15] By the same token, any intimation of black empowerment or defiance of white authority was vigorously banned from the screen; for instance, as Dan Streible points out, when African American boxer Jack Johnson clobbered a series of white opponents in the first decade of the century, "so great were white anxieties that many states and cities censored Johnson films in particular and the U.S. Congress banned interstate commerce in prizefight films in general" (170). If the early cinema inscribed the racist ideology of its time, it likewise expressed the racial anxiety at that ideology's core.

Given such precedents, it is unsurprising that the first generally acknowledged masterpiece of the cinematic form, D. W. Griffith's *The Birth of a Nation* (1915), is fundamentally committed to promulgating ideologies of racial separatism and violence. Michael Rogin, noting that "American movies were born . . . in a racist epic," critiques "celebrants of *Birth*'s formal achievement" for "either minimiz[ing] the film's racialist content or separat[ing] its aesthetic power from its negrophobia" ("'Sword'" 150). As with those who laud *Kong*'s special effects or stirring plot while forgiving its racism, admirers of *Birth*'s form, Rogin notes, all too often divorce the film from its ideology, as if in art there could be any other vehicle *for* ideology than form.[16] Yet not only was *Birth* directly (if unwittingly) implicated in the broader culture's assault on African Americans—the founder of the modern KKK timed the rebirth of the order to coincide with the Atlanta premiere of Griffith's film, which was subsequently adopted for Klan recruitment, training, and propaganda[17]—but the film itself, as Daniel Leab writes, materializes the racist arguments of its time: "The black is presented as a person lusting for white women, grasping for white property, and unwilling to accept a preordained station at the bottom of the social order" (25). To extol Griffith's film for its formal innovations while pardoning its noxious and unremitting racism is thus not simply unacceptable on ethical or theoretical grounds. More fundamentally, such a separation obscures the fact that *Birth* is definitive precisely *because* it crowned a cinematic tradition that had toiled from the start to construct an impregnable barrier between whites and blacks and to punish any who dared transgress it. That this project aroused white audiences not just in the South but throughout the land is suggested by an account of the film's Los Angeles premiere:

> Every soul in that audience was in the saddle with the clansmen and pounding hell-for-leather on an errand of stern justice, lighted on their way by the holy flames of a burning cross. . . . [At film's end,] the audience didn't just sit there and applaud, but they stood up and cheered and yelled and stamped feet until Griffith finally made an appearance. (qtd. in Simmon 104–5)

Sitkoff notes that theatrical venues had served as sites for actual violence against African Americans: "In 1911 the townsfolk of Livermore, Kentucky, purchased tickets to participate in the lynching of a Negro at the local theatre. Orchestra seatholders were allowed to fire as many bullets as they chose into the hanging black body; those in the gallery were restricted to a single shot" (18). That Griffith's film staged the spectacle of the black beast's lynching thus suggests that *Birth*, by detaching racist violence from local contexts and by permitting audiences to partake vicariously in the hunt and kill, was foundational for a white national identity, both on the screen and in the stands.

Griffith's film was also, in ways at once incidental and inescapable, foundational for another film that dramatized the death of the black beast: *Kong*. Clyde Taylor reports an anecdote told by Lillian Gish, one of the stars of *Birth*: "One day while we were rehearsing the scene where the colored man picks up the Northern girl gorilla-fashion, my hair, which was very blond, fell below my waist and Griffith, seeing the contrast in the two figures, assigned me to play Elsie Stoneman" (26). Though only a single remark by one of the company's players, Gish's terms are nonetheless suggestive: the association of the African American man with a gorilla, the revelation of blondness as the paradigmatic symbol of white womanhood, and the desire to exaggerate through this visual "contrast" the gulf between whiteness and blackness are all formative for *Kong* as well. Merian C. Cooper is reported to have used nearly identical terms in his instructions to Fay Wray, a natural brunette, when casting her for the role of Ann Darrow: "Of course you'd have to be a blonde. We've got to have that contrast" (qtd. in Ambrogio 135).[18] The contrast of white and black that Griffith and Cooper labored to institute was born from the threat of miscegenation, the ultimate abrogation of racial difference; the lynching of Gus, the black man who stalks the younger Cameron sister in *Birth*, is clearly a cinematic precursor to the gunning of Kong (a fact signaled by the similar spatial iconography of both films, in which the ascent to and fall from a height surround the act of violation and violence). In both instances, then, racial contrast is achieved through the thwarting of black male sexual predation; white superiority is secured in a violence both expressive of and validated by the fear that white identity has been pushed to its most tenuous contingency.

At the same time, Gish's comment links *Birth* to a set of films that represented another of the early cinema's most prominent takes on racial difference, a set of films of which *Kong* is itself the crowning achievement: "jungle" films, the exotic, location-shot (or at least putatively so) pictures on which Carl Denham built his reputation.[19] One of the hallmarks of these films was the contact—and contrast—between white civilization and the dark-skinned tribes of primitive lands, apelike men (or in many cases, actual apes) who craved the icon of whiteness, the golden-haired woman. In films such as *Tarzan of the Apes* (1918), *The Lost World* (1921)—in which O'Brien's stop-motion techniques first attained renown— *Bali, the Unknown; or, Ape Island* (1921), and *Ourang* (1930), the story line that *Kong* would make famous was played out again and again: the white woman abducted by, sacrificed to, or (implicitly) ravished by apes or by their barely more human black counterparts. In a cinematic climate in which "sex relationships" between the white and black races" were implicitly and (after 1927) explicitly tabooed,[20] what made such films possible—and profitable—was the subterfuge on which *Kong* would elaborate: though typically touted so as to play up the sexually suggestive nature of their plots, jungle films could at the same time sidestep miscegenation through metonymy, by displacing the fabled sexual aggression of the black male onto a figure sufficiently saturated in racist cliché to stand in for the black rapist, yet enough unlike that fantasy assailant to avoid the censure, or outright censoring, of the product. The jungle films, then, fulfilled both the salacious and the monitory requirements of white definition (and black defamation): whiteness could be pictured as so inherently desirable that even dumb, black brutes found it irresistible and yet, through the same means, it could be protected from defilement at the hands of the real-world dark-skinned figures whom whiteness both needed and dreaded.

What should be apparent from the preceding discussion is that the culture within which the early cinema operated was compulsively employed in staging intricate, intimate dramas whereby whiteness could be jeopardized yet championed, racism rehearsed yet disowned, pitch-black aggressors summoned yet thwarted just short of their final, foul victory. In some of these dramas—such as those confined to the cinema—African Americans were robbed of their dignity and decency; in others—such as those that spilled out into the streets—they could be robbed of their livelihoods and lives. The point, however, is that these dramas were continuous with one another, complementary manifestations of a pervasive cultural enterprise that took on such ubiquitous and variegated forms because it required their mutual reiteration and reinforcement to naturalize a black/white divide that was no more inherently given than the figment of race itself. *Kong* is but one fragment of the larger cultural drama; I do not claim any hallowed or exemplary status for it in this context, though I do maintain that, like *Birth*, it represents a culminating moment in the racist tradition from which it springs and thus is a useful instrument for disinterring and dissecting that tradition. Commenting on the difficulty of analyzing "the representation of whiteness as an ethnic category in mainstream film" due to the way in which "white power secures its dominance by seeming not to be anything in particular"

("White" 44), Richard Dyer notes that "the representation of white *qua* white begins to come into focus . . . in films in which non-white characters play a significant role. . . . What [such] films also share, which helps to sharpen further the sense of whiteness in them, is a situation in which white domination is contested" (47–48). In *Kong*, the domination of white culture—indeed, the survival of white civilization and of its most coveted symbol—is contested by a nonwhite character, a monster from the era's deepest racist fantasies, and through this process, the ideology of whiteness is rendered both visible and inescapable. In this sense, *Kong's* one-note theme might be said to reveal more than it knows: in a world reduced to black and white, it *is* the beautiful atrocity of whiteness that kills the black beast.

Kong: Race, Rape, and Revenge

King Kong tells of the awful consequences that transpire when the inviolable line separating black from white is violated. As such, the film labors to construct whiteness and blackness as inhabiting absolutely separate worlds, worlds that are twice contaminated by members of the other race (first, when the whites land on Skull Mountain Island, and second, when Kong is brought to New York), each time with equivalent and calamitous consequences. The Manhattan scenes that frame the island adventure portray a society utterly bereft of a black presence: in the soup kitchen line, in the diner, in the theater, in the elevated train—in every setting, Jim Crow arrangements are the unequivocal and unquestioned rule. Even in contexts in which one might plausibly expect to see an African American person—in the hotel as a porter, on the docks, or simply in the scenes of chaos in the streets after Kong's escape—the rule is ironclad: whites only. Though it cannot be claimed that *Kong* is unaware of national or ethnic diversity—the presence of the Italian fruit-stand vendor on the streets of New York or of the Chinese cook among the lily-white crew of the *Venture* suggests otherwise—blackness is specifically targeted for exile, placed wholly outside the world of white civilization. In a 1927 telegram, Will Hays had instructed filmmakers, "Inadvisable always to show white women in scenes with Negroes where there is any inference of miscegenation" (qtd. in Vasey 139). In *Kong*, the complete absence of black persons in the white world under normal circumstances makes plain that any black encroachment on the charmed circle of whiteness constitutes, by definition, such an "inference."

The world of Skull Mountain Island, accordingly, is as egregiously black as that of Manhattan is white. Clearly, if verisimilitude were desired, the islanders would be badly miscast; occupants of an East Indian island would not be black Africans (as they must be to have procured the gorilla hides so central to their ceremonial observances). But not satisfied with the difference of skin color, the mise-en-scène of the island pointedly heightens the contrast of black and white, the islanders' decorations—white face paint and feathers—accentuating the darkness of their skin. Too, the superficial visual similarities that critics have observed between Manhattan and Skull Mountain Island—with the Empire State Building paralleling Kong's mountain aerie, the biplanes recalling the pteranodon, and so on—only underscore the rock-bottom racial difference. In like fashion, Denham's quip when the islanders spy (and desire) Darrow, "Yeah, blondes are scarce around here," serves a purpose beyond its offhand and gratuitous racism. More fundamentally, the line functions within a persistent pattern in the pre-Kong sequences of establishing the contrast between black and white, a contrast asserted so regularly and rigorously that the anxiety beneath the apparently "natural" segregation of white and black worlds cannot be doubted.

Kong, of course, incarnates that anxiety, substantiating the racist nightmare of a creature (in Denham's words) "neither beast nor man," "monstrous," and "all powerful," that can overwhelm the blockades the white world has erected around itself, penetrating to the very heart of the white world by making off with its most visible and valuable icon. This understanding of Kong as the figuration of blackness threatening to burst into the protected zone of whiteness helps to explain the repeated instances in which his arrival on-screen is achieved by the leveling of a barrier: he first appears, for instance, after tearing down a thicket of trees positioned in the shot's left background, while Darrow, a gleaming white figure against the darkness of the forest and a symbol of helpless maidenhood bound to the natives' altar, occupies the right foreground. The breaching of the great wall, too, can be seen in these terms: though in demolishing this barrier Kong is of course entering the village of the blacks, his motivation (the recovery of Darrow) and the fact that the scene is played to emphasize the threat to the white heroes (the islanders reappearing only at Denham's behest) make it clear that what is at stake in the wall's stability is its virtue as a protective shield for whites. In the New York sequences after Kong's capture, similarly, this motif of forced entry repeats a number of times: once, briefly, in the shot of Kong battering down the theater wall to emerge into the street, and twice, in sequences filmed almost identically, with Kong's face appearing outside one bedroom window and his hand thrusting through another, when he steals first an unidentified woman and then Darrow from their hotel-room beds. In the latter two sequences in particular, the generalized threat of black penetration is infused with the sexual connotation that underlay or gave shape to white anxieties; for as Hellenbrand notes, the hotel scenes are "rape scenes, bedroom scenes in which miscegenation looms darkly in the shape of King Kong" (90). It is worth noting, along these lines, that the majority of the process shots that bring Kong into the human world strongly suggest the eruption of a foreign presence into a space he is not supposed to occupy. Thus what strikes viewers today as the lamentable crudity of Depression-era special effects techniques can more productively be seen as consistent with the film's discourse, its delineation of "white" and "black" spaces and its need both to pollute and to preserve that dichotomy. The technical tricks by which Kong and Darrow come into apparent contact—culminating in the elaborate spectacle of the disrobing scene—thus participate in the film's halting recognition that it is playing with fire: Kong never *really* touches Wray, yet it is imperative that the film produce the illusion that the boundary between black and white has been overcome.

For this reason, it will not do to protest, as some critics have, that Kong never behaves in an inappropriate manner toward Darrow—that he is a perfect gentleman, offering her no harm and, indeed, placing her out of harm's way while he takes the full force of the biplanes' bullets. Not only is such an argument historically inert—for as I have indicated, most of the African American men made to suffer for supposedly violating white women were in all likelihood innocent of any such act—but Kong's threat and punishment have no more to do with *actual* rape than did the accusations of rape regularly circulated by lynch mobs. What is at issue, rather, is Kong's participation in the more trenchant cultural trauma of whiteness threatened by an imagined black adversary, one who will stop at nothing to claim his prize, even if his pursuit of the prize means the tearing down of white civilization itself. That Kong appears to be succeeding in this quest is, of course, the gist of his Manhattan rampage, which visualizes the logic of racist ideology: for the black man to claim the white woman is for the privileges of whiteness—exemplified in the bright lights, top hats, and mink stoles of the theater audience and in the lofty symbol of the Empire State Building itself—to be, as it were, surmounted by a dark enemy, an invading army of one. As the film's white heroes huddle in the police station, listening to reports of Kong's trail of carnage through the city, a voice over the radio intones, "Kong is climbing the Empire State Building. That is all." Kong, the men conclude before first mate Driscoll dreams up the airplane gambit, has "licked us": he has absconded with the symbol of racial purity and supremacy, and as such the announcer's toneless "that is all" takes on the apocalyptic ring of civilization's doom.[21]

Thus Kong must die, must himself suffer the downfall with which he threatens white civilization—the downfall that claimed the life of the younger Cameron sister when pursued by the black ape of *Birth of a Nation*. There is, in this respect, a logical progression in the twin rescue operations that form the film's action sequences: whereas the Skull Island rescue has the look of vigilante justice—with the self-appointed protectors of the white woman, a ragtag posse armed to the teeth and led by Denham with his rifle, cowboy hat, and sheriff's vest, charging confusedly into the bush to save Darrow from ravishment at black hands—the Manhattan parallel provides official license to the lynch-mob feel of the earlier episode, as shots of screeching cop cars and references to "the riot squad" acknowledge the need for state authorities to engage in defeating the menace. These shots of the governmental response to Kong's threat are intercut with shots of Kong scaling the first of many buildings to locate a screaming woman, only to find a sleeping substitute whom, disappointed, he drops to her death. The effect of this sequence is thus to suggest that the wholesale assault on Kong, like the earlier Skull Mountain Island chase, is at bottom motivated by legitimate fear of the black beast's desire for, and violence against, white women. Moreover, if one considers the New York sequence as the culmination of an arc of violence begun with the first dinosaur kill on Skull Mountain Island, one perceives how the film gradually draws the audience into condoning the extreme measures of the final act of slaughter: selecting a stegosaur and an apatosaur—two herbivores who, bizarrely, seem to lust for human flesh—as the first animal antagonists, the film creates a perception of constant threat to white life, safety, and property, a condition that renders absolutely necessary the armed response of white men acting within—and without—the constraints of the law. Thus, by the time of the brief burst of violence that closes *Kong*, the audience has been so worked into a fervor for justified or defensive military operations that the question of *whether* to kill the beast never receives an airing, the only issue being *how* to do so—and as quickly as possible.

Up to this point, my reading of *Kong* has focused on the most notorious evidences of its alienating strategies. Yet *Kong*, in keeping with its form and function as a work of cinema, performs this act of alienation in more subtle, and in some respects more powerful, ways—ways that ultimately figure the great divide between white and black not as a construct in need of definition but as a constant that is defined simply by the nature of things. I refer here to the ways in which *Kong* figures the visual, the look. If, as I suggested previously, the early cinema supplemented the racial violence of its era by helping to assure the dominance of the white "look"—the white look *of* things and the white look *at* things—then a film so keenly oriented toward the visual, the spectacle, as *Kong* would seem an apt candidate to carry forward this cultural-cinematic enterprise. From the first to the last, *Kong* is a film steeped in the discourse of seeing. Denham, for instance, habitually judges the significance of his find on its visual mystery and allure: "I'm telling you," he comments to Driscoll and Captain Englehorn in one of many such pronouncements, "there's something on that island no white man has ever seen."

Moreover, even before the object of these speculations becomes visible, the film is structured to emphasize seeing; for example, as Denham roams the streets looking for a suitable female lead for his picture, the camera records the street scenes—the women in the soup line or, more pointedly, Darrow's face as her head falls back in a swoon—from his point of view. The most famous of such visual motifs is, of course, the shot/reverse-shot pattern involving Kong and Darrow, which emphasizes the power of the black, as opposed to the white, look. And indeed, it is precisely by *opposing* the white look to the black that *Kong* constructs black and white as if they are *not* constructed: rejecting Kong's look—the black look—in favor of identification with the proper—white—subject/viewpoint, the film grounds the opposition of black and white in the ostensibly natural medium of seeing rather than in acts of oppression and violence.

Toward this end, it is instructive to note that, just as seeing in *Kong* is a primary vehicle for audience involvement in a drama of racial difference, so is it a primary site wherein relations of power between the races are signified. This is expressed, for instance, in the line from Denham I quoted above, which construes the power to see (or the lack thereof) in terms of racial difference: "There's something on that island no white man has ever seen." On the beach, when the landing party approaches the islanders' ceremony, the racial quality of seeing is reiterated: announcing, "Wait till I see what goes on," the director peers through a screen of tall grass, affording him (and, from his point of view, the audience) a commanding view of the islanders, who under these conditions of unsolicited and unconscious inspection are objectified, transformed into an ethnographic tableau of primitive costume, tribal dance, and heathen ritual. That power between the races is in significant respects a representational matter, a function of the ability to constitute the black primitive through the camera lens without having that visual authority reciprocated or reversed, is underscored by Denham's lines. "If I can only get a picture before they see us," he utters hopefully, only to be disheartened a moment later: "Too late. They see us." Indeed, it is only when "they" see "us" that we—the viewing audience—first see from the point of view of the islanders; just as Denham had feared, the racial hierarchy is disrupted, inverted, by the natives' seeing. For the first thing we see through black eyes, at the very moment of their covetous look, is Darrow. In this initial moment of alignment with the black gaze, then, the audience sees the one thing that is most explicitly, by all the codes of the culture and of the film itself, forbidden: black desire for the golden woman. And as such, it becomes evident that the power of the black gaze inheres in its ability to break down not simply sexual segregation but all the barriers for which such segregation stood, barriers elaborately fabricated and violently defended to secure a precarious white identity.

Needless to say, this power will be recapitulated and amplified in Kong's gaze; if the islanders' licentious stares are both brief and vigorously contested by the white men present, Kong's look is constant, lingering, and (at least in his own, segregated territory) unchallenged. Indeed, with the notable exception of the disrobing sequence, one might say that all Kong does to Darrow *is* look at her. Yet as the first encounter between Kong and Darrow indicates, looking is in itself a violation of the line between black and white. Before he plucks Darrow from her pedestal, the camera tracks in on the eyes of the full-scale model of Kong's head, followed by a shot of the object of his look as she screams in terror. The life-size model's limited mobility notwithstanding, the flexing of its eyebrows suggests that Kong is, as it were, giving Darrow "the look"; immediately afterward, he cuts her loose and carries her off. As with the islanders, then, what this scene suggests is that the black being's look at the white goddess is a preliminary to, or even synonymous with, the act of seizure. In this sense, for all its hesitancy to name the violation for what it is, the disrobing completes a process through which the black gaze emerges as a direct threat to the barriers that define and defend whiteness against the dark assailant.

The movement of the film, accordingly, will be toward the recovery of the white woman as the object of *white* desire, white power, white authority. Most obviously, this movement will construct Darrow as the love object and sexual property of the white man, Driscoll. More generally, Darrow will be reified as the love object and proper idol of a white cinematic audience that has been terrorized into recognizing the potential loss of its most hallowed jewel. This recovery project, significantly, is troubled by the lack of any tangible difference between the black gaze and the white; since whiteness is, by the film's and the broader culture's own terms, visible only in its opposition to, and its threatened conquest by, blackness, the propriety of the white gaze can never be proved but can only be asserted insofar as it is *not* black. Thus it is telling that the film initially positions both Denham and Driscoll—the two white male competitors for Darrow's favors against Kong—in the same visual relation to Darrow as it positions Kong. For instance, in the restaurant after Denham has "saved" Darrow from the street vendor—his confessed motive, of course, being his designs to make her his cinematic property—the shot/reverse-shot pattern of Denham, on his feet and looking down at Darrow, and of Darrow, seated and looking up at Denham, bears an uncanny resemblance to the shot/reverse-shot sequences of Darrow and Kong, in which the difference between his looking *down* and her looking *up* is central. On the deck of the *Venture*, just before Driscoll and Darrow kiss—just before, that is, *he* claims her as his romantic property—the same differential is emphasized, with close-ups exaggerating her gaze upward and his downward.

That the vertical placement of the male look bears strong proprietary connotations can be measured not only by likening the white men's looks to Kong's but by contrasting the looks of all three to that of the *Venture*'s sole nonwhite crew member: the Chinese cook, who in his one major scene with Darrow decorously and doggedly looks *down*, engrossed in his menial (and effeminate) task of peeling potatoes, while she stands above him by the ship's rail. In this respect, though Denham swears to Darrow that he is "on the level," that no inappropriate desires lurk within his proposal, the fact that he delivers this line while he is, visually, *not* on a level with her suggests that the white male look at the golden woman, like the black male look, is one of lust and possession.

Yet in the end, the white look wins; in the end, Driscoll (once again positioned above Darrow as he cradles her on the Empire State Building's peak) and Denham (positioned such that he appears to be looking down at Kong lying dead below the reunited couple) gain mastery over the white woman and the black foe that had made off with her. That the white look has been constructed in terms similar to that of the black suggests that this victory inheres precisely in the fact that Driscoll and Denham *are* white (and Kong black); if his look is stigmatized and theirs legitimized, this must reflect a *racial* difference—a difference, moreover, that itself exists entirely through opposition. The film, in other words, inverts the causal relationship of violence to vision: rather than violence being seen as a means of enforcing white vision, white vision comes to seem a sufficient, indeed inevitable, justification for violence. Thus in the film's conclusion, Kong relinquishes the power of his gaze and is transformed into an object of white inspection, amusement, and retribution; reduced in the theater to what Denham calls a "mere show to gratify [the audience's] curiosity," the "greatest thing [their] eyes have ever beheld," he is further objectified on the Empire State Building's pinnacle by the tracking shots representing the biplane pilots' point of view as they close in for the kill. It is widely known that director Cooper and producer Ernest Schoedsack, delighting in the prospect of "kill[ing] the sonofabitch ourselves," made a spur-of-the-moment decision to play the fighters in the cockpit of the plane that brings Kong down (qtd. in Jensen 75). In this way, it is the white creators of *Kong* who definitively reclaim the power of the gaze that had been ceded to the black being—a cession that, as their eagerness to undertake the symbolic lynching implies, was at once threatening and invigorating to white authority and identity.

The year after one black beast was gunned down by his creators, another racist fantasy—this time, a real one—was played out; another black body was sacrificed to the needs of white power and subjected to the authority of the white look. The effectiveness of *Kong*'s strategies of containment, of ingenuous racism, can be gauged by setting it beside this real-world parallel, which took on, like *Kong*, the characteristics of a public spectacle to which "curious onlookers" rushed "because something unusual was happening" (Raper 12). In the aftermath of the particularly grisly 1934 lynching of Claude Neal, who was accused, in all likelihood falsely, of violating and murdering a white woman, one sees what *Kong* both could not and did show:

> Neal's body . . . was hung, nude, in the courthouse square. Live-wire photographers were on the scene early and took many pictures of the remains. They reckoned their business investment well, because some whites, who assembled after Neal's body was taken down early that Saturday morning, were so disappointed that they quickly bought up photographs for fifty cents. Fingers and toes from the corpse were exhibited as souvenirs. . . . Scores of aroused, curious people quietly paraded through the tension-filled jail in an orderly fashion to see the remains. (Howard 61)

Though indicative of the market that existed for acts of racist butchery—and for their spread through the photographic media—this direct viewing of the mutilated remains of an African American lynch-mob victim would, one imagines, have been too unsettling for the majority of white Americans, regardless of their deepest convictions about such measures of vengeance. Lacking distance from the spectacle and unable to derive consolation from an appeal to their own guiltlessness, viewers exposed to such an unspeakable display of brutality might have found it difficult to determine who in this festival of hatred represented beauty and who the beast. Indeed, as Grace Elizabeth Hale points out, the lynching of Neal—its gruesome details broadcast by the NAACP in an effective strategy of forcing into view racism's naked consummation—brought to an end the ritualized, theatrical, consumer-oriented "spectacle lynchings" that had marked the twentieth century's first three decades. But the end of spectacle lynchings, as Hale also insists, did not signal the end of the racist violence that fed them. Instead, "the image of the 'black beast rapist,' providing a foundation for the culture of segregation beyond the reach of rational discussion, remained" in the "representations of lynchings" that had taken the place of the "lynchings themselves" (227). *Kong* is one such representation, and it epitomizes the ways in which mimetic violence sustains what it seems to supplant: in *Kong*, the numerous displacements—from black man to ape, from reality to fantasy, from courthouse to movie house—work to purge atrocity, to shield audience members from their sanction of or participation in the act. The viewer of *Kong* experiences the satisfaction of racial victory without needing to reckon its costs—and in this way, *Kong* naturalizes the very violence whose place it appears to take. Ultimately, then, *Kong* offers perhaps the perfect emblem of 1930s America's racist culture, an emblem perfect because it captured the very image of the era's racism while allowing those who viewed that image to deny what they saw.

King Kong is exhibited onstage for the entertainment of a crowd. From *King Kong* (RKO, 1933). Courtesy of Photofest.

Before I conclude this chapter, however, I would like to raise two elements of *Kong* that complicate the prevailing racist ideology of the film; though neither can counteract the film's racism, both are indicators of the complexity of fantasy film's ideological operations. The first of these factors concerns the *Kong* audience; the second, the *Kong* artist. Given what I have said about the film—in particular my claim that in *Kong* the black gaze is allotted no place but rather is demonized and killed off—it might strike one as inexplicable that in addition to what Cynthia Erb terms "the earnest, extremely oppositional approaches that often characterize black responses to *King Kong*" (*Tracking* 160), by some accounts *Kong* was in its time—and remains in ours—remarkably popular among African American moviegoers. X. J. Kennedy reports:

A Negro friend from Atlanta tells me that in movie houses in colored neighborhoods throughout the South, *Kong* does a constant business. They show the thing in Atlanta at least every year, presumably to the same audiences. Perhaps this popularity may simply be due to the fact that *Kong* is one of the most watchable movies ever constructed, but I wonder whether Negro audiences may not find some archetypal appeal in this serio-comic tale of a huge black powerful free spirit whom all the hardworking white policemen are out to kill. (123)

There are numerous ways in which to explain the apparent allure *Kong* holds for black audiences without recurring to its "archetypal" power (or, for that matter, implying that African Americans are deluded into capitulating to hegemonic social ideologies). For instance, one might agree with Judith Mayne that the pathetic touches in the film's portrayal of its title character—his hurt expression when Driscoll stabs his finger, the crucifixion imagery of his New York premiere, his agonized reaction to the biplanes' bullets—encourage "the spectator . . . to identify with Kong in a basically sympathetic way" (377), even, as Erb puts it, to root for "the suffering black exotic" (*Tracking* 17). J. P. Telotte, indeed, considers such ambivalence central to *Kong*'s cinematic discourse; in the very shot/reverse-shot sequences that I have argued serve the film's racist ideology, Telotte suggests that "we find ourselves—like Kong—becoming the dual figure of menace and menaced, threatened subject and monstrous object. . . . Simply put, the movie clutches us and makes us play by turns victim and villain, the self and the other; it forces us to assume a shadow aspect we might not have suspected lay within us" ("Movies" 395). Along the same lines, if the visual parallels between Kong and Denham supplement the film's racism, at the same time these parallels between black and white "monsters" may support Rhona Berenstein's argument that such racism is at odds with itself: "Although steeped in racism, films like *King Kong* are built on faulty and often paradoxical premises intended to confirm white supremacy but destined to destabilize it as well" (*Attack* 196).[22] And if so, what this would suggest is that *Kong*, perhaps in spite of itself, is a far more liberatory film than I have allowed—a film, indeed, that extends an emancipatory promise (or premise) to the very race it assails.

Conversely, rather than assuming that it is within the "premises" of *Kong* that this liberatory potential lies, one might argue that African American responses to *Kong* attest to what Manthia Diawara calls the "resisting" character of black spectatorship: though in the case of *Kong*, as in Diawara's test case, *Birth of a Nation*, viewers are "drawn by the narrative to identify with the white woman" imperiled by black monstrosity, the African American viewer may "resis[t] the racist reading of the black man as a dangerous beast" (852). As with the question of *Kong*'s potentially ambivalent or multiform construction of race, such resistant identification ultimately reflects on my reconstruction of race in the cinema as a whole, as indeed it does on my reconstruction of race in the culture more generally. For as I said in the introduction, throughout this study I assume the perspective of the dominant—in this context, white—culture in the creation, circulation, and reception of fantasy films. I do not regret this choice, nor do I retreat from it here. Yet as I also said, any approach to alienation in fantasy film that selects *only* dominant social attitudes and readings is necessarily partial. Thus if, as I believe to be the case, reading fantasy film in terms of such attitudes is both necessary and justified, at the same time one must recall, as Diawara puts it, that "aspects of a dominant film can be read differently once the alternative readings of Afro-American spectators are taken into account" (846).[23]

With this thought of alternative readings in mind, I turn to the second of the two factors that may complicate the dominant tenor of *Kong*'s racism: the work of stop-motion artist Willis H. O'Brien. In O'Brien's case, the issue of identification once again becomes paramount; but at the same time, it becomes exceedingly furtive and elusive. O'Brien was, by all accounts, not only introverted and taciturn by nature but particularly reluctant to divulge the secrets of his trade; he worked almost invariably in private, kept no notes, permitted few photographs, and left only a single, sketchy description of his special effects processes, precious to trivia-starved fans like myself but, for the same reason, dispiriting when placed beside the wonders he wrought from the Kong figurine.[24] And yet, it seems reasonable to suggest that without O'Brien's having identified with Kong in ways surely different from, and perhaps even more profound than, that of *Kong*'s audiences, such wonders could never have been achieved. Because it relies on direct tactile engagement with the animated object, without the mediation of pen, paint, or keyboard, stop-motion (arguably to a greater extent than other forms of animation) transforms the animated being into an extension of the animator, infusing it with his or her identity—the animator's fingerprints, as it were, a fact literally recorded in the bristling of Kong's fur under O'Brien's hands. And in this respect, it is possible to see the animation of Kong—a black being—by O'Brien—a white animator—as itself a violation of the rigid codes of racial separatism that shaped 1930s America and 1930s Hollywood, codes that decreed that only through *opposition* to black could white identity be secured. In the case of O'Brien and Kong, by contrast, the identity of both animator and animated emerged through *collaboration* across the divide of race; in their case, one could indeed argue that the boundaries of white and black were overrun, yet that from this breaching of difference arose not chaos but creation.

The movements and personality that O'Brien imparted to Kong (or that Kong expressed for O'Brien) lend credence to this theory. Erb, noting the boxerlike motions with which Kong regularly confronts his animal and human antagonists, proposes that these mannerisms, viewed in light of O'Brien's enthusiasm for boxing (and his own brief stint in the ring), may signal the animator's identification with "the ethnic and class-based impulses of the sport" and in particular with African American boxers such as Jack Johnson (*Tracking* 117). Though I find this reading suggestive, I would prefer to say that O'Brien's animation of Kong is distinguished more generally and powerfully by self-projection or introjection: both in the character's overall design—most notably, Kong's eschewing of knuckle walking in favor of an upright posture and gait—and in countless pieces of humanizing action—the wrestling moves he performs on the tyrannosaur, the hand-over-hand motion he employs to haul the vine holding Darrow and Driscoll, the careful step-and-pivot he uses to navigate over a fallen tree—Kong is a material embodiment of the animator's ghostly presence, substance to the man's shadow. O'Brien's second wife, Darlyne, spoke of this mating of man and monster: "I could see [O'Brien] in every one of [Kong's] gestures and movements" (qtd. in Jensen 81). And though on the one hand, the transformation of Kong into a *human* presence heightens the racial menace, suggesting that he is not simply a dumb brute, much less a brute object, but a calculating sexual predator, on the other hand, the transformation breaks down, from within, the very threat it broadcasts. If Kong is O'Brien—if the black beast is not only *created* by the white man but *is* the white man, the behind-the-scenes manipulator and his dark self two parts of the same whole—then implicitly, in Kong, lies the understanding that only through embrace of one's supposed Other, not through violence against him, can one's self be secured, or even saved.

I raise this possibility fully aware that the process I have described—that of a white man inhabiting a black body—might itself be read in terms of the dominant racism of 1930s American culture and cinema, inasmuch as it might be seen as an elaborate form of blackface minstrelsy, which some scholars have identified as one of the principal means by which white Americans forged a distinctive identity through "public performances of torture inflicted on the black body" (Gubar 78). In this light, the Irish American O'Brien's "blacking up" as, or in his case "aping," the African American might be considered no more than a cynical act of appropriation—an act, moreover, that connects *Kong* once more to the racist fantasies of *Birth*, with its blackfaced predators of white women. If one reads the O'Brien-Kong relationship in this way—and there is certainly precedent for doing so, with gestures such as Kong's ubiquitous eye-rolling being characteristic of minstrel-show mannerisms—then one would have to say that their relationship is characterized not by identification but by exploitation, or by exploitation *through* identification. As Michael Rogin describes it, "blackface, whatever desire lay buried in the form, assaulted the people through whose mouths it claimed to speak" (*Blackface* 49). Moreover, "It passed immigrants into Americans by differentiating them from the black Americans . . . who were not permitted to speak for themselves" (56).[25] Kong would in this respect be O'Brien's "puppet" in the truest sense: a figure created and controlled by the white man so as simultaneously to mask and to make his own identity.

Loving *King Kong* as I do, however, I do not accept this portrait in its entirety; or, at least, I believe that the alternative construction I offered of the O'Brien-Kong relationship, one based (to use Rogin's terms) in "desire" rather than "assault," is equally persuasive. Yet at the same time, I must insist that to credit the positive potential of O'Brien's performance is neither to eulogize the man as a heroic individual rising above the prejudices of his time nor, conversely, to mourn the tragedy of his maverick, egalitarian vision having been sullied by the racism of his cultural moment. Neither of these characterizations will bear much scrutiny, and both, finally, miss the point. One cannot separate O'Brien's Kong from the film *King Kong*; even if one could prove that O'Brien meant to contest the racial climate of his era, his industry, his craft—and there is insufficient evidence for such a case[26]—what he produced was inextricable from the racial contexts within which he worked. Thus the very heart of *Kong* harbors a paradox not unlike that which I have maintained is formative for fantasy film as a whole: the man who, perhaps, loved Kong to the point of entering into a glorious fusion of souls with him was also the man who, through that very process, introduced into American culture one of the most resonant and undying images of its hateful racial legacy. That was one beast even beauty could not kill.

2

THE PROMISE OF MIRACLES Technology and Class
Conflict in *The Wizard of Oz*

What devices does Hollywood use to persuade moviegoers that it is satisfying their desires, to convince them that they are getting what they
want?—Margaret Farrand Thorp, *America at the Movies* (1939)

*N*ineteen thirty-nine was the year of the New York World's Fair, in which
corporate America triumphantly unveiled its "World of Tomorrow," a fantasized
future of prosperity through technological (and commercial) advance. It was also
a year of continuing Depression in America, with millions at the mercy of assembly lines and breadlines. The year before, Orson Welles had convulsed the
nation (or at least New Jersey) by fusing two mechanical invaders of the American home, the radio and the Martians. Two years earlier, the Roosevelt administration had issued *Technological Trends and National Policy* (1937), a blueprint for
curing the nation's ills through the salve of technological savvy. While art critics
Sheldon and Martha Cheney's *Art and the Machine* (1936) enthused over contemporary art forms that reflected the "peculiar beauty" (xi) of "machine-age speed,
precision, and efficiency" (97), artist and filmmaker Charlie Chaplin's *Modern Times*
(1936) portrayed the machine age as a peculiarly ugly realm of manhandling feed-
ing contraptions, devouring gears, and Big Brother bosses. While mass-market
periodicals such as *Popular Mechanics* pitched the latest gadgets, gimmicks, and
gewgaws, sci-fi pulps such as *Amazing Stories* painted grim pictures of automatons,
computers, and doomsday devices run amok. And amidst the hoopla and hysteria, the obsession with technology as messiah or nemesis, an event took place that
seems at first glance far removed from the technological climate of the 1930s: a
children's story came to the screen in glorious Technicolor and went on to become one of the best-known and best-loved movies of all time.

And yet, in one specialized but significant sense, Metro-Goldwyn-Mayer's *The Wizard of Oz* (1939) is quite overtly symptomatic of its era's technological utopianism, its faith in machine technology to lift the nation from the dire realities of the Depression to fantastic realms of wonder and plenty: from its deployment of the pricey and cumbersome Technicolor process to its spectacular cyclone effects, *Oz* represents a triumph of the technological, a high point in the history of the Hollywood cinema as (dream) machine.[1] Contemporary reviews, though stressing the film's appeal as otherworldly fantasy, were at the same time awed by its command of the technologies of this world: critics praised its "technical wizardry," lauded it as "a towering achievement in the technical magic of motion pictures," and pronounced it "one of the greatest technical feats the screen has to its credit" (qtd. in Fricke, Scarfone, and Stillman 173, 174, 183).[2] Like the Wizard of Menlo Park, widely regarded in *Oz*'s day as the originator of the cinematic apparatus and industry, the behind-the-scenes wizards of *Oz* were hailed as pioneers in harnessing technology for the welfare of the masses.

Yet at the same time, if *Oz* projects an image of technological wizardry, the images it projects recall the other strand of its era's technological thought: a cautionary or even apocalyptic tradition that charged machine technology with spawning isolation, dislocation, and dehumanization, and that promoted the core values of heart and home over the perilous phantasm of technological advance. In this chapter, I will argue that it is by placing *Oz* within the context of Depression-era debates over technology that one can begin to unravel the film's role in the processes of social alienation I have identified as central to fantasy film. Specifically, such a reading will reveal *Oz*'s part in defending structures of economic privilege against the putatively malcontent masses. To view *Oz* in these terms, I recognize, might threaten to overlook its genial tone and innocent posture; to do so also rejects the critical tendency toward removing the film from its historical context, whether by emphasizing its "archetypal" qualities or by suggesting that it offered "escape" from the pressing realities of its time.[3] I wish, however, to follow another road to *Oz*, to reconnect its historical-material relationship to technology with its representation of technology and in so doing to illustrate that even this seemingly most escapist of fantasy films is historically resonant and, more particularly, relevant to the processes of alienation I am tracing.[4]

To be sure, the shift from *King Kong* to *Oz* marks a corresponding shift from the raw, graphic force of an alienating racial ideology to the subtle, delicate workings of an alienating economic one: there are, to put it simply, no giant gorillas in *Oz*. There are, nevertheless, monsters—and not merely the Witch and her Kong-like host of winged monkeys. Rather, *Oz* embodies Depression-era anxieties concerning the legions of the poor—the vagrants, idlers, and thugs (as they appeared to those in power) who, time and again during the 1930s, besieged the symbolic and literal centers of technological society. In 1932, tens of thousands of World War I veterans—a force fantasized as "undesirables—thieves, plug-uglies, degenerates," a "criminal fringe" of "invaders" (qtd. in Cowley 89)—camped out in the nation's capital to demand immediate payment of their war-time bonuses, only to be met by government tear gas and bayonets. The next year, the cross-country Hunger March, composed of thousands of poor and rural folk, once again descended on Washington, incarnating for some nervous leaders "the nightmare that hungry mobs would take over the streets . . . loot the downtown stores and seize the White House" (Cowley 129).[5] In stark contrast to *Kong*, these monstrous outsiders do not take physical form in *Oz*; the film keeps them, as it were, down on the farm. Yet for all that, I will argue that *Oz* participates in the processes of alienation I have begun to reconstruct for the fantasy film genre; I will suggest, indeed, that in its gentle, winning way *Oz* may ultimately be a more powerful vehicle of alienation than *Kong*. In his study of machine-age sci-fi movies, J. P. Telotte argues that since film, by definition, relies on advanced technology, the cinema is "more fundamentally invested in the technological, more implicated in its cultural construction, than [is] literature; it has more at stake" (*Distant* 18). What is at stake in the technological discourse of *Oz*, I wish to argue, is not merely technology's role in motion pictures; more significantly, it is the fact that technological society sanctions the monopolization of wealth by the few and the alienation from wealth of the many. That this fact gives birth to monsters, the history of fantasy film amply illustrates: a precursor of the increasingly sophisticated, technologically oriented fantasy films of our day, *Oz* "gives the people what they want" in terms of technological spectacle and splendor, while at the same time defining "the people" as monstrous threats to the very technologies that enable the cinema to conjure utopian fantasy into fulfillment.

The Machine Stops: The American Depression

Technological utopianism and dystopianism, as scholars such as Leo Marx have demonstrated, are deeply rooted in American culture.[6] In respect to the 1930s, however, it is impossible to overstate the pervasiveness and urgency of techno-logical thought: America of the 1930s was not only suffused with machinery but steeped in a mechanistic worldview, predisposed to visualize society itself as both product of and analogue to the machine. "We are all machinists today," industrial designer Walter Dorwin Teague asserted at decade's close, "the geometry of the machines themselves has gotten into our minds and into our eyes and affected all our preferences and tastes" (90). Teague's affectionate summary is retrospective; it looks fondly back at a decade in which his knack for machine-age product design was in high demand. But if the logic and lines of the machine had indeed radically transfigured society, then that logic also applied prospectively, delineating and delimiting blueprints for social reform. Just as the onslaught of the Depression seemed to signify that "the machine as a whole" had "overspeeded, stripped its gears, and c[o]me to a standstill" (Mumford 283), so did technological discourse provide Depression-era Americans a way both of comprehending their plight and of envisioning possibilities for recovery.

For simplicity's sake, one can identify three strands of 1930s technological discourse: the strictly utopian, the strictly dystopian, and a middle ground most identified with, though by no means limited to, the Roosevelt administration's ideal of technological engineering. The strictly utopian view held that technology itself was capable of addressing the temporary maladjustment signaled by the Depression; that it was due to a lack of individual preparedness that so many had suffered from this setback; and that the only power needed to steer the machine back on course was that which had mustered the forces of machine technology to begin with: corporate capitalism. "There is no stopping it," Henry Ford wrote in an essay, "Machines as Ministers to Man," printed in the 1939 World's Fair section of the *New York Times*. "It is instinct in man's nature. Despite every restriction that can be placed on it by so-called 'reformers' the quest will continue—invention will go forward" (70).[7] Ford's scoffing remark that "there are still in this world men who actually believe that machinery is a menace and a curse" (10) was, moreover, consistent with the theme of the fair itself, which forecast, in the words of its science director, Gerald Wendt, a "world of tomorrow in which science will advance as now but in which the citizens of a democracy . . . will realize that change is inevitable, that the conditions of life can be almost indefinitely improved . . . and that the attitude of science expresses the highest reaches of the human spirit" (307). A particularly spectacular manifestation of 1930s technological utopianism, the fair offered sunny visions of a mechanized world both on a grand scale and of a more homely sort. Most impressive were the massive Trylon and Perisphere, the looming pyramidal tower and glistening sphere at the fairground's center, within the latter of which was housed the General Motors "Futurama," a seated tour of an enormous model cityscape. At the same time, unremarkable because so pervasive were the inescapable, streamlined products—irons, televisions, blenders—offered for perusal and preorder. What linked the disparate displays was an unrestrained optimism about technological progress: at the dawn of the Depression's second decade, the World's Fair announced that paradise was not only close by but ready at hand, tangibly present in the form of machine-made commodities, machine-run homes, farms, and cities, and machine-minded citizens.[8] One visitor, though awed by the display of technological grandeur, found in this vision of a future fabricated by men like Ford a cause for alarm:

> The co-operative movement in this country is now twenty years old and is making the most rapid growth it has ever experienced. Will that pattern of life be represented at the Fair only as it looks to some exhibitor who opposes it? Who will speak for the consumer at the Fair? Who will speak for labor, for the farmers . . . ? Will organized business do all the interpreting of this future . . . ? Amid the million watt lights . . . and the cascades of sound and color with which this greatest of World's Fairs will dazzle the country, it is not too much to hope that the average man's interest in the future will be remembered. (Harding 137)

An example of the tendency of 1930s thinkers to conceptualize the technological fantasia of the World's Fair in terms befitting the motion picture—perhaps an unsurprising tendency, considering that film was one of the technologies showcased there[9]—this skeptical appraisal expresses a concern that, like the Great Oz, the masterminds who orchestrated the glitz and worked the levers might be seeking to bewitch the audience into mute submission. The fair, this writer sensed, did not simply pitch technological progress; at the same time, it staged a spectacle in which the "menace and curse" of the people whom technological society had left behind might be quelled.

The reference to the cooperative movement, moreover, sounds a note that would be echoed by many Depression-era social critics—no less technological utopians than the vendors at the fair, but considerably less sanguine about technology's ability to run the show on its own. To those who championed this middle-ground position, technology could honor its utopian pledge only when brought under what economist Stuart Chase termed the "directing intelligence" of its operators (qtd. in Pells 28). Elaborating on this point in the campaign literature for his abortive presidential bid in 1933, Upton Sinclair reasoned, "Here we have this enormous machine, the most perfect ever constructed in the history of our planet. . . . Our problem is to take all this productive machinery and make it into one machine: to organize it and systematize its processes, making one process with one purpose" (55). Though Sinclair went down to third-party defeat, the alarm his platform set off in the minds of Ford and company was anything but allayed: following Roosevelt's election to a second term, the National Resources Committee's Subcommittee on Technology issued the report *Technological Trends and National Policy* (1937), which recommended the formation of "a permanent over-all planning board" to encourage, chart, predict, and manage the interface of technology and social welfare (x).[10]

A more fantastic plan for a coordinated technological utopia was the "short-lived but momentous affair known as Technocracy" ([J. Carter] 56). A political movement that recommended handing over social control to the technicians—and, indeed, calculating social productivity and prosperity in terms of *ergs*, or units of energy expended—Technocracy promised to bring about an era of prosperity for all. "Every man in a technocracy," wrote party booster Harold Loeb, would "have his material wants generously satisfied," while "no man would be given extraordinary power because he had the luck or the shrewdness to obtain paper possession of some energy source provided by nature" (54).[11] Even at the World's Fair, a planned technological society was conjured by one of the grandfathers of science fiction, H. G. Wells, who wrote the lead article for the *Times* preview: "Steadily in the near Tomorrow," Wells intoned, "a collective human intelligence will be appearing and organizing itself in a collective human will" (61). The rationalist technological utopia divined by these and other prophets differed substantially from its corporate counterpart: collectivist and socialist in tenor rather than individualist and capitalist, the reformist school understood machines themselves not as an unrelieved benefit but as essentially neutral, potential blights or boons, depending on the conscious choices and priorities of their handlers. If, then, the fair sought to still the demons technological inequality had bred, the cooperative movement kept before the public (and corporate) eye the vision of technology as contested goods, a common birthright to be wrested from the hands of those who had monopolized its treasures.

For a third school of 1930s technological thought, however, the distinction between corporate and collective control was ultimately nugatory. In the words of the southern authors of *I'll Take My Stand* (1930), both the puffers and the planners were mere "apologists" for technology, proposing remedies that were "always homeopathic. They expect the evils to disappear when we have bigger and better machines, and more of them" (Twelve Southerners xiii). For this third, dystopian set, technology was not only the source of the problem in an immediate, material sense—for the mechanization of urban and rural life, these critics charged, had rendered much human labor expendable—but in the larger, almost impalpable sense that machinery had so infected the minds of creators and consumers alike that it had taken on a life of its own. "The machine," Lewis Mumford wrote, "has undergone a perversion: instead of being utilized as an instrument of life, it has tended to become an absolute. . . . The machine has been valued because—it increased the employment of machines" (281).[12] Jeremiads such as this were literalized in the pulp science fiction of the day, as in Henry

Hasse's 1936 tale of a future in which humanity has succumbed to the machine's soulless protocols:

> As far as I could see in every direction were huge, grotesque metal structures and strange mechanical contrivances. . . . [N]owhere was there the slightest evidence of any human occupancy, no controlling force, no intelligence, nothing save the machines. . . . Yet . . . there was no confusion at all as it had seemed at first glance, but rather was there a simple, efficient, systematic order of things. . . .
>   Endless chains of machines delved deep into the earth, to emerge with loads of ore which they deposited, to descend again.
>   Huge hauling machines came and transported the ore to roaring mills.
>   Inside the mills machines melted the ore, rolled and cut and fashioned the steel.
>   Other machines builded and assembled and adjusted intricate parts, and when the long process was completed the result was—more machines! (760–61)[13]

To dystopian thinkers like Hasse, it was futile to imagine that state or corporate regulation could avert technological Armageddon—for at a basic level, humans had become adjuncts to their machines. Rather, radical dystopianists argued, it was necessary to eliminate contemporary technology in its entirety and hence return to a pastoral estate before the values of home, family, and selfhood had been polluted by the machine. "A comfortable home in which to labor and to play," as Ralph Borsodi, a leader of the back-to-the-land movement of the 1930s, described this bucolic ideal, "with trees and grass and flowers and skies and stars; a small garden; a few fruit trees; some fowls, some kine, some bees . . . and I, at least, have time for love, for children, for a few friends, and for the work I like to do. More the world can give to no man, and more no man can give the world" (462).

It is with this third school that *The Wizard of Oz* identifies itself: Dorothy's odyssey from the seeming wasteland of her Dust Bowl farm to the seeming wonderland of Oz, and then back, duplicates the dystopianists' counsel of flight from the glittering illusion of the technological megalopolis to the safety and stability of the preindustrial homestead. Yet it is central to an understanding of *Oz* as dominant social fantasy to note that it employs dystopian discourse not to assail the most obvious adversary—the laissez-faire, technophilic buoyancy of Ford and his ilk—but to burlesque the collectivist technological planning advocated by such bodies as the architects of the New Deal. To appreciate the significance of this move, one must recall that however *Oz* may rail against technology in its narrative operations, the narrative exists by virtue of a medium that thoroughly exalts technology in its ravishing, breathtaking visions: one cannot divorce the film's dystopian fantasy from its utopian realization. The wizardry of *Oz* is thus akin to that of the World's Fair: in both cases, the energy expended to keep the monsters of the social imaginary in check produces the shimmering spectacle of the whole. If, then, the fantasized antagonists of Depression-era economic discourse—the angry mobs lusting for their share—do not appear in the film, the film nonetheless supports the dominant social ideologies of its time, upholding discourses of economic alienation through the lens of the technological.

Monsters, Magicians, and Machines

What *Oz* offers in the opening Kansas sequence is, first, a penetrating image of a world impoverished beyond recall; and second, a correspondingly implicit argument to embrace the technological utopia the Land of Oz will turn out to be. Yet this argument never materializes; rather, the film will insist that, wonders notwithstanding, Oz is unattainable and undesirable as a reality. How the film endeavors to steer audience identification away from Oz and back to Kansas is at once remarkably involved and stunningly simple, hinging on a fairy-tale standard in which technology becomes the wicked stepmother, the impediment to the protagonist's self-realization. Unraveling this simple opposition, accordingly, will disclose the film's immense investment of labor in determining Dorothy's choice and thereby containing the threat of lower-class revolution that her "Ozdyssey" implies.

Consider at first, then, the ways in which the film suggests the failure of the technological in Kansas. Dorothy's homeland hovers somewhere between L. Frank Baum's turn-of-the-century Kansas and the midwestern Dust Bowl of the 1930s. Though the failing farm, cropless fields, and swirling clouds of dust that ride the cyclone's trail were clearly recognizable to contemporary audiences from such photojournalistic essays as Dorothea Lange and Paul Taylor's stark portraits of Dust Bowl poverty, *An American Exodus* (1939)—and though Aunt Em's curt reminder to Hunk, Zeke, and Hickory that "three shiftless farmhands" may find themselves "out of a job before they know it" reinforces the visual references to the Depression—the only functional technologies are distinctly nineteenth century: telegraph wires, horse-drawn wagons, kerosene lamps. Lacking such nearly universal symbols of the 1930s as motor vehicles, telephones, and radios, the Gale farm is, at the least, a far cry from utopian constructs such as the Electrified Farm exhibit of the 1939 World's Fair, itself forecast in the following address from 1930:

> The home on the farm will have all modern comforts and conveniences. . . . Television will soon project Grand Opera and other

forms of entertainment on a screen in the farmer's living-room. The automobile has already eliminated distances and added much to the social and community life. All these are products of the engineer's mind and the next few years will see even greater wonders. Hard labor and drudgery will be entirely eliminated. (Campbell 174).

The Gale homestead, it seems, remains untouched by the technological forces transforming the nation—forces, notably, symbolized in this passage by the presence of the "screen" in the bosom of the family home.

Such insularity is, however, only apparent; even in Dorothy's technological backwater, the machine remains insistently in view. For instance, as the camera follows Dorothy in her dash onto the Gale property, it fleetingly picks up an automobile tire dangling from a tree centered in the farmyard: the sine qua non of Ford's machine age so needless here that it can serve only as a child's toy. Moreover, with the exception of Professor Marvel, the principal Kansas characters are all introduced through some relationship to the technological. For Dorothy's immediate circle, however, that relationship is limited in range from sour—as it is for the farmhands, whose struggles to repair a wagon result in a crushed finger for one and a scolding from Aunt Em for "tinkering with that contraption"—to despairing, as it is for Aunt Em and Uncle Henry, who distractedly and distressedly flutter over an "old incubator" that has "gone bad." Though the couple could easily be describing themselves—for they have, in Dorothy's eyes, "gone bad" as nurturers of her and Toto—the line also implies that technology, for all its promises, has proved inadequate as a giver of life. Along these lines, it is noteworthy that Dorothy perches atop a rusted, tilting reaper, a grim enough symbol of technology gone bad, as she sings her signature utopian song, "Over the Rainbow." In Kansas, the only piece of machinery that works, a bicycle, is owned and operated by Miss Gulch, whose rigid posture, robotic features, starched uniform, helmet-shaped hat, and pistonlike pedaling transform her into an extension of the machine. Miss Gulch's arrival thus registers not merely the intrusion of the state into the privacy of the family haven but, more particularly, the encroachment of technological power on a failed pastoral bereft of, and at the mercy of, the machine.

Yet however the Kansas frame may suggest a land that has declared a moratorium on technological progress, no sooner does Dorothy enter Oz than the film musters its energies to send her back. Indeed, a principal strategy by which Oz achieves this feat is its insistence that there simply is no alternative to the place Dorothy has just left. For one thing, by positioning Dorothy's journey as a dream—one of its few systemic liberties with Baum's book—the film denies the very possibility of escape for which it is often lauded. At the same time, the film's visual language repeatedly reinforces that Oz is but a shadow-Kansas, not an alternative but a mirror image. The most-often cited parallel lies in the doubling of roles: the farmhands as the Scarecrow, Tin Man, and Lion; Miss Gulch as the Wicked Witch, whose theme music carries over from Kansas as well; Professor Marvel as the Wizard, who is, of course, an "old Kansas man" himself. Implied character parallels are also evident. Both Aunt Em and Glinda, for example, are women who, though apparently not biological mothers, act as protectors of the children entrusted to their care; thus it is telling that it is Glinda who teaches Dorothy how to return to the woman whose seeming indifference first kindled her desire to flee. Then, too, numerous shots from the Kansas sequence are duplicated in Oz. Most overtly, the first shot in the film after the credits and dedication, a high-angle shot of a road stretching to the horizon, lined with a fence and punctuated by a single scraggly tree, into which Dorothy rushes from below screen, reappears numerous times in Oz: once when Dorothy turns to wave good-bye to the Munchkins; once at the end of each segment in which she gains a new traveling companion; once before she and her friends enter the poppy field en route to the Emerald City; and once after they exit.

Less ideologically charged than this Depression-era symbol of ambiguous escape (an analogous shot appears at the end of Chaplin's *Modern Times*), countless seemingly casual correspondences between Kansas and Oz footage help to cement the two locales. For instance, the shot of Dorothy wiping tears from the Lion's eyes on their first encounter precisely inverts the shot of Dorothy poking fun at Zeke after her tumble into the pigsty; in the Oz shot, Jack Haley, Ray Bolger, Judy Garland, and Bert Lahr line up screen left to right, while in Kansas the four pose, in that order, screen right to left.[14] Even the colors of Kansas, or lack thereof, are revived in the Land of Oz; so accustomed are viewers to recalling the Oz segments as vibrant Technicolor murals that one forgets that only one sequence, the scene of revelry in Munchkinland, departs markedly from the monochromatic scheme introduced in Kansas. In the Emerald City, of course, the dominant color is green; in the Witch's forest and castle it is gray-blue; in the poppy field it is pink; and so on. Moreover, the fact that the color scheme becomes increasingly monotonous as Dorothy's sojourn progresses, with Munchkinland the apparent chromatic antithesis to Kansas and the Witch's castle nearly duplicating Kansas in lifelessness, lowering skies, and dark-hued gloom, visually draws the viewer back to the starting point.[15] Nor is Munchkinland so foreign as it initially appears: a place of thatched huts, horse-drawn carriages, simple folk, and dizzying cornfields, it is sufficiently reminiscent of Kansas before things "went bad" to lend humor to Dorothy's legendary line, "Toto, I've a feeling we're not in Kansas anymore." And lest one doubt that Dorothy *is* in Kansas even here, the moment she begins to skip down the Yellow Brick Road is marked by the sight of her humpbacked, drab-hued house, yet another visual reminder that escape is never truly possible, that Kansas is never far away.

If, however, the Land of Oz is not an achieved fact, it is an apparent future: a potential Kansas revamped by the powers of machine technology. The audacious and still-startling jump to Technicolor that initiates the Munchkinland sequence announces the relationship Oz bears toward Kansas to be a prospective or projected one; indeed, for audiences unused to color films, the marketing of color itself as a futuristic feat of technical skill signals the utopian nature of the Oz sequences. As *Oz* was finalizing production design in 1938, an interoffice memo advised:

> The whole background should be more modernized than it is in the book. . . . When L. Frank Baum wrote this story . . . there were no autos, no radios, no airplanes and I do believe if he had written it today he would have in some manner made it a little more acceptable to the audience on a basis of using some of the modern contrivances that we use today. I think our *Wizard of Oz* background should be a Fairy-land of 1938 and not of 1900. (qtd. in Scarfone and Stillman 102)

Notable for its reminder of how readily Depression-era thought identified *modern* with *technological*, this quote might nonetheless seem puzzling when placed beside the finished film; for no actual autos, radios, or airplanes appear in the Land of Oz. The absence of 1930s contrivances, however, turns out to be only apparent; not only the grand design of Oz's realm but any number of individual plot elements draw immediate parallels to contemporary technologies.

The most obvious representative of this technological presence is the Tin Man, who incarnates the decade's fascination with robots. That Dorothy reacts with considerably greater amazement to "a man made out of tin" than to a talking Scarecrow or bipedal Lion—and this before she discovers the Tin Man to be animate—acknowledges the contemporary sense of manufactured beings as marvelous yet not utterly fantastic. The Tin Man's singular nature is enhanced by his dance sequence; with the Scarecrow's extended number scrapped in the editing phase, the Tin Man is the only character who retains a dance independent of his theme song, a fact that, coupled with cutaways to a beguiled Dorothy and Scarecrow during his dance, calls attention to the miracle of metal moving like a man. But the Tin Man is as much a vehicle for dystopian arguments as for the reverse. His tendency to rust, for instance, is reiterated so frequently as to form a structural motif: not only does the audience witness him rusting in the poppy field but he is reminded twice not to cry for fear of the same fate. It may be needless to remark, too, that the Tin Man's missing heart invokes a pivotal dystopian accusation, that of the machine's lack of, and assault on, emotion. But it should be noted that the film underscores this lack by having Dorothy and the Scarecrow echo, quite needlessly and in exaggerated disbelief, the Tin Man's announcement that he has "no heart." (Again, one might contrast this with Dorothy's equanimity in the presence of a literate lion.) And it is further intriguing that though the Tin Man has soul enough to feel his lack, the film hedges in granting him full humanity: as his song phrases it, he's "presumin'" that he could be "kinda" human if he only had a heart.

The Tin Man's ambivalent commentary on technology is, however, more than countered by two figures, the Wicked Witch and the Wizard, who point up the film's technological dystopianism. The Witch has so regularly been pictured as a classic Halloween horror—perhaps because the film has so fixed this figure in viewers' minds—that the topical and narrowly technological aspects of her character have been overlooked. Yet these aspects, in keeping with the film's generally concrete signifying practices, are manifest enough. Along with her Stygian comings and goings, which connect her to the industrial heritage and infrastructure of the machine age—the factory and, in particular, the steel mill—the Witch wields powers that do not rely, like those of the "good" witch, Glinda, on the traditional magic wand but on an array of technological intermediaries. Her crystal ball, for example, makes an immediate contemporary reference to television (the original models of which had circular screens); not only did many Americans' first exposure to television occur at the RCA exhibit at the 1939 World's Fair but commercial TV broadcasts began on the fair's opening day. The Witch's skywriting broomstick, meanwhile, could not but recall the airplane, its association with far-deadlier feats than skywriting accentuated by her exploding hourglass, strongly evocative of a hand grenade. Her ruby slippers, too, are wired with electricity—hardly a revolutionary technology for most Americans in 1939, but as the absence of electric power on the Gale farm suggests, still not a reliable source of energy for rural areas. None of these technologies—indeed, no technology—was viewed without ambivalence in the Depression; yet in the film, all of these technologies inherit the overwhelmingly negative cast of the Witch herself. Thus it is telling that in the end, the Witch succumbs not to the equally ambivalent technologies wielded in the haunted forest by Dorothy's companions—the Tin Man's giant factory wrench, the Lion's poison-spray fumigator, and the Scarecrow's gun—but to two vestiges of the preindustrial era, both strongly identified with a romanticized pastoral state: her plot is spoiled by the family dog, her fire quenched and her life taken by cleansing water.

Yet if the Witch is overtly a technological terror, the mysterious power to whom Dorothy appeals turns out to be yet another technological force, and as such, a potentially dangerous and ultimately disappointing ally: the Wizard. That the Wizard is conceptualized in terms more fitting the technician than the magician is implicit in Dorothy's pronouncement that he will "fix everything"; that technology can indeed fix everything appears confirmed in the first, imposing prospect of the house that Oz built. The grand edifice that is the Emerald City, its gleaming, leaf-green, curvilinear towers framed by trees and bordering an immense meadow when first beheld, typifies what Howard Segal views as the technological utopianists' dream of fusing the best of pastoral and urban estates: "The utopians would resolve the tension [between country and city] by the modernization rather than the abandonment of the garden, by transporting it out of the wilderness and relocating it in the city—a city itself to be transformed from a lethal chaos into a healthy order" (*Technological Utopianism* 24). Indeed, not content to dream of such Edens, the Depression set about building them: the planned communities, such as the Greenbelt Towns, subsidized by the Roosevelt administration; the World's Fair pavilions based on the schematics of Walter Dorwin Teague and Norman Bel Geddes; the yet more ideal Radiant Cities illustrated by visionary designer Le Corbusier. One such urban utopia appeared in *Amazing Stories* as "a city of curves and streamlines, of sweep and rounded beauty," a "mecca of peace, quiet, and contentment, and a wonder-house of science and industry and mechanical coordination" (qtd. in Meikle 186).[16] Obviously analogous to these utopian communities, the Emerald City, with its wide, clean, lustrous marble streets, parklike terraces, star-shaped design elements of burnished steel and glass, and joyful populace, appears to fulfill the dream of technology not only enhancing life but taking on its qualities: in color, form, and integration, Oz's kingdom is more organism than mechanism.

Then, too, if the Emerald City bears a resemblance to a factory,[17] as in the scene in which Dorothy and her friends are groomed, assembly-line fashion, for their audience with the Wizard, it is a factory lacking in the disorder, drudgery, and despair of the day. There is no unemployment, and neither is there any fear of the foreman's prying eyes, for as in the Technocrats' planned communities, "all [workers] are bound together by belonging to the same enormous, nationwide industrial undertaking" (Loeb 142). The only machines visible, such as the noiseless, spotless wheel that polishes the Tin Man, are designed solely for comfort and cosmetics. The lyrics to "The Merry Old Land of Oz," moreover, announce that labor has been transformed into play: "We get up at twelve and go to work at one; / Take an hour for lunch and then at two we're done. / Jolly good fun!" Segal's summary of 1930s technological utopias neatly captures the film's fantasy: "Despite its basis in modern technology, technological utopia was not to be a mass of sooting smokestacks, clanging machines, and teeming streets. The dirt, noise, and chaos that invariably accompanied industrialization in the real world were to give way in the future to perfect cleanliness, efficiency, quiet, and harmony" (*Technological Utopianism* 123). Rendering literal the mechanical metaphors so widespread in 1930s America, the Emerald Society runs like a well-oiled (though oil-less) machine.

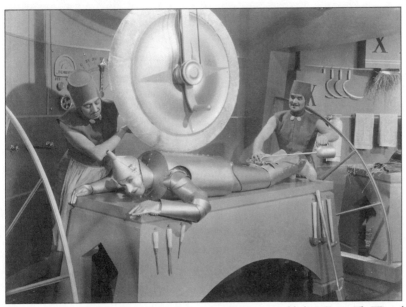

The Tin Man (Jack Haley) goes through the Emerald City assembly line. From *The Wizard of Oz* (MGM, 1939). Courtesy of Photofest.

It might appear odd, then, that in a variety of ways, *Oz* draws correspondences between the apparently benign technological force represented by the Wizard and the irremediably malevolent one represented by the Witch. There are, for instance, a number of visual parallels between the two: the Witch's and Wizard's similarly green faces (a face that Oz, of course, wears only in his masquerade as technological power);[18] the crystal balls to either side of Oz's throne, which remind the viewer not only of his Kansas persona but of his supposed adversary; the fire jets and orange smoke that accompany the arrival of each. Then, too, the film's editing twice links the Witch and the Wizard: once when the Witch heads for the Emerald City, at which point a dissolve superimposes the turrets of her castle over the spires of Oz's palace; and once after the Witch's death, when another dissolve to the Wizard's throne room briefly suggests that it is his fire blooming from the singed broomstick Dorothy holds. In particular, this tendency of the film to equate both the Witch and the Wizard with fire, and through fire with each other—a tendency that extends even to the identical sound effect backing their flames—suggests a more significant affinity, a more fundamental sense in which both technological powers are linked and both limned as potentially sinister.

For as *Oz* constructs it, the promise of technological utopia represented by the Emerald City portends precisely what dystopianists forewarned: the subordination of personal autonomy to the heartless directives of the machine. Where middle-ground utopianists idealized the collective as the apex of human evolution, envisioning the city of the future as "an efficient and beautiful center for the great bureaucracies whose total administration of society would bring . . . order and harmony" (Fishman 164), dystopianists saw in such institutions a totalitarian technology reducing all "to mere cogs in a gigantic industrial machine" (Borsodi 14). Thus, if the Emerald citizens' being all alike—green-clad, chipper, and incapable of initiative—seems an innocent enough exaggeration of the Technocrats' dictum that "the residents of each technological community would tend to be more homogeneous" than the norm (Loeb 135), the film's other example of collectivism—the Witch's similarly identical (and enslaved) monkeys and guards—casts the Emerald City in a considerably less festive light. The folk of Oz, it seems, are "merry" *because* mindless; they form a society in which all act "in response to the will of a corporate mind as fingers move and write at the direction of the brain" (Segal, *Technological Utopianism* 128). This totalitarian, technophobic nightmare was staged by Hasse in a scene anticipating Oz's throne room, the abode of the machine as God:

> There in the center of the single spacious room was the Machine of all Machines: the Cause of it All; the Central Force, the Ruler, the Controlling Power. . . . It was roughly circular, large and ponderous. It was bewilderingly complicated, a maze of gears, wheels, switchboards, lights, levers, buttons, tubing, and intricacies beyond my comprehension. . . . The result was a throbbing, rhythmic, purposeful unit. I could imagine invisible waves going out in every direction. . . .
>   It was the Brain. (764)

Oz, of course, is exposed as considerably less than *deus*, or even *machina*: the imposing throne-room persona gives way to the ineptitude of third-rate huckster, a man capable of mounting a spectacular show when no more is called for than lights and whistles, but incapable of harnessing the simplest technology for practical, desirable ends. Thus his "hazardous and technically unexplainable voyage into the upper stratosphere" degenerates into the image of the bumbling showman sailing off without his passenger, tangled in the ropes of his balloon and howling, "I can't come back! I don't know how it works!"

In its unveiling of the sham Wizard, the film thus admonishes not only the hollowness of technological society but, just as important, the willful blindness of those who worship it: most evidently the Emerald citizens, who are all too eager to relinquish personal responsibility to an invisible, mysterious machine, but Dorothy as well, who, Glinda chides, "always had the power" to direct her fate but needed to learn her lesson before she believed it. "What have you learned, Dorothy?" the Tin Man asks, his asking a means of emphasizing not only the film's moral precept but its disciplinary imperatives. Dorothy's famous answer— "If I ever go looking for my heart's desire again, I won't look any further than my own backyard, because if it isn't there, I never really lost it to begin with"— need not be dwelt on just yet; what must be explored first is how the film's ideological operations construct that inevitable (if illogical) answer in the service of technological dominance and alienation.

In exploring this issue, it would, of course, be reckless to ignore the ways in which *Oz* differs from kindred fantasies of the 1930s; notably lacking in the urgency and irony that animate most technological dystopias, *Oz* presents itself as no more than a moving picture-book or, at most, a tongue-in-cheek satire of contemporary trends. Yet the film's antitechnological discourse helps one to see the satire, however frothy, as considerably more complex and politically grounded than it is normally credited as being. The film's material relationship to the technological society it fantasizes, that is, proves central in identifying its ideological relationship to the technological society of which it was a part. And in this respect, to excuse *Oz*'s ideology on the grounds that the film is an innocent fantasy is to accept precisely the means by which that ideology seeks to operate unremarked and unchallenged.

One way to explore *Oz*'s cultural work—the most readily apparent way and one that will open up other, yet more productive avenues—is to locate its antitechnological discourse within the narrow context of 1930s Hollywood's struggles for control of its own technological future. "The existence of cinema," as Steve Neale writes and as *Oz* amply illustrates, "is premised upon the existence of certain technologies" (*Cinema* 1); the film industry is not simply reliant on but inseparable from technological knowledge, structures, and processes that seemed to audiences in 1939, and continue to seem to audiences today, representative of a utopian covenant. And it was during the 1930s that Hollywood's version of technological utopia came under assault by another version: the New Deal government's ideal of technological planning, which it attempted to impose on the film industry, as on other industries, through a battery of legal challenges and executive actions. In 1935, for example, the Wagner Act made possible the union-ization of Hollywood's technical personnel, a revolution the major studios fiercely but unsuccessfully resisted.[19] The following year, the Roosevelt administration undertook to requite the corporate interests that had discovered the polemical uses of film; the 1936 "message" film *The Plow That Broke the Plains*, which fin-gered unregulated corporate technology for despoiling the nation's heartland, can usefully be placed beside *Oz*, with its final image of Kansas as a preindustrial Arcadia.[20] In 1937, meanwhile, though Roosevelt's Subcommittee on Technol-ogy did not specifically name Hollywood as being among those industries that were overripe for federal supervision, the following passage from the subcom-mittee's report could not have been more pointed: "When to the spoken word is added the living image, the effect is to magnify the potential dangers of a ma-chine which can subtly instill ideas, strong beliefs, profound disgusts, and affec-tions. There is danger from propaganda entering the schools, and perhaps much greater danger from the propaganda entering the home" (Gilfillan 32–33). And finally, in 1938, capping an investigation into Hollywood's protectionist distri-bution system—the year of *Oz*'s release, 99 percent of the movies shown in MGM-owned theaters had been produced by the five major studios (MGM, RKO, Paramount, 20th Century Fox, and Warner Brothers), effectively barring independent production companies from exhibiting their films[21]—the Justice Department filed an antitrust suit against the majors.[22] Hollywood, in short, was engaged throughout the 1930s in defining and defending its vital interests in technology against federal legislation, litigation, and competition. Thus one way to view the dystopianism of *Oz* is to attribute it to the film industry's hostility not toward technology as such but toward planned applications of technology, toward the "governmental machinery" of the New Deal (American Liberty League 56), "the mechanics of collectivism" (Mills 57), and the Brain Trust "wizards" (Dennis 10) whose supposed goal was an "all-embracing Totalitarian State in which the citizen is but a robot" (Desvernine 2), all expressions that conserva-tive critics used to characterize and caricature the Roosevelt administration.

Such a reading can lead even more deeply into the film's ideological work, beginning with the observation that the vision of centralized technocracy against which *Oz* testifies, however it might have applied to the New Dealers' projected society, applied flawlessly to 1930s Hollywood, which Charles and Mary Beard described in 1939 as a system of "huge financial corporations with expensive mechanical devices at their command" (619). Indeed, the Emerald City itself might be considered a work of sardonic self-reflection: with its perpetual sun-shine, groves of manicured fruit trees, lovingly ersatz sets, costumed extras roam-ing the streets, and great and powerful movie moguls hidden behind the scenes, giving the people what they want (or telling the people that what they want they already have), the Emerald City tableau closely plays off (industry-orchestrated) images of Tinseltown such as those to which audiences were exposed in prefeature shorts. More generally, the Land of Oz is marked by strongly cinematic valences, what Helen Kim terms its "artificial, mediated, or constructed" nature, as opposed to the "natural" and "unmediated" realm of Kansas (221). Consider, in this light, the multitude of ways in which Munchkinland announces its artifice: the choreographed movements of the characters, which reach their most elaborate realizations in the ensemble musical numbers but which are evident even in minor details, such as Dorothy's slow, carefully plotted retreat from Glinda's bubble; the active camera, which cranes high over the village, swoops low to exaggerate the Munchkins' tininess, tracks in and out during dance numbers, and snakes through the streets to follow the crowds, thus distinguishing itself *as* a camera rather than the neutral or even invisible recording device that the stationary medium-to-long shots in Kansas suggest; the soft-focus lenses used in close-ups of Glinda, which audiences of the 1930s knew to expect of glamorous stars like Billie Burke; the transformation of natural objects, such as the clam shell that doubles as a carriage or the flowers that sprout from Munchkin clothing, into highly designed decorative motifs; the Munchkins' abnormally high-pitched voices, an obvious recording effect. In a broad sense, then, the land of Oz proclaims itself as filmworld, avatar of the cinema's technological operations.

More pointedly, this technological presence is announced in those elements of the film that most powerfully manifest the utopian capabilities of the cinema. J. P. Telotte argues that the invocation of the technological in sci-fi film "always carries a potential for demonstrating [a film's] *movieness*: for reminding us of film's technological base" (*Distant* 167). Thus it is noteworthy that numerous effects shots in *Oz*—shots, that is, that most patently attract attention to themselves as technical constructs—directly invoke, in Rob Latham's words, "the articulations of the cinematic apparatus" ("There's" 50). For instance, to deposit actors within the cyclone and superimpose the Witch's face on her crystal, the technical crew utilized rear and front projection rather than mattes or double exposures, thereby creating, in effect, miniature films-within-the-film. The most telling instance of this self-reflexivity occurs in the Wizard's throne room; projecting footage of Oz's face against the billowing clouds of smoke, the filmmakers link the technological power *in* the film with the technological power *of* the film, or of film itself. Following this argument, then, one might suggest that *Oz* should be read as Hollywood's complexly self-referential depiction of its own technological base, its critique of governmental tampering in the technology of cinema, and its attempt to shape popular perceptions of the cinema and the state in the film industry's own best interests.

To account fully for the alienating ideology of *Oz*, however, this reading must be refined somewhat. For the Oz-as-Hollywood theory as I have presented it thus far runs the risk of being confused with two theories I declined in the introduction: the intentionalist (indeed, in this case conspiratorial) and the reflectionist. As such, it is important to clarify that I am not suggesting that the technological discourse of *Oz* exists because "they"—the MGM brass, director Victor Fleming, the screenwriters, whoever—had a gripe with New Deal technological planning and, consciously or not, crafted a product that reflected their disgruntlement.[23] Such a conclusion would be flawed in any number of ways: for example, even if the studio heads wanted to make such a product, some of the people involved in production, such as the technical personnel, might have wanted to make something entirely different. But more important, such a conclusion would move one away from the role of fantasy film as social ideology and, in particular, as a vehicle that both bodies forth and produces dominant assumptions about social insiderhood and outsiderhood. As Stephen Heath writes, "Cinema does not exist in the technological and then become this or that practice in the social; its history is a history of the technological and social together, a history in which the determinations are not simple but multiple, interacting . . . in which the ideological is there from the start" (227). In this regard, just as the Wizard's imposing head and booming voice are but smokescreens for the man behind the curtain, the man nobody has seen ("not nobody, not nohow!"), so is the film itself an example of what Telotte, writing of the World's Fair, terms "a nearly impenetrable wall of . . . images so alluring that . . . we really did not wish to see behind them, to view the mechanism that allowed both their artifice and our dreams to converge and flourish" (*Distant* 177). And that mechanism, I would argue, is not merely the conservative, corporate ideology of Hollywood but the ideology of American capitalism itself: the pervasive, underlying structure of beliefs about social order and privilege so deeply ingrained that it normally appears invisible, but that underwent such severe strain during the Depression that for millions of Americans the promise of technological utopia became visible as a fantasy, if not an outright deception.

For these disillusioned, outraged Americans, it is perhaps needless to say, *Oz* has a hopeful word, a comforting fantasy: a promise that with patience and fortitude, they will live to see better days. Consider the following snippet of conversation from the Scarecrow's cornfield:

> *Scarecrow:* There goes some of me again!
> *Dorothy:* Does it hurt you?
> *Scarecrow:* Oh no, I just keep picking it up and putting it back in
> again.

A suggestive exchange for audiences who had lost much of themselves in the Depression, these lines submit that no loss is beyond recovery if one will only trust in one's own strength, wits, and good cheer. In similar fashion, the song of the Cowardly Lion, "Courage," issues a lyrical challenge to audience members: its question-and-answer format, with the answer to each question being "cour-age," literally *en-courages* the audience to become the answer for which the song calls. In moments such as these, the film veers away from external, societal an-swers such as those represented by the Wizard toward personal attributes that reside within and, in the case of the Lion, visibly upon the individual's breast.[24]

Yet if the film renders visible the ideology of pluck and stick-to-itiveness, in so doing it obscures not only institutional, systemic problems within technologi-cal society but the cultural animosities and anxieties these bred during the De-pression. For as I have indicated, simmering just beneath the stiff-upper-lip pro-nouncements of texts such as *Oz* was a palpable fear: that a society that promised so many wonders and delivered so few to so many was imminently and intimately vulnerable to chaos, to class warfare, to revolutionists—the Bolsheviks, the work-ers, the farmers—rising up against the masters of technological society. In re-sponse to that fantasized fear, Hollywood took full advantage of its own techno-logical (and fantasizing) capabilities to mold public opinion. Some of these actions could be transparently clear: in 1934, for instance, to aid California Republicans in their campaign against socialist gubernatorial candidate Upton Sinclair, MGM loaned out its cameras and extras to film a supposed "Okie" invasion of the West Coast (Manchester 101). More generally, Depression-era Hollywood responded to the hallucinatory threat it had helped spawn by throwing the weight of its tech-nological power into producing films that thoroughly demean the technologi-cal, films that present displaced persons such as Dorothy and her traveling com-panions as deluded, pursuing a fruitless technological dream that, however paradoxically, Hollywood wizardry had itself whipped up for them. In *The Day of the Locust*, published the same year *The Wizard of Oz* was released, onetime screenwriter Nathanael West mirrored back these fears of popular revolution in a climactic scene of riot at a Hollywood premiere:

> Although it was still several hours before the celebrities would ar-rive, thousands of people had already gathered. . . . The police force would have to be doubled when the stars started to arrive. At the sight of their heroes and heroines, the crowd would turn demoniac. Some little gesture, either too pleasing or too offensive, would start it moving and then nothing but machine guns would stop it. Indi-vidually the purpose of its members might simply be to get a sou-venir, but collectively it would grab and rend. . . . It was a mistake

to think them harmless curiosity seekers. They were savage and bitter . . . and had been made so by boredom and disappointment.

All their lives they had slaved at some kind of dull, heavy labor, behind desks and counters, in the fields and at tedious machines of all sorts, saving their pennies and dreaming of the leisure that would be theirs. . . . They realize that they've been tricked and burn with resentment. Every day of their lives they read the newspapers and went to the movies. Both fed them on lynchings, murders, sex crimes, explosions, wrecks, love nests, fires, miracles, revolutions, wars. . . . Nothing can ever be violent enough to make taut their slack minds and bodies. They have been cheated and betrayed. They have slaved and saved for nothing. (154–57)

Not solely in its title's Dust Bowl reference does *Day of the Locust* connect with MGM's musical. However distant Dorothy's pilgrimage to the Emerald City might seem from the lurid, nightmarish vision of "poor devils who can only be stirred by the promise of miracles and then only to violence" (165), one might profitably consider *Oz* a realization of West's vision: a vision of the poor storming the citadels of technological (and cinematic) power to demand their share.

One might ask, of course, what threat Dorothy, the small and meek, poses to the edifice of economic inequality and its technological base. It is easy enough to see such a threat in West's bleak novel or in an earlier technological dystopia, the German film *Metropolis* (1926), which, like *Oz*, was filmed during a period of economic crisis and, also like *Oz*, is a film of great technical sophistication. In this film, the abused and enraged proletariat, vowing that they will "wait" for deliverance "only a little longer," ultimately smash the machines to which they live in thrall, bringing down the lords of technotopia in the process. By contrast, Dorothy apparently lacks the power to liquidate technological society. All she possesses is the power of exposure, the power to reveal that the man behind the curtain, the workings of capitalist ideology within the nucleus of technological might and authority, is a fraud: "If you were really great and powerful," she scolds the Wizard, "you'd keep your promises!" But in a sense, Dorothy's power of exposure trumps the power of demolition—or one might say that the former is the necessary precondition for the latter. When the palace guard tells the Emerald citizens that "everything is all right," that they can "go on home," they meekly obey; they cannot imagine an alternative to Oz's word. Thus to expose that word, to track ideology to where it hides in plain sight in the configurations, contraptions, and contrivances of capitalist society, and in so doing to reveal that despite its promise of prosperity through technological advance, there isn't, as Dorothy says, "anything in that black bag for me," is perhaps more decisive in the overturning of capitalist ideology than the violence of *Day of the Locust*, in which potentially revolutionary energy is leeched away through impotent acts of desperate adulation.

Thus the film's obsessive need to return Dorothy to Kansas, where the revolutionary threat is annealed, if not annulled: the monsters of the dominant social imaginary are cut down to size. So too the film's concluding message of contentment and quiescence; as her family and friends throng into the rural retreat of Dorothy's room, crowding the borders of the film frame and thereby barring not only escape to but awareness of what lies beyond, she approves such sequestration by promising, "I'm not going to leave here ever, ever again." In the end, the film restores the technology of alienation: the future of technological power vested in the Land of Oz and in the hands of those whose machines made the Land of Oz possible, a sentimentalized, preindustrial heartland reserved—or dictated—for Dorothy and for her kind in the film's audience.[25] In this respect, in performing what Richard Dyer terms the musical's function of "working through" social contradictions "in such a way as to 'manage' them, to make them seem to disappear" ("Entertainment" 185), *Oz* quite closely corresponds to Max Horkheimer and Theodor Adorno's critique of the culture industry:

> The principle [of film] dictates that [the consumer] should be shown all his needs as capable of fulfillment, but that those needs should be so predetermined that he feels himself to be the eternal consumer, the object of the culture industry. Not only does it make him believe that the deception it practices is satisfaction, but it goes further and implies that, whatever the state of affairs, he must put up with what is offered. . . . The paradise offered by the culture industry is the same old drudgery. Both escape and elopement are predesigned to lead back to the starting point. (142)

To pair the somber polemic of *Dialectic of Enlightenment* with the vivacious fantasy of *The Wizard of Oz* may itself seem fantastic.[26] But as I have argued from the start, fantasy and ideology are, in reality, interdependent: social fantasy at once magnifies and mystifies social ideology. *Oz* is thus a significant film in the fantasy tradition not only because it so powerfully, with such apparent seamlessness, renders the culture's dominant ideology at once inevitable and invisible. At the same time, its status as classic has shaped perceptions of fantasy film that function to this day as obstacles to historical and cultural analysis, that blunt the impulse to view such films as representatives of the ideology of alienation. For what are megahits such as *Return of the Jedi* (1983), *Jurassic Park* (1993), *Independence Day* (1996), and a host of others but endless sequels to the tradition pioneered by *Oz*, films that marshal multimillion-dollar machine-generated images in increasingly strident, jam-packed homages to the sheltered enclaves of the pastoral park and the bourgeois family? And what if not the same displaced fears of the monstrous mob can account for the persistence of this duplicitous fantasy? Like its title character in his throne room/projection room, *The Wizard of Oz* continues to wield the forces of technology in an attempt to impose on its audiences a distant and deferential relationship toward the power that lies behind the screen.

3

MONSTERS FROM THE MIDDLE EAST
Ray Harryhausen's Sinbad Trilogy

It is Europe that articulates the Orient; this articulation is the prerogative, not of a puppet master, but of a genuine creator, whose life-giving power represents, animates, constitutes the otherwise silent and dangerous space beyond familiar boundaries.—Edward W. Said, *Orientalism* (1978)

*I*n the realm of movie special effects, the achievements of stop-motion animator Ray Harryhausen admit no equal. For over three decades, from his breakthrough role on the Willis O'Brien vehicle *Mighty Joe Young* (1949) to his swan song, the mythological epic *Clash of the Titans* (1981), Harryhausen not only masterminded individual cinematic visions that remain unsurpassed in style, imaginativeness, and splendor but helped found whole schools of fantasy film to follow: *The Beast from Twenty Thousand Fathoms* (1953) spurred the radioactive-monster-on-the-loose craze. *The Seventh Voyage of Sinbad* (1958) breathed life into the swords-and-sorcery genre. *First Men in the Moon* (1964) paved the way for *Star Wars* and its kin. Conducting the animated portions of his films alone in all but *Joe Young* and *Titans*, equipped solely with optical technology, and backed by budgets typically in the thousands of dollars, Harryhausen brought to life the kinds of otherworldly spectacles that vast teams commanding million-dollar digital machines are presently employed to assemble. And arguably, his effects not only stand up to but surpass those of the present; eerie simulacra of the living, his stop-motion beings cast a dreamlike feel over the whole that is lacking in the literalist reproductions of computer-generated imagery. (Only in one particular, the irksome matting of live actors into location settings, do his films lose credibility; *Jason and the Argonauts* [1963], by many considered the jewel in Harryhausen's crown, outshines the rest in part because its heftier budget enabled the crew to film the principals on location, obviating the process shots that look so fishy to modern eyes.) Given the ever-burgeoning scale of effects units, moreover, Harryhausen is certain to remain the only individual artist working in feature-length film whose contributions so powerfully account for the films' appeal; no other body of work mates the qualities of humanity, personality, and grandeur so perfectly as Harryhausen's.

Though all of the sentiments I have expressed thus far are sincere, none is particularly original; similar claims have been made by everyone from Harryhausen's lifetime pal Ray Bradbury to his faithful filmographer Jeff Rovin to the founders of his many popular Web sites. What I find remarkable, however, is that such an important and enduring figure, one so essential to the development of fantasy film, has been so disregarded outside practitioner and fan communities, his works erased from critical discourse save for a handful of throwaway references. (For instance, *Earth Versus the Flying Saucers* [1956] crops up now and again in surveys of alien-invasion films, while *Beast* makes the odd appearance in studies of *Godzilla* [1954].)[1] Though the people who create and cherish fantasy film have long paid tribute to Harryhausen's legacy in the form of retrospectives, interviews, and—as with the restaurant named "Harryhausen's" in *Monsters, Inc.* (2001)— intertextual nods, those who study the cinema have seemingly considered his films beneath notice.

This snubbing of Harryhausen, I suspect, has something to do with the belief that fantasy film is a subcinematic, adolescent genre unworthy of serious attention, and that Harryhausen's films, as the most unabashed of the type, must be particularly lightweight. More specifically, critical discourse on the Harryhausen films has been derailed by two interrelated tendencies fostered by his fans and by the artist himself: the first, the tendency to consider his films solely mediums for his stop-motion art; and the second, the tendency to pigeonhole his films as purely escapist fare. In a recap of Harryhausen's career, Ted Newsom evinces both trends: "The films of Ray Harryhausen are entertainment, pure and often simple. . . . Indeed, in Harryhausen's case, the effects *are* the picture. But *what* effects!" ("Ray Harryhausen Story" 25).[2] By these standards, Harryhausen's films can be assessed only by the authenticity of their illusions: if, as most agree, the animation transports us to realms of wonder, the films are marvels; if not, as a few skeptics charge, they are flops. By these standards, one is left with two equally unsatisfying options: to divorce Harryhausen's virtuosity from the total system of his films—a schism between style and substance that, as I have argued, is particularly suspect in the analysis of fantasy film—or, what is in practice the same thing, to make his artistry stand so completely for the total film that they are reduced (or exalted) to transcendent feats of special effects bravura. By these standards, finally, even the most characteristic approach to fantasy film—the archetypal approach—is doomed to fail, for by these standards the Harryhausen films constitute a charmed bubble, a hermetically sealed realm of fantasy as its own absolute and self-sufficient justification.

Self-evidently, I reject this quarantining of Harryhausen's films. I believe that his films, like all fantasy films, can and should be restored to the specific social ideologies within which they operate. The purpose of this chapter, then, is not simply (or even mostly) to redress Harryhausen's absence from film analysis. More vitally, I address Harryhausen's works to round out my claims about the alienating function of classic fantasy films—even when those films appear purely escapist, vehicles solely for spectacular cinematic illusions. As such, the Harryhausen films on which I will focus are those that have been the most acclaimed for conjuring thoroughly fantastic worlds: the Sinbad trilogy, comprising *The Seventh Voyage of Sinbad* (1958), *The Golden Voyage of Sinbad* (1974), and *Sinbad and the Eye of the Tiger* (1977). I will argue that these films, far from existing outside their cultural contexts, engage in the dominant discourses of their time, discourses of the Arab world as a mysterious, monstrous threat to the West. Indeed, I will illustrate that the Harryhausen Sinbad films are not only compatible with the social-historical approach but especially potent arguments for it: though they may appear simple illustrations of otherness as monstrosity, they turn out to be particularly productive of mobile, historically determinate ideologies of alienation concerning the Middle East.[3] In this respect, the Harryhausen Sinbad films speak for the importance of applying a fine touch to the analysis of fantasy-in-history; the hammer approach, which treats all monster movies as vehicles for demonizing the universal Other, will not work here.

In this respect, too, the Harryhausen Sinbad films are not merely exemplars of a fantasy film tradition of social alienation but are representative of comparable trends within American cinema as a whole. Critics have amply demonstrated that, throughout the history of American motion pictures, no region of the world has been so regularly identified with the exotic and evil as the Middle East. In his encyclopedic survey of Arabs in American film, Jack Shaheen documents over nine hundred films that represent Arabs, the barest handful of which either challenge stock characterizations—oil barons and sexual Lotharios, fundamentalists and terrorists, bedouins and belly dancers—or produce a balanced portrait of Arab nations in their internal or international aspects.[4] Yet despite film scholarship's attention to the cinema's overwhelmingly negative portrayal of Arab peoples, the Sinbad trilogy has, again, escaped notice; with that peculiar passion for purity that marks so much discourse on fantasy film, Harryhausen's Sinbad films are lauded as works of "pure showmanship" (Mandell 80) and hence removed from the messy, impure world of politics and power. Perhaps, as Leslie Sharman writes of Disney's hotly contested *Aladdin* (1992), this denial of the ideological character of Harryhausen's films reflects the fact that most "think it ludicrous to expect cultural accuracy" from fantasy films (13). Yet as Sharman further notes, one might argue that it is "precisely because of its medium" that such films "should be questioned," for "animation is a highly effective tool for propaganda, its cosy, innocuous image having a special power to palliate unpleasantries and validate stereotypes" (13).[5] Indeed, the void Harryhausen has left in film scholarship may be the best measure of his animated fantasies' reign. To employ Edward Said's terms, viewers and critics alike have been so awed by the master's "life-giving power" over his articulated effigies, they have failed to consider how this "genuine creator," in surpassing the "familiar boundaries" of cinematic space, inscribes the all-too-familiar boundaries of Western power over a "silent and dangerous" non-Western world (57).

Orientalist Fantasies

The awful events of September 11, 2001, rekindled a deep-seated distrust and hatred of the Arab world that has permeated the West for centuries. As Edward Said documents in his groundbreaking *Orientalism* (1978), hostility toward Arab peoples has its roots in the conflicted relationships of exploitation and interdependence the West has long entertained toward the Middle East: "The Orient," by which Said connotes the Middle East, "is not only adjacent to Europe; it is also the place of Europe's greatest and richest and oldest colonies, the source of its civilization and languages, its cultural contestant, and one of its deepest and most recurring images of the Other" (1). "European culture," he goes on to say, "gained in strength and identity by setting itself off against the Orient as a sort of surrogate and even underground self" (3). Born in the medieval vilification of Islam as Christianity's demonic adversary, Orientalism in its modern form deploys religious difference as only one facet within a network of oppositions: "The Oriental is irrational, depraved (fallen), childlike, 'different'; thus the European is rational, virtuous, mature, 'normal'" (40). In Said's view, Western discourse on "the Orient" is at once self-justifying and hallucinatory, establishing its "presence . . . by virtue of its having excluded, displaced, made supererogatory any such *real thing* as 'the Orient'" (21). To employ the model I have used throughout this study, then, Orientalism renders *as if real* ideologies that are founded in social fantasy. And accordingly, though one may cite seemingly "positive" factors within the Orientalist aegis—the Middle East as a land of mystical beauty, deep antiquity, sexual liberty, and so on—what distinguishes Orientalism as a device for the alienation of Arab peoples is its assertion of absolute difference: like the black/white divide of *Kong*, Orientalist fantasy defines the Arab world as inherently foreign, inferior, and threatening to the West.

Like all foundational works, Said's has not escaped criticism. The principal thrust of revision concerns the book's implication that Orientalist fantasy transcends history, that it is impervious to individual, cultural, or geopolitical circumstances. John MacKenzie, for instance, charges *Orientalism* with furthering the very ideology it critiques, a totalizing ideology that effectively erases Arab peoples—not least by disregarding the creative cross-fertilizations that traversed, transgressed, and transformed the East/West divide. In a related vein, Melani McAlister questions the applicability of a unified, invariant Orientalism to all times and places: "In the last fifty years, the meanings of the Middle East in the United States have been far more mobile, flexible, and rich than the Orientalism binary would allow" (270).[6] These are significant considerations, the more so when one recalls that in Said's own analysis, it is the removal of "the Orient" from history that undergirds the binary of East and West: "The Orientalist attitude," he writes, "shares with magic and with mythology the self-containing, self-reinforcing character of a closed system, in which objects are what they are *because* they are what they are, for once, for all time, for ontological reasons that no empirical material can either dislodge or alter" (70). As such, challenges to Said's thesis should be seen not as a means of denying the existence of the Orientalist binary but as a means of subjecting that binary to history, revealing its diverse sources, shapes, and uses in the formation of cultural artifacts.

In this light, if Said's work remains vital in providing a framework for excavating the material character of colonial texts, it may be criticized for overlooking its own insights into the reciprocal relations of text and context: "The period of immense advance in the institutions and content of Orientalism coincides exactly with the period of unparalleled European expansion" (41), Said argues. However, "to say simply that Orientalism was a rationalization of colonial rule is to ignore the extent to which colonial rule was justified in advance by Orientalism" (39). This model of the mutually sustaining intersection of textual and material sites is particularly amenable to the approach I have adopted in this study, an approach that considers cultural productions to be both constituted *by* and constitutive *of* their historical contexts. Applying this approach to the subject of the present chapter, two points become clear: first, that the tendency to read Harryhausen's films as "pure" fantasies is dangerously reductive in part because it reinscribes the Orientalist flight from history; and second, that the Orientalist binary alone cannot sustain an analysis of films implicated in complex, postwar American attitudes toward the Arab world. Rather, as with the binaries black/white or technical/pastoral, the films' Orientalism must be located within an elaborate interplay of text and context, with the "fantasy" of Orientalism and the "real" of history not distinct or opposing but interrelated and interpenetrating.

Such a claim is consistent with current readings of Orientalist cinema on the whole. On the one hand, there can be no question that cinematic discourse on the East has proved remarkably durable; indeed, as Robert Stam and Louise Spence argue, "since the beginnings of the cinema coincided with the height of European imperialism" (637), it is unsurprising that the cinema itself should have become both analogue to and instrument of Western power:

> The cinematic and televisual apparatuses, taken in their most inclu-
> sive sense, might be said to inscribe certain features of European
> colonialism. The magic carpet provided by these apparatuses flies us
> around the globe and makes us, by virtue of our subject position,
> its audiovisual masters. It produces us as subjects, transforming us
> into armchair conquistadores, affirming our sense of power while
> making the inhabitants of the Third World objects of spectacle for
> the First World's voyeuristic gaze. (636)[7]

Within the compass of this panoptic authority, the Orientalist cinema's master-narrative takes shape, as summarized by Ella Shohat in terms perfectly suited to the basic plot of all three Sinbad films: "Heroic status is attributed to the voyager . . . come to master a new land and its treasures, the value of which the 'primitive' residents had been unaware" (27). Furthermore,

> The colonial films claim to initiate the Western spectator into an
> unknown culture. This is valid even for films set in "exotic" lands
> and ancient times that do *not* employ Western characters . . . yet
> whose oriental heroes/heroines are played by Western stars. . . . Any
> possibility of dialogic interaction and of a dialectical representation
> of the East/West relation is excluded from the outset. The films thus
> reproduce the colonialist mechanism by which the Orient, rendered
> as devoid of any active historical or narrative role, becomes the ob-
> ject of study and spectacle. (31–32)

Yet for all the power and persistence of this master-narrative, it cannot be mapped intact onto Orientalist films arising from diverse periods and circumstances. The risks of doing so are implicit in Shohat's synopsis—for as she makes plain, the Orientalist project relies precisely on the illusion that its own discourse is time-less and monolithic, rather than being embedded in the particularities of an imperial history. Therefore, even when the Middle East is imaged as, in L. Carl Brown's words, "a strange, never-never land" with "little or no impact on what

Americans [see] as the 'real world'" (20)—an image that had its bellwether in the 1921 Valentino production of *The Sheik*, and that persists in films such as *Ishtar* (1987) and *The Mummy* (1999)—to circumscribe these films within "the domain of fantasy, pure and simple" (22) is to reproduce the films' own discourse, to minimize their intricacies and dull their cultural instrumentalities. (One has only to recall the climactic scene in *The Sheik*, which eerily echoes *The Birth of a Nation* in picturing the white-robed minions of the "good"—European—sheik riding to deliver the heroine from defilement at the hands of the "bad"—dark-skinned—desert bandit, to locate this seemingly escapist romance in the specifics of 1920s American discourse on race and difference.) As Matthew Bernstein sums up, "simplifying films to a structured opposition between East and West cannot account for these films' specific articulation of power relations [or] for their compelling appeal to audiences" (11). However Orientalist cinema may attempt to distance and dismiss, close reading of individual films enables one to excavate the tensions, emphases, and ellipses within these films and in so doing to reveal their placement within the shifting dynamics of American-Arab relations and representations.

A brief history of U.S. involvement in the Middle East during the period of the Sinbad films' production will help ground an analysis of postwar Orientalist cinema as a situated, interested activity, one that both reproduces and produces American discourse on the Arab world.[8] Prior to World War II, though the United States had long looked to the Middle East as a fertile ground for trade and missionary labors, in the eyes of most Americans the region seemed, as Burton Kaufman writes, "a strange and alien place with which the United States had far less contact than with Europe" (1). In the interwar years, ceding control over the region to Britain and France, the United States remained, in Barry Rubin's words, "far more spectator than actor in the Arab world" (247). For a number of interrelated reasons, however, the end of World War II marked the genesis of a profound change in the United States' relationship toward the Middle East. To begin with, the battle over the creation of the state of Israel tested the nation's claim to moral leadership in the postwar period. At the same time, the shift from contesting the Axis Powers to containing the Soviet Union began to bring the strategic importance of the Middle East into focus; due to its geographic proximity to the Soviet Union, its evident political instability, and its seemingly limitless oil reserves, the Middle East appeared a likely battleground in the struggle between capitalism and communism. This possibility was heightened by the gradual withdrawal of the region's colonial overseers, which created a power vacuum that, in the eyes of leaders such as Dwight D. Eisenhower, "must be filled by the United States before it is filled by Russia" (qtd. in Fraser 73). At the dawn of the Cold

War, the Middle East was thus positioned to assume a significance undreamed of in the prewar period.

Yet this new vision of the Middle East did not coalesce immediately. For a variety of reasons—the nation's need to recover from the trauma of world war; its policing of the more evident threat in North Korea; and, frankly, its suspicion of what seemed the byzantine nature of Arab politics—there remained, in David Lesch's words, "a good deal of confusion" over "what exactly [American] policy toward the Middle East should be" (80). Thus during much of the 1950s, a wariness of entanglement in the Middle East marked the nation's policy. For instance, though the United States granted Israel immediate recognition after its 1948 declaration of statehood, significant military aid to the Jewish state was not forthcoming until the 1960s. Then, too, through much of the 1950s, the United States sought ways to act within the protective embrace, or under the cover, of its wartime allies. For example, 1950 saw the signing of the Tripartite Agreement, by which the United States, Britain, and France agreed to limit the buildup of arms in the region. In 1955, meanwhile, though the United States may well have been instrumental in engineering the Baghdad Pact, a military alliance between Britain and the so-called northern tier of the Middle East (Turkey, Iraq, Pakistan, and Iran), the United States itself remained conspicuously absent as a signatory. That America's leaders were watchful of developments in the Middle East is proved by the nation's covert support of the 1953 revolt against Mohammad Mossadegh, the nationalist leader of Iran; that such actions remained fitful suggests a wariness of arousing anti-American sentiment, an uncertainty over the workings of power in the region, and a hope that the European presence might render sustained intervention unnecessary.

The 1956 Suez crisis at once exemplified and ended this policy of selective detachment, as it made plain what the United States had been reluctant to admit: the former imperial powers had lost their ability to police the region. The seeds of the crisis were sown in 1952, when a military coup led by General Muhammad Naguib overthrew Egypt's King Farouk. Naguib was succeeded in 1954 by Colonel Gamal Abdel Nasser, who displayed the traits that America and its European allies most feared: an unflinching support of Arab self-determination and a willingness to court favor and cut deals with the Soviet Union. At the center of nationalist and Pan-Arab movements for the next fifteen years, Nasser took a dramatic step toward curtailing Western influence in the Middle East when he nationalized the Suez Canal Company on July 26, 1956, an act calculated both to defy and to drain a European community deeply dependent on the flow of oil through the Suez. Within months, Britain and France, in concert with Israel, had launched an attack on Nasser's nation; had the United States backed the offensive, Egypt would certainly have been forced to yield. But despite Nasser's links to the Kremlin, despite a growing impression among U.S. policy makers that the Egyptian president was, as John Foster Dulles saw him, "an extremely dangerous fanatic" bent on regional domination (qtd. in Freiberger 167), the United States refused to enter into the conflict, seeking instead to negotiate a peaceful resolution and, failing that, to bring economic pressure to bear on its allies in order to end the hostilities. The United States' motivations for this course of action were complex and far from consistent; though the desire not to rouse anti-American emotion dictated prudence, the belief that world socialism stood behind Nasser's regime might have seemed to call for an armed response. That such a response did not develop indicates that, as late as 1956, the conception of the Middle East as deadly nemesis had not yet become fully ingrained in the American cultural imagination.

Ironically, however, by exposing the pretense of British and French ascendancy, the United States catapulted itself into the position whereby its own nascent fears of Middle Eastern instability and extremism began to be realized. In 1957, less than a year after the Suez crisis, the United States took two actions that revealed its anxieties about the volatile nature of the Arab world: on the one hand, the CIA backed a Syrian military coup against a procommunist government; on the other, the Eisenhower Doctrine, which promised economic and military aid to Middle Eastern countries threatened by Soviet influence, was signed into law. Within the next year, the United States had twice applied the doctrine, once by activating sea forces during a Jordanian monarchical crisis and once by deploying ground troops to Lebanon during that nation's civil war. Within the next few years, the United States had further alienated the Arab nations by stepping up financial and military support of Israel. By the early 1960s, America had thus committed itself to the course of action most likely to confirm its own monstrous image of the Arab world: taking on the role of diplomatic, economic, and military heavy in the Middle East, the nation had played a part in igniting the passions that are still felt, and in increasingly terrible forms, to this day.

Thus it was that, as T. G. Fraser notes, the 1960s and the early 1970s "saw the Middle East develop from an area where the United States had interests but no deep commitments into one of Washington's main priorities in foreign policy" (77). The nation's already hazardous position in the region was exacerbated by a number of developments during the 1960s: the birth of the Organization of Petroleum Exporting Countries (OPEC) in 1960; the growth of the Palestine Liberation Organization (PLO) from 1964 to 1968; and the Arab-Israeli war of 1967, by which Israel dramatically increased its territory, military dominance, and reputation for imperialism. A year after the war, Lyndon Johnson drew an ominous parallel: "Today in two areas of danger and conflict—the Middle East and Vietnam—events drive home the difficulty of making peace" (qtd. in Spiegel 119). In part, this difficulty was occasioned by the United States' new role as Israel's largest supplier of arms; the trade-off in securing Israel as a partner was, in Kaufman's words, "further polarization of the Arab world, further Arab militancy, further Soviet influence in the Middle East, and further erosion in American relations with most Arab nations" (64). In the eyes of U.S. policy makers, the early years of the 1970s produced yet more evidence that the Arab world represented a mortal threat to the United States and its principal Middle Eastern ally: the 1970 hijacking of airliners and the 1972 kidnapping of Israeli Olympians by Palestinian militants added the random ingredient of terror to the already explosive mix. The nadir of U.S.-Arab relations arrived in 1973, the year in which Syria and Egypt launched devastating military strikes against Israel in what is variously termed the Yom Kippur, Ramadan, or (more neutrally) October War. Not only did this conflict place the United States and the Soviet Union on full nuclear alert but the ensuing OPEC oil embargo of 1973–74 meant that all three tenets of the nightmare vision Leon Hadar identifies as the "Arab bogeyman" scenario had fallen into place: "Washington was programmed to expect that, without American military and diplomatic leadership, any Middle Eastern crisis might lead to a world war, an oil embargo, or the destruction of Israel" (10). Whereas in the 1950s the Middle East had been to a great extent an enigma, by the early 1970s developments in the region were routinely magnified into potential global conflagrations.

Not surprisingly, this period also saw the rise, or the hardening, of anti-Arab stereotypes throughout American society; if during the 1950s Arabs had lurked as strange, vaguely hostile figures on the margins of American consciousness, during the late 1960s and early 1970s the market was saturated with high-profile images casting them as public enemy number one. At the most restrained, Arabs were chided for pursuing policies of "oil warfare," their "strategy of squeeze" indicative of "the rise of Arab power" ("Arabs'" 88). Far less charitably, letter-to-the-editor writers cursed Arabs as "the rulers of the world," who threatened to turn the nation into "an Arab lackey licking the oil off their feet," and whose actions led one writer to long for the good old days of Western domination: "I understand more clearly now the rationale of imperialism."[9] In (pseudo) scholarly discourse, meanwhile, throwbacks to eighteenth-century Orientalism proliferated. Cast as "a human type which readily and frequently throws off the restraints of discipline and . . . is likely to go on a rampage" (Patai 162–63), Arabs were constructed as the West's absolute antithesis: "The Westerner is stupefied by Arab violence. After a Palestinian terrorist attack he will say, 'But it's all so senseless!' This is to expect something logical from the fundamentally irrational. When projected outwards Arab violence is non-selective; the identity of the victims is immaterial. For the Arab, violence in itself is consolatory" (Laffin 131). Such convictions were echoed throughout the canons of visual culture: pictured as vulturous, turbaned sheiks in political cartoons, reduced to rifle-toting, kaffiyeh-swathed terrorists on evening news clips, Arabs became synonymous with mad acts of murder and mayhem. Following the trend, feature films such as *Network* (1976; portraying an Arab takeover of network news), *Prisoner in the Middle* (1974; depicting Palestinian terrorists), and *Black Sunday* (1977; still more Palestinian terrorists, this time at the Super Bowl) reinforced the predominant image of Arabs as monstrous threats to the nation's values and safety, indeed to its very life.

If, however, the immediate issue of early-1970s events was a torrent of anger and recrimination against Arab peoples, this period also produced two more sanguine results: a less lopsided assessment of Arab claims and, along with it, a deepening sense of urgency to resolve the region's conflicts. The history of these developments was multifaceted, one factor being the changing face of events in the region itself: when PLO chairman Yasser Arafat movingly addressed the United Nations General Assembly in 1974, or when Israeli military units strafed Palestinian refugee camps the same year in retaliation against alleged terrorist attacks, it became increasingly difficult for some Americans to determine who was friend and who was foe. Such qualms might not have arisen, however, if not for concurrent seismic shifts in the nation's own political landscape: with the civil rights and anti–Vietnam War movements having sensitized the nation to the fate of oppressed peoples at home and abroad, many Americans were prepared to view the plight of the Palestinians, and the grievances of their Arab supporters, in terms other than the absolutist framework of U.S. (or Israeli) moral rectitude. Perhaps most decisive in deepening America's resolve to mediate the Middle East conflict, however, was the palpable evidence that continued turmoil in the region would mean continued danger, discomfort, and unrest in the United States; no longer a faraway prospect the nation could safely put off, peace within the Arab world had come to seem intimately and imminently entwined with America's very survival. American diplomatic successes during this period were limited (though they were crowned by the Camp David Peace Accord); the failure to secure a lasting Pax Arabia need hardly be belabored. My point, however, is not to second-guess from a present-day vantage. Rather, it is to argue that the latter years of the 1970s saw a change in American relations toward the Middle East perhaps as profound as that which had transpired toward the close of the 1950s: marked by aggressive, anxious diplomacy and cautious (if, once again, anxious) optimism, this period saw the effort to forge a more comprehensive, balanced settlement of the region's conflicts than had hitherto been attempted.

To simplify considerably, then, one may trace three overlapping but identifiable stages of American involvement in the Middle East during the three decades following World War II: limited engagement, wholesale commitment, and hopeful mediation. At the same time, the changing fortunes of the United States in relation to the Middle East correspond roughly to three dominant images of the Arab world: as an unfathomable vortex into which the nation is reluctantly and ineluctably drawn; as an inherently evil, personalized menace; and as a more ambiguous, ambivalent power, still treacherous yet potentially treatable. It is my contention that the three Sinbad films, in sequence, parallel these three geopolitical stages and, as such, that their dominant tenor accords with each stage's representations of the Arab world. Such parallels may be difficult to extract from the films, overlain as they are with the more obvious Orientalist master-narrative. At the same time, I would not wish to contend that the differences among the films are clear-cut or absolute; to confine each film to a single ideological niche—especially when two of the three appeared within three years of each other—would drastically schematize the nature of historical-cultural productions. I do wish to argue, however, that close examination of each film will reveal significant differences among their narrative and representational strategies; if in their broad outlines the Sinbad films suggest an Orientalist freedom from history, in their particular features they prove considerably more subtle—and as such, more potent, if problematic—vehicles of social alienation than the simplistic fantasies they are routinely understood to be. In my readings of the Sinbad films, I am guided by two beliefs: first, that because the Orientalist metanarrative is so pervasive throughout American culture (including film culture), it may actually be, however paradoxically, *more* responsive to current events than the norm; and second, that because this narrative is so resistant to scrutiny, it may, again paradoxically, provide a particularly congenial environment for clandestine—by which I do not imply intentional—commentary on the real. The Sinbad films, then, enable one to observe not only the complex ways in which cultural productions participate in the histories that produce them but, more specifically, the ways in which, as McAlister writes, "representations of the Middle East . . . helped to make the area and its people meaningful within the cultural and political context in the United States" (2).

Before elaborating on this thesis, however, two further caveats are in order. First, though I will insist on locating the Sinbad films within the history of United States-Arab relations, at the same time I will resist reading the films as forthright political allegories, with Sinbad as the United States, the kingdoms he protects as Israel, Sokurah as Nasser, Koura as OPEC, Zenobia as the PLO, and so on. An exaggerated reaction against the tendency to divorce these films from history, such clever matching of text and context actually leeches the films of their polymorphous power. For similar reasons, I must abjure any notion that the Sinbad films, by virtue of the fact that they are set in the Middle East, are either *more* representative of Middle Eastern conflicts than other concurrent films or *solely* representative of such conflicts. It would be quite possible to demonstrate that films seemingly remote from the Middle East are implicated in pervasive cultural desires and anxieties concerning the region; conversely, it would be possible to read the Sinbad films in terms wholly distant from the arena of international power relations, or in terms of other such relations (most obvious being the nation's disastrous military legacies in Korea and Vietnam).[10] My point, then, is not to enshrine or confine the Sinbad films within any static cultural niche. My point, rather, is to illustrate that of the countless productions in which U.S. concerns about the Arab world came to be focused, the Sinbad trilogy is one such site, an intriguing and fertile one but neither a definitive nor a conclusive one. Reading this site opens up the possibility not only of examining how diverse and far-flung are the manifestations of history within popular culture, but more specifically of affirming even the most fantastic of films' affinities with particular histories of social alienation.

Mystery, Menace, Mediation: Sinbad in the Middle East

Toward the close of the extended introduction that sets up the main adventure in *The Seventh Voyage of Sinbad*, the princess Parisa, betrothed of the film's hero, utters the following line: "The world has grown very large overnight." It is a suggestive snatch of dialogue in the context of the American 1950s, a comment that bespeaks the United States' awakening to its role, risks, and responsibilities in a new global order. In the narrower U.S.–Middle East nexus, it is a line that underscores national anxieties over the meaning and significance of the Arab world, a world that was only haltingly being integrated into America's mental map and that was, according to the producers of the film, unfit for location shooting (they chose Spain instead) due to its "unsettled conditions."[11] Were Parisa's line spoken in virtually any other fifties-era film, its historical resonances would be unmistakable.

Spoken as it is in a Ray Harryhausen Sinbad film, however, the political implications of Parisa's line have passed unnoticed and unremarked. That this is so may be attributable to the cinematic packaging with which the line is surrounded, or swamped. For one thing, the line in its immediate context is meant as a whimsical, if painful, joke: it is not in fact the world that has grown larger, but Parisa who has grown smaller, reduced to doll size by the malevolent magician Sokurah. For another, a special effects shot—the matting of the miniature princess into the life-size setting occupied by Sinbad—fills the screen while her line is spoken; intent on the magic of this image, viewers are presumably paying little attention to the lovers' banter. The result of these devices is that Parisa's tantalizing words are obscured beneath a heavy veil of Orientalist distancing, not to say trivializing, effects. To say this is not to imply that Harryhausen, or anyone involved in the film, wished to produce an underground morality play and so designed the shot in such a way as to parry its ideological thrust. It is, rather, to say that during the era in which the film was made, few Americans—including the filmmakers—were prepared to recognize their own historically situated anxieties within the film's presumably pure, innocent Orientalist trappings.

Indeed, as I have said, the Sinbad films' deployment of the conventional tricks of the Orientalist cinema's trade continue to deflect attention from their historically concrete discourse regarding the United States and the Arab world. Since in this generic respect the three Sinbad films are roughly similar, I will limit myself to touching on the Orientalist master-narrative at this point, suggesting its appearance in *Seventh Voyage* before moving on to explore the insufficiency of this narrative alone in accounting for each film's cultural work. The opening credits of *Seventh Voyage* key the Orientalist master-narrative: playing over images, somewhat in the manner of an illuminated map, of monstrous creatures on rocky isles alternating with the most readily identifiable of markers (bedouin tents and camels, walled cities with spires and minarets), the credits begin the work of distancing this world from the viewer's own. Bernard Hermann's sprightly, Middle Eastern–flavored music completes this initial encounter with the foreign: guided by the score's driving rhythms and by the roaming camera, which dissolves from one corner of the visible area to another, the viewer realizes the parallel fantasies of complete physical separation from, and complete visual authority over, this outlandish land.

Within the film-world, the mise-en-scène operates to confirm the fairy-tale nature of the proceedings; the standard turbans, scimitars, gongs, dancing girls, sedan chairs, and other icons of Hollywood's Middle East reinforce the impression of the film existing within the eternal fantasy of Orientalist film alone. As one minor indication of this persistent, even audacious, otherworldliness, when Parisa first appears, she is carting a brightly colored parrot, an inexplicable companion but for its hopeful attempt to ensure that the unmistakably Anglo actor who plays the princess will not be taken as such. A more prevalent, and considerably less playful, illustration of the film's investment in the Orientalist narrative of absolute difference involves its depiction of the crew of convicts Sinbad raises for the return voyage to the island of Colossa. Not only are these men the most physically stereotyped members of the cast, with dark skin, black pointed beards, golden earrings, and thick accents, but their behavior typifies the cowardice, mendacity, gluttony, inconstancy, and depravity for which the screen Arab was renowned: criminals to begin with, they attempt to steal Sinbad's ship (only to plead for his help when they hit rough waters), guzzle wine from the island's enchanted stream and slay the baby roc to glut their bellies, and foolishly linger amidst the Cyclops's treasure horde, draping themselves in jewels and provoking another armed conflict with their abstemious captain when he tries to reason with them. The convict crew, moreover, provides a pretext for the film's most objectionable moment: when one careless sailor falls to his death, the pious captain intones, "Allah knows many ways of dealing with hungry men." The film's only reference to the divine beyond a few perfunctory prayers, this pearl is presented as if it were a proverb, characteristic of the low value the Muslim world places on human life.

Moreover, the film's special effects are quite in keeping with, indeed indispensable to, its Orientalism. To begin with, as the principal site of spectacle, the effects provide an impression of mastery over the Orient akin to Harryhausen's own mastery over his articulated puppets; most stunningly realized in the sequence in which the blinded Cyclops gropes after the hero, the film offers its audience unilateral, unencumbered vision and control over the Orient. At the same time, the monsters exemplify the discourse of absolute difference, their utterly fantastic nature removing them from contact with the viewer's reality. Indeed, in the case of the Cyclops, the film takes a further step toward ensuring difference by depriving the (articulated) creature of articulation: the Cyclopes "have no speech," Sokurah assures Sinbad, and thus the magic lamp "is useless to them." This is, of course, unlikely: the horned giants, who craft cages, clubs, and stools, who make fire, and who cook their meat, would almost certainly possess some form of spoken language. But beyond the extreme difficulty of creating a convincing illusion of speech with latex stop-motion puppets—a problem Harryhausen circumvented in *Clash of the Titans* by employing a live actor for the speaking parts of the animated character Calibos—depriving the denizens of the non-Western world of their voice is a hallmark of the Orientalist project. As David Spurr writes, there is a long-standing

> rhetorical tradition in which non-Western peoples are essentially denied the power of language and are represented as mute or incoherent. They are denied a voice in the ordinary idiomatic sense— not permitted to speak—and in a more radical sense—not recog-

nized as capable of speech. . . . The incoherence of the Oriental, in this view, is related to an incapacity to enter into the basic systems of thought that make civilized life possible. (104)

Taken as a whole, then, *Seventh Voyage* strives to produce a Middle Eastern fantasy world as far from the realities of "civilized"—Western—life as possible.

Ultimately, however, the Orientalist master-narrative proves inadequate to achieving its goal. Orientalism, I have noted, asserts the West's absolute authority to construct the East, an authority most readily secured if the East can be so fully fantasized as to seem to exist outside history. Yet as Sharman notes, this retreat from history must itself be placed within history: the making of Orientalist films "during a time when the Middle East is so politically volatile suggests an underlying nostalgia for orientalist narratives which offer heroes and villains rather than the morally ambiguous characters" who dominate the world stage (11). In this light, for all its proclamations of power over the fantasy land of the Orient, *Seventh Voyage* turns out to be awash in the anxieties over authority that marked American views of the Middle East during the postwar period. From 1950 to 1958, regional instability fostered by the withdrawal of the European powers, the growth of Arab nationalism, and Western (including U.S.) counterinsurgency against Soviet-backed governments brought down King Abdullah of Jordan, King Farouk of Egypt, Mohammad Mossadegh of Iran, Shukri el-Kuwatly of Syria, and King Faisal II of Iraq. Under these "unsettled conditions," American attempts to forge partnerships and alliances—or even, in the case of *Seventh Voyage*, to secure location footage—were both erratic and, more often than not, bootless. Within the film-world of *Seventh Voyage*, the chronic instability and insecurity of the time take the form of a profound suspicion concerning the origin, nature, use, and usefulness of power in the Middle East. In this respect, rather than representational power over the Arab world becoming the film's uncontested province, the uncertainty of power within the Arab world becomes a principal subject of the film's representations. This does not mean that *Seventh Voyage* is not an Orientalist film. It does mean that the film's illusion that its Middle Eastern discourse exists outside history is just that—an illusion, one that strives unsuccessfully to cloak the historical grounds within which it arose.

The uncertainties concerning the West's position in the Arab world operate from the film's first sequence and do not relent by its last. *Seventh Voyage* opens on a shot of a ship at sail, gliding slowly through a nighttime mist as an ominous note plays on the sound track. This shot is, of course, a standard Orientalist opening; a daytime version appears, for example, in a key pretext for *Seventh Voyage*, Alexander Korda's 1940 film *The Thief of Bagdad*. At the same time, however, this opening shot activates the historically rich image of the nation-as-vessel, an image reinforced by the following shot of the stalwart (and turbanless at this point, notably Western) captain standing at the wheel, staring intently into the dark. When Sinbad calls for a sounding, his crew expresses mistrust: "If there was land, it would be such that no man would dare set foot upon." The surprising discovery of land underscores both the captain's prescience and the unpredictable conditions of his world. Likewise, the first mate's prayer that "we may find nothing more" than food and water on the island of Colossa captures both the irresolute nature of the common (Middle Eastern) seaman and the inadequacy of such fervent prayers—for of course, what they find on Colossa dictates the entire course of the adventure to follow. The dialogue that caps the opening scene, in which Parisa's lady-in-waiting berates Sinbad for "taking [Parisa] from the comfort and safety" of home and in which the princess defends her lover, claiming that he is "not responsible for the mysterious winds that blew us off course," heightens the dominant note of this expository sequence: the unpredictability of events when one departs home port for lands unknown, sailing (in Sinbad's later words) "uncharted waters" in the company of a "doubtful crew" and with an even more doubtful mission or end.

This discourse on the perilous nature of foreign entanglements deepens as the film progresses. On Colossa, Sinbad, brave but headstrong, nearly leads his crew into mortal danger: marveling at the stone face carved into the cliff, which he likens to the work of "some ancient civilization," and determined to "see where that stone mouth leads," he is narrowly saved by, of all persons, the magician who will turn out to be his foe, the man's emergence from the cave preventing Sinbad from literally walking into the mouth of the beast. That Sinbad applies the term *ancient civilization* to the monument connects the Valley of the Cyclopes to the Middle East, the "ancient civilization" from which the West was born and to which, as colonizers and self-designated saviors of the region's supposedly half-bestial peoples, the West has regularly returned. That Sinbad has been chastened by his near-fatal encounter with this backward world is evident when he steadfastly refuses to aid Sokurah in recovering the lamp and its "weird power": "The Cyclops will be on guard now," he warns, and in any event "we are on an important mission for the Caliph of Bagdad. Our presence there means the difference between war and peace. I'll not risk that by turning back." Unswayed by the magician's offer of "a king's ransom" in jewels—which he empties over a map, so that monetary and territorial interests are visually linked—Sinbad expresses the nation's hesitancy to become involved in an alluring and alarming land of fabled wealth, sudden violence, unaccountable beings, and weird power.

The lull in the action after the escape from Colossa serves to establish character relations, to flesh out the back story, to situate the viewer more fully in an

Orientalist milieu, and to provide audience and animator alike a breathing spell (though it does include one of Harryhausen's flashiest creations, the snake-woman). At the same time, however, this period of relative quiet permits the aura of anxiety cultivated in the prologue to mount, not only as regards the film's manifest conflict—the magician's monomaniacal quest for the lamp—but in respect to other, less insistent elements of the action. For instance, in the scene of the banquet honoring Parisa's father, the Sultan of Chandra, the film identi-fies multiple threats to the safety and stability of the land. The sultan himself, an Orientalist caricature constantly muttering maledictions beneath his beard, serves as a reminder of the ferocity lurking below the polished, glamorous sur-face of Middle Eastern opulence and decadence. Similarly, Sokurah's counter-feited prophecy—according to which "mysterious and evil forces are at work" to produce "great disaster," a regional war instead of a royal wedding—recalls the precarious, hair-trigger quality of war and peace in this land. For even if Sokurah *is* bearing false witness to achieve his dastardly ends, his prophecy nearly comes true: finding the shrunken Parisa the following day (and, like everyone else, improbably never suspecting the magician of the misdeed), the sultan threat-ens Bagdad with the very fate Sokurah had "foreseen."

Indeed, pursuing this line of inquiry, it is intriguing to note that, as Sokurah himself pleads when Sinbad floors him for his lie, he was *asked* to prognosticate; if he prevaricated instead, the sultan and the caliph had engineered the condi-tions for his fib. (Given the sultan's volatile temper, moreover, to foresee the collapse of the peace process hardly constitutes a whopper.) The fallout from Sokurah's prophecy further suggests the razor-thin difference between lie and truth, war and peace: in the brief scene preceding Parisa's enchantment, as even the stalwart Sinbad expresses anxieties about Sokurah's prophecy, his lover reas-sures him by crooning, "I'll dream of the dangers he predicted, so you can res-cue me." Their kiss dissolves to the scene of Parisa in bed, where "the dangers [Sokurah] predicted" do indeed come true; the "evil dreams" he foresaw are re-alized. In this regard, even the most dreamlike, fantastic element of the Bagdad sequence, Harryhausen's wildly imaginative snake-woman (whom the sultan and the caliph do indeed call a "dream"), becomes part of the overriding sense of anxiety over foreign affairs: seduced into performing by Sokurah's promise of "power," Parisa's handmaiden becomes a monstrous fusion of unlike parts that cannot coexist peacefully but must rebel against each other. The snake-woman thus dramatizes the dangers of trusting in unknown powers or bedfellows, as she embodies the fear of literal entanglement within the beast's coils.

The portrait that the early movements of *Seventh Voyage* draw, then, is one of a world marked by inexplicable forces, doubts over the validity of one's perceptions and judgments, and, above all, reservations about the location, extent, and uses of power. It would be tempting to attribute these features to flaws within the film's script or to its desire to flay the "inscrutable Oriental" hobbyhorse. However, not only is each of these dismissals a mere excuse packaged as an explanation, but both overlook the fact that the film's incongruities, far from being quirks, are so consistent—and insistent—that they constitute the very texture of the film's discourse. Consider, for instance, how often the film raises questions about power: "Who's in command of the great crossbow?" a sailor asks. "I do not understand the power of this lamp," Sinbad says. And moments later, he asks Sokurah, "What protects your castle from [the Cyclopes]?" Consider, too, how frequently expectations are reversed: Confident that the convicts "can do nothing" against him, Sinbad is proved wrong—almost dead wrong—in the very next shot. Conversely, twitting Sokurah's curse aboard ship, the rebellious convicts are nearly destroyed by the Harpies in the scene that follows. Given the film's outward candor—the fact that much of what the characters find wrapped in intolerable obscurity the audience can plainly observe—the prodigies that suffuse *Seventh Voyage* cannot be passed off as the necessary atmosphere for an exotic, quixotic Sinbad film. Rather, the aura of dark intimation serves the function, is the medium, of the film's unmistakable disquiet over the conditions of the real.

Toward this end, it is notable that the most fantastic elements of *Seventh Voyage*—the magician Sokurah, the genie Barani, and the animated monsters—not only enable the anxieties about power to be most fully activated within the filmworld but resist penetration or resolution by the audience as well. Of the villains in the three Sinbad films, Sokurah is the most enigmatic; his motivations throughout the film, though they may appear straightforward, are in truth notably murky. After his initial rescue, as he attempts to bribe Sinbad into returning to Colossa, he announces, grimly and with finality, "There is nothing I would not do to regain [the lamp]." Yet as he speaks this line, his face, in close-up, passes into shadow, an indication that his motives, if evil, are oddly unaccountable. Sinbad attributes the sorcerer's desire for the lamp to a kind of madness—"his life is distorted with this single, driving wish"—but this explanation simply rephrases what is readily observable: Sokurah wants the lamp very, very much. At another point, Sinbad terms him "ambitious." But ambitious for *what*? Again, for the lamp. Yet with all the film's focus on the lamp, it is worth asking what Sokurah plans to *do* with the lamp if he should regain it. He is already a remarkably powerful figure, with the ability to effect dramatic physical metamorphoses with the mere application of a potion (as in the transfiguration of the snake-woman) or the mere look of his eyes (as in the animation of the skeleton). And the lamp, as he himself has announced, has merely "protective" powers: "The man who holds this treasure

then, is a mixed blessing; not only is it subject to the pattern of reversals I noted previously, with the appeal to its power followed immediately by that power's defeat, but it is an awkward and inconstant ally at best.

For the lamp's resident, likewise, its power is neither absolutely certain nor absolutely desirable; like the genie of Disney's *Aladdin*, Barani provides a point of focus for what Alan Nadel terms an "anxiety and confusion about the source, use, and legitimacy of power . . . in the Arabian world" (190). On the one hand, though Barani arguably possesses the greatest power in the film, he is merely a child unsure of his abilities: "I shall try, master, I shall try" is his doubtful refrain whenever he is commanded to act. On the other hand, whatever his power, rather than being liberated by it, he is oppressed and confined by it; though it may be true, as he tells Parisa, that "a genie knows many things," he lacks basic understanding of his own condition, possessing only the undecipherable riddle that illuminates his prison wall and that must, in its lack of illumination, torment him daily. It is, indeed, perhaps because Barani has lived with (or under) great power, seen its effects and limitations, and experienced its inequities and paradoxes that he is so uncomfortable with its exercise; initially reluctant to teach Parisa the invocation that will call him forth, saying falteringly, "I like you, but it's a great power to grant," he yields only when Parisa promises to bind herself to him in joint obligation. Too, freeing the genie itself involves speculation and risk: Parisa has no certainty that the lava pit truly represents the "fiery rock" of Barani's impressionistic poem, and in casting the lamp into the pit, she places herself and her lover in continued danger from the magician, the dragon, and (as it turns out) the second Cyclops. Thus the role of Barani reinforces the notion that, whatever one's perceived obligations, in a world of uncertain power one's actions arise within, or from, a radically incomplete perception of their ramifications.

Turning to Harryhausen's animated creations, a similar air of ungraspable power, promise, and threat prevails. Again, the film's principal animated figure, the Cyclops, may serve as a point of entrance to these issues. By Harryhausen's account, the pop-eyed, grimacing giant was designed to resemble *The Thief of Bagdad*'s Conrad Veidt, whom the animator considered "the very incarnation of evil" (qtd. in Mandell 78). Yet far from being an incarnation of evil—or of anything—the Cyclops, like Sokurah, is motivated by much more complex, even arcane, impulses than may initially appear. At first, the Cyclops seems but a lumbering, bellowing brute, motivated, one assumes, by nothing more subtle than animal hunger. Yet this impression is belied by Harryhausen's subsequent development of the character. When, for example, the Cyclops captures the lamp, it cradles the prize to its chest, looking jealously over its shoulder in a fine piece of animated acting—and a piece that raises doubts about the character on the whole.

Does the Cyclops, in fact, *desire* the lamp? And if so, why? Simply because, like the other treasures it has collected in its cave, the lamp is a bright, shiny object? Or does the Cyclops recognize that the lure of treasure will bring one of its sources of food, human beings, within its reach? That the lamp serves only as bait, however, seems unlikely; when the Cyclops is roasting Haroufa on the spit, it deserts a meal already in hand to investigate the clattering it hears in its treasure chamber. Can it be, then, that the Cyclops is far more human than Sokurah recognizes or grants, that the creature is, like the greedy, gluttonous sailors, torn between conflicting desires for gold and for grub? (How else to explain the complete human skeletons dangling in one of its cages, captives not eaten but left to die?) Or can it even be, on the outer edge of possibility, that the Cyclops, for its own obscure reasons, longs to bring Sokurah within its power, and that its seizure of the lamp was designed for just that purpose, the capture of Sinbad's men being only a salutary by-product of its scheme? These questions are impossible to answer—and, in fact, I am not suggesting that one attempt to answer them, to settle on what motivates a mass of rubber and ball bearings. I am suggesting, however, that rather than viewing the incongruity of the Cyclops in negative terms—as when Harryhausen's creatures are accused of occupying "walk-on" roles, their relation to the plot less keen than their occasion for the master to work his will—the uncertainty of the creature's motivations should not be isolated from *Seventh Voyage* as a whole. Rather, the opacity of this central animated figure is consistent with the film's skepticism regarding the stability or clarity of power, identity, and causality in the Arab world. If Harryhausen's monsters are central to the film's deployment of the Orientalist binary, at the same time they are crucial in extending the film's historically resonant discourse.[12]

   That discourse is not hushed by film's end; for all the genre pressures to wrap the adventure tidily, a sense of unsettledness lingers. The concluding image, for instance, inverts the opening shot: this time, the ship sails away from the camera, so that resolution is achieved through renunciation, not only of Colossa but of the narrative itself, which merely returns to the point at which it began. The world of Colossa, moreover, remains terra incognita; the best the captain can do is bid it farewell, sailing away from the bad dream that had haunted him and his fiancée. And yet, the destiny to which the couple sails is still uncertain: Bagdad and Chandra remain a single mishap from war, the wedding has not been consummated, and, at that, the vista into which the voyagers sail is amphibious, legible as either a sunrise or a sunset. The conclusion of *Seventh Voyage* thus epitomizes 1950s-era discourse on the Arab world as a place of inscrutable powers and uncertain commitments: retaining no obligations to the world they leave behind, its only legacy being the accidental attainment of the material wealth the hero had initially resisted, Sinbad and his bride-to-be reserve toward the isle of Colossa a stance neither of surety nor of overt hostility but of suspicion and a fiercely guarded neutrality.

By the time of *The Golden Voyage of Sinbad*, the Arab world had changed drastically in American eyes; far from seeming a nebulous, distant peril, it had come to appear a direct and immediate threat to American safety and sovereignty, a land of random terror and, with its vast oil reserves, terrible power. At the same time, the United States' role in the region had become far more complex and intimate; American military and economic power underlay to a great extent Israel's security, while American diplomacy sought throughout the late 1960s and the early 1970s to achieve a resolution to the region's conflicts. These twin changes in perception and preoccupation are evident in the second Harryhausen Sinbad film, as both the nature of the villain and the activity of the hero differ strikingly from those of its 1958 prototype. The drama of a conflict between the necromancer Koura and the steward of the kingdom for which Koura lusts, *Golden Voyage* is distinguished from the first Sinbad film not only by a more somber setting and creature design but also by an abiding atmosphere of veiled yet imminent menace, of barely contained violence, and of potentially cataclysmic outcomes looming in the near future.

The most evident difference between the two films lies in *Golden Voyage*'s portrayal of the evil sorcerer Koura, the counterpart (and, indeed, phonetic double) to Sokurah. To begin with, where the bad guy of the 1958 film evoked no particular stereotype of the modern-day Middle East, his bald head, ornately trimmed black doublets, and indeterminate accent locating him more in the realm of fairy tale than in any contemporary milieu, Koura combines elements of the region's two most instantly recognizable villains: in his first appearance, his features are swathed in a veil like a cloaked terrorist; while in later scenes, his turban and sharply pointed beard invoke the cartoon symbols of the rapacious sheik. Moreover, where Sokurah's motives are notably unclear, Koura's could not be plainer: he is, the grand vizier states, "dedicated to bringing this domain under his power." His means of doing so are likewise more straightforward and violent than those of Sokurah: while the latter has to rely on the roundabout stratagem of shrinking Parisa to fulfill his desires, Koura tries both direct terror attacks, sending "a great ball of fire" to ravage the vizier's map chamber, and the longer-range but nonetheless frontal assault indicated in the vizier's claim that "our country is being choked alive" by the magician. Though the film fails to visualize the devastation Koura has wrought, allowing the vizier's disfigurement to stand for the land's presumably crippling sorrows, the language of being "choked alive" unmistakably parallels early-1970s accusations that the Middle East's economic and political rulers were, as Gerald Ford and Henry Kissinger put it, bent on the "strangulation" of the West (qtd. in Spiegel 222).

Moreover, in his relationship to Harryhausen's monsters, Koura differs significantly from Sokurah. Indeed, the difference lies largely in the fact that he *has* a relationship to virtually every monster in the film, and a fundamental one at that. In *Seventh Voyage*, as I have indicated, the motivation of many of the creatures is obscure at best: the Cyclops's actions are beyond the characters' or viewers' penetration, while the parent roc too acts cryptically, snatching Sinbad in apparent retribution for the death of its chick yet simply dropping him in its abandoned nest thereafter. One can, however, at least be certain that these beings are to a large degree independent agents rather than pawns; even the snake-woman, though created by Sokurah, rebels against his creative powers for reasons the magician apparently did not anticipate and the audience is left to ponder. Of the two creatures that are undeniably motivated, given life and direction, by Sokurah—the dragon and the skeleton—only one acts according to plan. Though the dragon does obey the magician's command to "follow"—in several shots, looking goofily like a giant dog trotting after its master—the trainer's authority turns out to be illusory, as the beast, slain by the man's own giant crossbow, falls and crushes him. The skeleton alone is motivated both in the cinematic sense—visible in early shots of the magician's laboratory, it does not, like so many of the film's creatures, simply appear out of thin air—and in the sense of its being Sokurah's killing machine: close-ups of the magician's face with eerily glowing eyes, shots of his hands gesticulating as if manipulating a puppet, and his orders to the being to "kill!" all signal its dependence on his animating force. In keeping with the first film's doubts concerning the source of power in the Middle East, the acts of the majority of the figures at the center of this (as of every) Harryhausen production cannot be traced to any single culprit or design.

In *Golden Voyage*, conversely, every hostile creature is cast in the mold of *Seventh Voyage*'s skeleton, each having at least an implicit, and in most cases an absolute, dependence on Koura's motivating power. The homunculus, most obviously, is the man's literal extension: vivified by his blood, serving as his long-distance eyes and ears in the vizier's map room, and sending a pang through its master's body when it is killed in the chamber of the oracle, the creature has no independent existence whatsoever. But both the ship's figurehead and the statue of the goddess Kali, if not actually fashioned by Koura, are utterly reliant on him for motion and motivation. The scene with the figurehead, for instance, is filmed to emphasize Koura's controlling power. Beginning with a low-angle shot that zooms in to an extreme close-up of the dark prince's gleaming eyes, the scene dissolves to Sinbad's ship, leaving the afterimage of those eyes briefly superimposed over the figurehead just before its arm moves. As the sequence unfolds, crosscutting between shots of Koura performing anticipatory gestures and the figurehead duplicating his motions accentuate his authority over the figure. That Koura's incantation involves the repetition of his own name further implicates the man in the monster. Likewise, when he orders the creature to "return" and it pauses uncannily, listening, and then retreats at his beckoning, the film makes plain that this apparition is in truth an embodiment of the sorcerer.

The other animated figures in the film follow a similar logic. In the case of Kali, not only does the idol's spectacular dance signal Koura's authority, but the model substitutions for which Harryhausen is justly renowned tightly bind the maestro and the many-armed being he orchestrates: when the live-action Koura throws his sword and the stop-motion Kali snatches it from midair, the two are joined even more intimately than Sokurah and his skeletal marionette. Even the centaur, though not strictly under Koura's control, does seem to be in his camp: at the Fountain of Destiny, when Koura implores the dark powers to come to his aid, the centaur reappears, armed this time and ready to attack at Koura's word. That the one figure beyond Koura's·control or even awareness—the heroic gryphon—is, as many critics have pointed out, the least plausibly motivated of Harryhausen's creations in this or any of his films underscores Koura's centrality: actuated not by the magician but by some unknown source, the gryphon ends up seeming completely arbitrary and irrelevant. In sharp contrast to its predecessor, then, *Golden Voyage* links virtually all otherworldly events directly to its villain; he is truly the film's puppet master or manipulator, the one who forces plot, characters, and creatures to revolve around him. Paul Jensen argues that Harryhausen's penchant for presenting magician figures who grant motion and apparent volition to inanimate objects suggests the artist's commentary on his own craft: like Aeetes, master of the hydra's teeth in *Jason and the Argonauts*, Koura "creates [the monsters] or brings them to life, and they do his bidding, just as an animator controls his models" (141). While I find this a valuable point, it is nonetheless notable that in *Golden Voyage*, the theme of an animate, malevolent, all-controlling power does not simply operate in a handful of showy set pieces but suffuses the film as a whole. And in this respect, Koura's power is consistent with the era's belief that malign forces emanating from the Middle East held the world in a grip of fear and incapacity.

At the same time, if *Golden Voyage* reenvisions the villain in accordance with its historical moment, so too does it remodel the hero to represent America's drastically altered role in the Middle East. From the start, rather than casting Sinbad as a reluctant player, dragged into the conflict only when he has no choice, the film fashions an active, committed—even impetuous—captain who plunges into the affairs of Marabia (*Arabia* with an *M*) as if they are his own. Indeed, the film itself plunges into these affairs instantly: In the opening shot, no sooner does the watch call out, "A fine clear morning, and all is well" than the film cuts to the homunculus in flight, initiating the chain of events that will engage Sinbad and his crew in the fate of the nation. The captain's first act, his recovery of the portion of the amulet that falls to his ship's deck, signals his commitment; though his mate urges him to cast it away, the captain binds himself to the talisman by stringing it around his neck. Again, when the storm blows his ship off course to Marabia, he is neither dismayed nor distracted; convinced that "we've been brought here by some mysterious force," a force that he must "follow," he goes (literally) overboard, unwilling to wait even for the ship to anchor. On shore, his unwillingness to relinquish the amulet to Koura indicates once more that this is a Sinbad who believes himself to be embroiled in the conflict from the start, even though he is not at this point certain as to the conflict's nature or extent.

His encounter with the vizier, who offers a full account of the conflict, affirms Sinbad's commitment. Indeed, the vizier's greeting—"We have waited for you a long time"—underscores the notion that the captain's presence in the besieged city is less a freak occurrence than a providential unfolding. The two interlocking parts of the amulet are emblematic of the interdependence between Sinbad and the kingdom to which he has come; like the amulet—the two portions of which, significantly, join to produce a map, both parts being necessary to chart the shape and reaches of geographic authority[13]—Sinbad and Marabia are united, in the vizier's words, as "allies against the same enemy." That the secret the amulet promises to unlock concerns "power to rid this land forever of Koura's black and ugly ambitions" connects the film obliquely but powerfully to the geopolitical conflicts of the period. And that the risk the heroes run involves Koura himself gaining the amulet's power and thereby dispossessing Marabia "forever" of "freedom and happiness"—a risk heightened by the vizier's uncertain claim to the land, which he rules unauthorized by lineage or antiquity—underscores the urgency and anxiety of American interests at this time. No longer an island of obscure, embryonic significance, the Middle East of *Golden Voyage* is one in which unlikely allies confront a great and manifest evil for control of contested land, resources, and birthright.

This discourse on America's role in the struggle for power in the Middle East is developed even in that element of the film that seems to serve the Orientalist project of dehistoricizing: the theme of fate, or destiny. Sinbad, as noted above, believes that he has been brought to Marabia by "some mysterious force." Once he meets the vizier, that force receives a name: "Only destiny could have brought you here." Harryhausen, discussing the role destiny plays in the film, characteristically stresses its timeless origins and nature: "The movie was based on the Middle Eastern point of view of Destiny: that everything is the will of Allah. You're not your own free-will agent; there's some sort of pattern. The whole of life is plotted out ahead of time" (qtd. in Rovin 234). Yet what this précis misses is that the film's hero largely *rejects* such determinism. His saying, "Trust in Allah—but tie up your camel," repeated three times during the film, suggests not only that Sinbad is (again) a "Western" hero—a partisan, as it were, of the "free" world rather than a pawn of Eastern superstition or despotism—but that while destiny may have a positive flavor when it tastes of "commitment," considerable wariness attaches to the notion of destiny as compulsion, forced obligation, or fate. Throughout the film, when others are content to place their futures in the hands of the Almighty, Sinbad innovates, improvises, intervenes; he feels his way through the sea of mists, leaps onto the centaur's back to deliver the death thrust, and fashions an arrow and rope from a brazier and turbans to escape the temple of the oracle. Indeed, the oracle itself appears to subscribe to Sinbad's philosophy; though the seer does speak of destiny, it concludes that "the deeds of weak and mortal men" will turn the tide. The firmest advocate of fate in the film, tellingly, is Koura—yet not only does he have a great deal to gain from believing that his takeover of Marabia is foreordained, but his brand of coercive power is precisely that which the film renounces. Taken as a whole, then, the film's meditation on fate and free will arrives at an understanding less in keeping with any putative Middle Eastern mysticism than with the geopolitical context of its era, one in which America's perceived commitments to the Middle East were compelling in two distinct respects: they arose from deeply-rooted animosities into which the United States was drawn as if by dark powers beyond its control, and they reflected the nation's self-interest in interceding to avert a final outcome engineered by those powers.

Toward this end, it is intriguing that the Fountain of Destiny—the "final place," as Koura calls it, where the struggle over the land will be resolved at last— itself sustains this geopolitical discourse. Visually, though the ring of monoliths surrounding the fountain is evocative of Stonehenge, an ancient mystery presumably beyond time and human ken, it would not take much of a leap of the cultural imagination to perceive in the bubbling geyser that turns first to blood and then to gold the prototypical Western image of oil, seen at the time of the film's release as the principal source of the Arab world's potency, promise, and peril. It is in this suggestive setting that "the forces of good and evil battle eternally." During the round of battles that concludes the film's action, frequent close-ups of the fountain rivet attention on this wellspring, this font of conflict as well as of "untold riches," this mysterious power that, Koura vaunts, will grant him boundless and inexhaustible "energy." It is in this setting too that Koura at once gains his greatest apparent advantage and suffers his ultimate defeat; rendered invisible by the power of the fountain and taunting Sinbad that "for all your strength, you are helpless; I can kill you at any time," Koura is slain when, stepping within the heart of the gushing fountain, his shape becomes visible. The climactic struggle of *Golden Voyage* is thus not merely an "eternal" one between Good and Evil. Rather, it is a struggle for material, political, and geographic hegemony waged against the free world by an invisible instrument of terror who is finally revealed within the very source of his iniquitous and ill-gotten might.

Unlike *Seventh Voyage*, then, *Golden Voyage* has little doubt as to the source, extent, and corrupting effects of Middle Eastern power. Like its predecessor, however, the second film conveys considerable uneasiness about the exercise of, or association with, such power. However committed Sinbad may be throughout the film, once the villain is vanquished, he abdicates the prize—the crown to the kingdom of Marabia—that appears on his head in the vision reflected in the fountain's waters. To Margiana, he explains this decision in terms befitting the romance plot that the film grafts onto the fantasy adventure: "I value freedom," he says, and "a king is never truly free," not even to marry whom he desires. Yet in light of the associations *freedom* has carried throughout the film— associations concerning the hazard of the free world's entanglement within the web of Middle Eastern intrigue—Sinbad's renunciation of power can be said to signal a continued American hesitancy to become embroiled in the Arab world's internecine conflicts. In *Golden Voyage*, power is a dangerous commodity: not only does it consume Koura, racking his frame and twisting his mind, but it devours the keeper of the oracle's flame, leaving nothing but an empty cloak and a pile of ash. The closing shot of the film—a shot that, as with its precursor, flip-flops the opening, Sinbad's ship sailing away from the camera where before it had forged ahead—suggests a desire to remain unscathed by the fire brewing in the Middle East. Subduing the region's demons, *Golden Voyage* expresses a wish for an end to the hostilities in which America had become, so it seemed, fated to play a central role.

And yet that wish could not have come true—for a mere three years later, the total time needed to produce a Harryhausen film, Sinbad set sail for another and, due to the animator's advancing age, final voyage. The release of a third Sinbad film so close on the heels of the second can, of course, be explained simply in terms of the profit motive: both prior installments had done good box-office business. But films are never profitable merely in dollars and cents, and the appeal of *Sinbad and the Eye of the Tiger* in 1977 had much to do with the sense that the nation still had unfinished business of another sort to conduct. Reproducing the plotline of the second Sinbad film in narrating the sorceress Zenobia's assault on a wounded nation, while recalling the first installment in having Zenobia hex a member of the royal family to seal her wicked design, *Eye of the Tiger* reveals once again both the continuities and the transformations in American attitudes and policy toward the Middle East. With a kingdom yet hanging in the balance—and with John Wayne's son in the title role—the third Sinbad film is characterized by a heightened urgency for the cowboy to ride to the rescue, as well as by an increased hopefulness that the Western adventure-hero might at last shepherd the conflicted land away from savagery and toward civilization.

These two qualities—urgency and hopefulness—pervade American discourse on the Middle East during the period of the film's production. In 1977, for example, when Egyptian president Anwar Sadat took the unprecedented step of visiting Jerusalem, *Newsweek* described his trip in a cover story that could barely contain either the exultation or the anxiety attending the event:

> Anwar Sadat, the President of Egypt, had come to the homeland of the Jews in one of the most remarkable and dramatic pilgrimages ever made. . . . Sadat's journey was an event of epic proportions. . . . In one totally unexpected step, Israel and Egypt had broken their diplomatic stalemate, adding a hopeful—if unpredictable—new dimension to the search for peace in the whole Middle East. (Steele 36–37)

Several years earlier, during the Geneva Peace Conference held after the close of the October War, Secretary of State Henry Kissinger delivered an opening address marked by the mingled optimism and foreboding that would characterize the Middle Eastern diplomacy of the late 1970s:

> We are convened here at a moment of historic opportunity for the cause of peace in the Middle East and for the cause of peace in the world. . . . All of us must have the wisdom to grasp this moment— to break the shackles of the past and to create at last a new hope for the future. . . . We are challenged by emotions so deeply felt—by causes so passionately believed and pursued—that the tragic march from cataclysm to cataclysm, each more costly and indecisive than the last, sometimes seems preordained. Yet our presence here today, in itself a momentous accomplishment, is a symbol of rejection of this fatalistic view. Respect for the forces of history does not mean blind submission to those forces. . . . Let us resolve here today that we will overcome the legacy of hatred and suffering. Let us overcome old myths with new hope. (44–45)

Disavowing, yet not altogether suppressing, the "fatalism" that vexes *Golden Voyage*, Kissinger's statement may be viewed as prescient for *Eye of the Tiger*, a film that suggests the efforts of the Middle Eastern nations and their American brokers to rise above what may have seemed a fated course of violence, to resist succumbing to the baser passions, and to appeal to the higher powers of reason—or to an even higher power beyond the human world—in order to overcome a "legacy of hatred and suffering."

Eye of the Tiger opens on a shot of fireworks exploding against a night sky. It is a telling image, given what follows: for in their sudden, brief burst across the darkened screen, the explosions may be read either as signs of celebration or of war. The sequence that plays during the opening credits helps to situate the viewer, but not to resolve the ominous aura: the scene of a coronation, this evidently auspicious event is marred by shots of eyes glancing anxiously to the side, hands gripping knives, whispered warnings, and, just as the crown is placed on the new ruler's head, a burst of fire and a woman's terrified scream. The camera cuts to a shot of Sinbad and his men coming ashore, where the crew's jibes to their impatient captain—"The city will not vanish," they assure him—and their complaints, on hearing that a plague has descended upon the city, that "every time we reach a port, some misfortune strikes us," could be said to express American anxieties over the progress of peace in the Middle East, the fear that hopeful beginnings might be undone by the unforeseen act of some anonymous agent of terror.

That agent is, of course, Zenobia, the wicked stepmother who casts a spell over Prince Kassim to free the throne for her son, Rafi. Yet what is intriguing about the third Sinbad film is that, in contrast to the first two, the visible, human agent of evil becomes tangential rather than central to the narrative as it unfolds: though Zenobia sets events in motion, and though the early portions of the film seem to establish her in the traditional role of the Sinbad villain—even to the extent of having her animate the film's first two threats, the ghoul host and the bronze Minoton—she becomes irrelevant to a far more compelling conflict that dominates the film as soon as Sinbad sets sail with the enchanted prince. Rather, what commands the film's energies during its principal act is an *internal* threat or enemy: the conflict within Prince Kassim, who has been transformed by Zenobia into a baboon, between his human and bestial selves. In the scene in which Sinbad's first mate discovers the baboon and Princess Farah playing chess, for example, the debate concerns whether Kassim is, like a true baboon, "savage." The Prince reveals his humanity—and as such, at least in the terms the film has allowed thus far, his triumph over savagery—by writing his name on the wall of the ship, making him the only Harryhausen creature before or since to express himself in written language. Similarly, the brilliantly acted sequence in which Kassim scrutinizes and subsequently weeps over his reflection in the mirror of Melanthius, the wise hermit to whom Sinbad appeals for aid, emphasizes the defeat of bestiality: "A true baboon," Melanthius glosses Kassim's actions, "would have attacked its reflection, thinking it an enemy. It would not have recognized itself and been moved to grief." From a purely technical perspective, these two scenes vindicate Harryhausen's decision to use an animated rather than a real baboon: since, in the animator's words, baboons are "apparently very intelligent in their own way, but they're also very vicious" (qtd. in Rovin 249), his art alone made possible the revelation of the man within the beast. At the same time, these sequences suggest the nature (and the potential resolution) of conflict not only within the individual but within the wider world of the Middle East: if in the playing out of the deadly international game of chess, violence derives from a refusal to acknowledge the Other whom one sees in the mirror—or across the border—thinking it, rather, an enemy, then the peace process begins with an act of self-recognition, in which one is "moved to grief" over the monster one has oneself become.

The struggle expressed most powerfully through Kassim—a struggle between violence and compassion, bestiality and humanity—extends, moreover, throughout the film. For example, the monstrous Minoton—half-human, half-bull—loses, or apparently never engages in, the struggle between human and animal

Princess Farah (Jane Seymour) and the bewitched Prince Kassim play a game of chess. From *Sinbad and the Eye of the Tiger* (Columbia, 1977). Courtesy of Photofest.

halves: entirely beholden to Zenobia's corrupt power, the heartless monster not only obeys her command to ram the royal guard's ship but, looming impassively above the captain of the guard as he flails in the water, skewers the man and casually tosses his dead body overboard. Then, too, Zenobia herself is not fully human: initially distinguished as bestial by the cat eyes that replace hers when she works her baneful spells, she becomes increasingly dehumanized as the film progresses, forfeiting first a single foot when her potion fails to restore her from the form of a gull and then, in the film's climax, renouncing her humanity altogether when she inhabits the body of the saber-toothed tiger. Functionally, this final transformation spares the hero the ignominy of slaying an unarmed woman; ideologically, it is consistent with the film's exploration of personal/political conflict and violence. Even some of the film's heroic figures are only partially human: the giant troglodyte, most notably, is not only apelike in appearance but is equipped with a rhinoceros horn, a Darwinian abomination but a significant touch in light of the film's thematics. That the Trog and the baboon are nonhuman (or semihuman) primates reinforces the film's discourse on the choice between savagery and civilization; that the Hyperborean hominid is the sole Harryhausen model, the sole "foreign" creature, in this or any film with whom the heroes communicate—a process, moreover, that takes the form of a diplomatic parley, with Kassim interpreting between the Trog's grunts and the humans' words—suggests again the film's investment in a narrative of conflict resolution and international cooperation.

These hopeful signs are, however, shadowed by parallel developments that complicate the film's discourse on peace and violence, civilization and savagery. For instance, asked what became of the people who carved the imposing rock cities in which Melanthius resides, Dione, the sage's daughter, explains that her predecessors "became too civilized and destroyed each other," yielding to their "primitive" descendants—a bitter commentary on the equation of civilization with power and on the inability of peoples to overcome primal hatreds. Indeed, that the tendency to resolve conflicts violently may be innate to humankind—rather than a function of a spurious "civilizing" process—is suggested by the Trog. This inhabitant of an Edenic valley carries a club, in one rear-projected shot mirroring the armed and bare-chested Sinbad, and the creature avidly exchanges its "primitive" weapon when the opportunity presents itself to trade up for the slain Minoton's bronze pike. If, moreover, the Trog seems to be undergoing an accelerated evolutionary upswing, from the Stone Age to the Bronze Age—becoming perhaps "too civilized"—his companion, the baboon, is experiencing a retrograde movement, becoming in turn too savage. As Melanthius explains, not once but twice, dire hazard attends Kassim's continuing in his simian state:

The longer the transformation is delayed, the more likely is Kassim to lose those human qualities that still remain to him. . . . Time is our enemy on all counts. At the moment, Kassim is still in possession of some human qualities. But the longer the transformation is delayed, the more he'll revert to a baboon's natural behavior: more aggressive, savage, dangerous. He will never be Kassim again.

In this respect, if the film's central conflict concerns the risk of dehumanization, of becoming the "savage" that time, circumstances, or fate appear to have decreed, it seems that such a risk is heightened if intervention does not occur soon. Yet the difficulty lies in the fact that even if the heroes *do* restore Kassim—make him civilized—there is no certainty that his harrowing encounter with the savage within will have liberated him from that condition; like the Trog, he may simply begin anew a civilizing process that ends in destruction. As such, though I am inclined to agree with Frank Jackson that *Eye of the Tiger* is unified by a discourse of "primitivism," I am less convinced than he that the film celebrates "modern man overcom[ing] primitivism" (26). Rather, the ambiguous nature of the primitive/civilized dichotomy suggests the film's disquiet, despite or because of its hope, regarding the race's ability to overcome past (and present and possibly future) barbarity.

That this is so may help explain the feature of *Eye of the Tiger* that has always troubled viewers and reviewers of the film: its incoherence at the level of plot. There are simply too many journeys in the film—from Charak to Casgar, Casgar to the Arctic, thence to Hyperborea, and finally to the temple of the Arimaspai—and in consequence, the film seems particularly protracted and disjointed. At the same time, the numerous impediments Sinbad and his crew meet during the various legs of their journey seem to serve little purpose but to prolong the quest and delay its outcome: The whole business with Zenobia's boarding Sinbad's ship to spy on their destination seems contrived (and necessitates for interest's sake the introduction of one of Harryhausen's least inspired creations, the giant wasp). Sinbad's boat won't fit through the ice tunnel to Hyperborea and is unable, as the captain laments, to "make headway" against the icebergs, so the heroes must take the overland route instead (another dull interlude spiced up only by a second Harryhausen walk-on, the giant walrus). The gates to the valley won't open until the Trog lends a hand. The chains that operate the cage within the temple are momentarily jammed. The temple's power flickers. And so on. That this film suffers from drift—that many of Harryhausen's creatures seem mere window dressing—can, of course, be attributed to poor scripting. I would suggest, however, that the lurching feel of the third Sinbad installment is indicative of the film's uncertainty concerning its direction. Like the Middle East peace process, appropriately dubbed a "step-by-step" process during Kissinger's years of shuttle diplomacy, *Eye of the Tiger* proceeds falteringly from one episode to the next, with each episode marked by roadblocks that seem to threaten derailment, only to be overcome with unrealistically little effort. That the hero has very little to do in the drama to which he lends his name—that he is reduced to Melanthius's gofer, a fact Zenobia recognizes when she instructs Rafi to kill not the sailor but the sage in the temple of the Arimaspai—is another sign of the film's reluctance to celebrate prematurely. Unable to effect a transformation in the region's conflicts single-handed and admitting that the struggle "requires skills far greater than mine," the Sinbad of this film is a signally impotent hero, who must appeal finally to a power utterly beyond this world for deliverance.

That power—the unearthly force contained within the temple of the Arimaspai—is itself consistent with the era's Middle Eastern discourse. The fact that the temple is shaped like a pyramid may seem only a touch of Orientalist trimming; but considering the moves toward peace inspired by Anwar Sadat in the 1970s—moves that would culminate in the Camp David Accord the year after *Eye of the Tiger* appeared—it seems far from fortuitous that this most instantly recognizable symbol of Sadat's nation should be so prominently displayed.[14] On the map of Hyperborea in Melanthius's hermitage, the pyramid first appears: "the source," the wise man announces, as his hands cup the image to freeze attention on it, "of all their extraordinary power," which enabled them "to change or transform the nature of matter." When the great gates to the temple open, the pyramid appears, centered between the doors, with the mystical northern lights playing above it like a halo. Similarly, when Zenobia and her son approach the shrine, a low-angle shot of the edifice towering above them reinforces this image of the pyramid as deity, the one chance for a final and lasting transformation not achievable by human hands. Within the shrine itself, recognizably Egyptian images of pharaohs and birds are carved into the walls; sarcophagi, across which the camera pans, line the central chamber. And the power of the shrine itself—a beam of blue light descending from on high, with the magic to turn a monkey into a man—completes this image of a benign force, to which the titular hero can serve only as handmaiden, residing within the site that was at once the most ancient dreamland of Orientalist fantasy and, in the late 1970s, the most heralded prophet of international harmony.

The shrine, of course, fails; having achieved its one service, it succumbs to the breach forged by Zenobia's creature—her "army," as she calls the Minoton—and through that breach, darkness and winter descend upon the valley of the wise. The final Sinbad film, like the first two, ends where it began: with the closing credits playing over the coronation that was interrupted during the opening credits. Yet in this film, a final touch casts doubt over the already dubious consolation of returning to the place one has left: in the dark depths of a brazier of coals on which the camera rests, Zenobia's cat eyes open suddenly and remain on the screen as it fades to black. The beast, it seems, still lurks within the heart of humanity; it has been stilled but not stifled. And indeed, as the real-life sequels to *Eye of the Tiger* make plain, the film's ultimately pessimistic conclusion was warranted: events including the 1983 bombing of the U.S. embassy in Beirut, the 1990 Gulf War, the atrocities of September 11, and the retributory wars against Afghanistan and Iraq attest to the failure of the Middle East peace process in our time.

There is, at that, a moment near the end of the film that indicates perhaps *why* this process has failed: jubilant in the temple of the Arimaspai after Kassim's remission, the heroes cluster at the top of the stairs, leaving Zenobia alone at its base, huddled over the broken body of her dead son. As with the history of Middle Eastern strife within which this film took shape, the only solution the film presents is absolutist: *either* Kassim rules *or* Rafi does. That Rafi, like Kassim, is related to Farah—Zenobia is her stepmother, so Rafi is presumably her stepbrother—makes this solution even more troubling: to reclaim one brother, Farah must permit, encourage, and celebrate the death of another. And that Rafi is slain by Kassim—that the Prince's increasing "savagery" turns out to be the key to recovering his kingdom—leads one to doubt the film's moralizing, particularly when one notes that the dead brother is physically identified with the Middle East, the surviving one with the West. As Melanthius remarks of the Trog, this film, "like all primitives," is "afraid of the unknown"; or to recall Kissinger's words, the film cannot "overcome" the "old myths" of Orientalism, cannot envision a resolution to an aeons-old "legacy of hatred and suffering" except through further hatred and suffering. Blindly submitting to the fatalistic philosophy it seems to renounce, *Sinbad and the Eye of the Tiger*, like its pretexts on screen and off, fails to be moved to grief at its own monstrous visage.

4

DRAGON LADIES Fantasy Film and "Family Values"

We're all just meat to them.—A male complaint, in *Surrender* (1987)

*T*he Sixty-fifth Annual Academy Awards ceremony, broadcast in late March of 1993, was dedicated, according to a much-publicized preshow blitz, to 1992's "Year of the Woman." The hype notwithstanding, the show revealed the resistance with which Hollywood—a bastion of male power and an inexhaustible purveyor of regressive images of women—confronted the mere suggestion of social or cinematic gender equality.[1] The opening montage was telling: though it began with a send-up of Snow White warbling "Some Day My Prince Will Come," and though it did excerpt films that buck the Snow White image, including *Norma Rae* (1979), *Private Benjamin* (1980), and *Thelma and Louise* (1991), the bulk of the sequence was devoted to films, past and present, that portrayed women in their traditional roles: love objects, femmes fatales, and mothers. Similarly, though the show was peppered with references to Hillary Clinton, the nation's newly anointed first lady, the presence of not one but two ensemble numbers featuring scantily clad, buxom exotic dancers fortified host Billy Crystal's quip that, in the Year of the Woman, the "most talked about parts" in film were those of women's anatomies.

The awards portion of the program was, if anything, even less heartening. The parade of female presenters and homages to women's past achievements could not hide the fact that in the Year of the Woman, by far the majority of nominees were men. Of the ten nominees in the screenwriting categories, only one was a woman; of the thirty or so nominees in the categories of effects, sound, score, cinematography, and director, none was. The only non-gender-specific categories in which women fared well were a pair that embraced traditionally female activities: costumes and design. Even the Best Supporting Actress Oscar, the first award to be handed out, was in keeping with an overall tone of women being sidelined and silenced. Snubbing veterans Vanessa Redgrave, Joan Plowright, Judy Davis, and Miranda Richardson, the academy conferred the Oscar on nubile newcomer Marisa Tomei, whose role in *My Cousin Vinny* epitomized the shallowness of the show's rhetoric: a faux-feminist Snow White, who speaks her mind solely to further her boyfriend's career so he will wed her before her barely postpubescent "biological clock" stops ticking, Tomei's character defined the ideal—supporting—woman as young, self-effacing, and driven not by material aspirations but by maternal ones.[2]

Two months later, Hollywood unveiled, or unleashed, another fantasy woman, the apparent antithesis of the jiggly twenty-something hausfrau enshrined at the Oscars; her film went on to make box-office history. This woman was a far cry from the industry's childlike, housebound ideal; she was old—sixty-five million years old, to be precise—and so powerful she had to be caged to prevent her from roaming at will, chewing the scenery and everything else in her path. She was far from silent; in fact, she roared, and her thunderous voice literally froze grown men in their tracks when it wasn't (again literally) scaring them shitless. She was anything but nurturing; her designs on moppets involved not her womb but her gullet. In only one respect, her overwhelming lust to propagate her kind, did this woman resemble her sister. But where the biological clock of characters like Tomei's was timed to maintain traditional gender hierarchies, the doomsday drive of the other woman tolled that men's—or Man's—reign on earth had run out. In the half-wistful words of the only adult (human) female to share the screen with her, "Dinosaurs eat man. Woman inherits the earth."

The biogenetically engineered *Tyrannosaurus regina* of *Jurassic Park* (1993) was only the most eagerly awaited and attended of a slew of monstrous women who ruled the nation's movie screens in the 1980s and 1990s. The two decades brought forth dozens like her: the rapacious queen of *Aliens* (1986), the scheming sea-witch Ursula of *The Little Mermaid* (1989), the ravenous undead (and unwed) Lucy of *Bram Stoker's Dracula* (1992), the predatory breeder Sil of *Species* (1995), the sultry and insatiable Santanico Pandemonium of *From Dusk 'til Dawn* (1996); one might even include the bass-voiced but ruby-lipped Venus mantrap Audrey II of *Little Shop of Horrors* (1986), the chromosomally male but reproductively female behemoth of *Godzilla* (1998), or the looming, phallic-gunned mother ship of *Independence Day* (1996). Fantasy films have, of course, long been drawn to monstrous women: the cyborg Maria in *Metropolis* (1926), the fright-wigged intended in *The Bride of Frankenstein* (1935), and the mountainous missus in *Attack of the Fifty-Foot Woman* (1958) are but a few of the more memorable. And yet, the late twentieth century's seemingly unquenchable thirst for monstrous-woman films—not to mention for the genre's only slightly less fantastic soror-ity, the nuclear-family nightmares of *Fatal Attraction* (1987) and its interminable spin-offs—betrays the era's fear and fascination with the figure of the uncoupled, uncontrollable woman: the woman impelled by her own desires and designs, imperiling traditional structures of authority and, at the conclusion of many of the films named above, impaled by the heroes in a transparent reassertion of male potency. And in turn, this fixation with the matriarchal menace suggests that fantasy film provided a site within which widespread anxieties about changes in traditional gender roles, family configurations, and sexual power relations could be at once dramatized and contained.

It would be cheering if at this juncture, as I move from fantasy films of the golden age to those of the modern period, I could announce a seismic shift in the fantasy film genre, from the dark ages of social alienation to an era of equal-ity and acceptance. Such, however, is not the case; the alienating trends of the past survive, indeed thrive, right up to the present. One way of illustrating this continuity would be to return to the themes of this book's first three chapters to show their persistence in the modern cinema. Such a project would, unhappily, yield many examples. To cite only the most obvious case, the vilification of the Middle East endures in such films as *The Phantom Menace* (1999), with its rapa-cious Sandpeople, despotic Hut overlords, and hook-nosed slave traders oppos-ing the pure-white heroes of the civilized republic, or in the execrable remake of *The Mummy* (1999), with its ancient curse, craven bandits, and mindless fellahin hordes leagued, once more, against the sprightly, wisecracking Western good guys. In order to illustrate how widespread and diverse the forms of alienation within fantasy film are, however, I have chosen not to go over the same ground but to focus instead on a new set of issues, a new host of monstrous others, in the films of the modern period. I ask, therefore, that readers perform for themselves the act of projecting into the present the monsters I have identified in the films of the past, and that they perform a comparable act of rear projection as I focus on issues of alienation prominent in fantasy films of our own time (though present as well in those of an earlier era).

Topping the list in the modern-day cinema's culture of social alienation is the figure of the monstrous woman. Of all the beings discussed in this study, none has received more than a small fraction of the critical attention lavished on this figure: the release of *Alien* in 1979 touched off a flurry of scholarly activity on monstrosity and femininity that has not abated in the years since.[3] In accord with the dominant preoccupation of both feminist and fantasy film scholarship, critical discourse on this body of films has been strongly slanted toward the psychoana-lytic; the films have been read less in light of social or historical factors than in terms of men's universal, axiomatic, and unvarying dread of female sexuality. Studies of *Alien* provide a case in point. In her influential book *The Monstrous-Feminine: Film, Feminism, Psychoanalysis* (1993), Barbara Creed writes that "it is the notion of the fecund mother-as-abyss that is central to *Alien*; it is the abyss, the cannibalizing black hole from which all life comes and to which all life returns that is represented in the film as a source of deepest terror" (51). Likewise, Lynda Bundtzen believes that the alien "literally embodies woman's reproductive powers," arousing "primal anxieties about woman's sexual organs" and the "phallic mother of nightmare" (14). And though Judith Newton notes that "hostility and anxiety over the erosion of traditional gender roles [are] also present" in *Alien*, she concludes, "the alien is a potent expression of male terror at female sexuality and at castrating females in general" (85).[4] The "in general" overshadows *Alien*'s crucial position on the cusp between the women's movement of the 1970s and its unintended, unwelcome spawn, the 1980s counterattack of so-called family values.

I concur that the monstrous-woman films' manifest obsession with sexuality warrants psychoanalytic analyses. I believe, however, that such analyses may be refined, sharpened, and enriched—and their remedial potential thereby enhanced—through closer attention to the particular social histories within which the films operate.[5] To provide a single illustration of the limitations of psychoanalytic readings: Though Creed is certainly correct in noting that "when woman is represented as monstrous [in these films] it is almost always in relation to her mothering and reproductive functions" (7)—among the latter-day monstrous women I have enumerated, it is Ursula alone whose horror does not inhere in her hunger to perpetuate her seed, whether her clutch be dinosaurs, aliens, or vampires—Creed is on considerably shakier ground when she concludes that it is "the female reproductive/mothering capacity *per se*" that "is deemed monstrous" in *Alien* and its brood (51). In particular, such a conclusion glosses over the fact that in all these films, it is *unregulated* female reproduction, female reproduction that operates outside the patriarchal nuclear family, beyond male control or (in most cases) without willing male partnership—and *not* female reproduction per se—that is the monstrous woman's special scourge. It is as if the perversions of mothering that motivate these films embody the whole range of anxieties about personal, familial, and social maladjustments that changes in gender roles had ostensibly spawned; the films' accusations that women have become too big, too wild, and too free home in on women's defiance of sanctioned reproductive protocols. And in keeping with this social-historicist reading, it is notable that these films indict not only the monstrous woman but the host of male characters who are too ineffective, cowardly, or unscrupulous to prevent her from multiplying willfully—men who, in contrast to the paterfamilias heroes, forsake their immediate and broader families to dally with the monstrous—Other—woman.

In this chapter, then, I read *Jurassic Park* as representative of the era's monstrous-woman films, films rooted in the advocacy of patriarchal power that came to be defined, in a coup for conservative cant, as the "defense" of "family values." I say that *Jurassic Park* is representative, and so it is; but I should also say that it is not the *most* representative of its type. That dubious distinction likely falls to *Species*, a relative latecomer to the matriarchate that benefits both from audience conditioning and from its own determination to outstrip its predecessors in generic horror and formulaic perfection. But because it is so clearly riding the "womonster" bandwagon, *Species* is less suitable for extended treatment than *Jurassic Park*, which shows how deeply imbued with the era's hallucinatory gender fantasies were even those films that appear no more than sci-fi action adventures or showcases for cutting-edge special effects. I focus on *Jurassic Park*, then, relegating more obvious cases to supporting roles, in the belief that such an emphasis will illustrate the scope of the issues these films both espoused and engendered.

Fantasy Values

Family values was one of the most pervasive, yet evasive, concepts in American national discourse of the 1980s and 1990s. Overtly, advocates of the family-values movement were candid enough: spearheaded by New Right conservatives within or close to the Reagan White House and by televangelists such as Jerry Falwell of the Moral Majority, the campaign gained ground thanks to what many perceived as an evident upheaval in the philosophies and composition of the nation's families. From divorce to day care, pornography to perversity, aborted fetuses to absentee fathers, the families of the 1980s and 1990s seemed beset by a welter of moral failings, some of their own devising, others attributable to agents provocateurs (feminists, liberals) whose poisonous ideologies had contaminated both the private and the public well. Ultimately, the rhetoric of family values claimed the power to dominate debates over a range of issues, from welfare reform to television ratings; to divide (if never decide) presidential elections, particularly the Clinton-Bush race of 1992; and to shape representations of the nation's troubles and trials throughout the popular media, from mass-market magazines to mega-blockbuster movies.

Just as remarkable as the ubiquity of family-values rhetoric, however, is its elusiveness. Though a search through the literature of the era—political treatises, sociological essays, journalistic squibs—turns up references to *family values* too voluminous to begin to count, the same search turns up no outright definitions of the term and few attempts to define it at all. To an extent, this shiftiness was integral to the campaign's rhetoric, which generated the watchword *defense* when the modus operandi was attack, and which spun an aura of nostalgia, conservatism, even reactionism when its agenda was radical, visionary, even revolutionary. In the case of the campaign's lead term, however, fuzziness was not merely strategic but intrinsic; whatever forms it took at the level of policy or action, at the level of discourse family values was less a bounded set of beliefs than a capacious abstraction enabling the culture to give a range of misgivings about familial, social, and cultural change a local habitation and a name. And consequently, family values served also as ideological Red bait, a means of luring out of their lairs all the beasts ranged against what "true Americans" held dear, even if those Americans knew what they were holding only because someone or something threatened to snatch it away.

The contours of the campaign, accordingly, become crisp only when one shifts from the center to the margins, from family values to its foes. The most overt and invariable target of family-values diatribes was the supposed derangement within the bosom (and bedroom) of the family; singled out for profaning family values were those women and men who had been duped, seduced, or coerced into ignoring, repudiating, or sabotaging traditional gender roles. In *Backlash: The Undeclared War Against American Women* (1991), Susan Faludi meticulously excavates one pillar of this rhetoric: the 1980s assault against the women's liberation movement, an assault that both demonized and terrorized working women, childless women, and single women in a culturewide effort to "push women back into their 'acceptable' roles—whether as Daddy's girl or fluttery romantic, active nester or passive love object" (xxii). Toward the close of the 1980s, however, the thrust of family-values rhetoric shifted, in Judith Stacey's words, "from laments over the social hazards unleashed by miscreant moms to those caused by missing dads" (51); the retooled campaign declared itself aggrieved not only by aggressive women but by the impotent men who, in the face of the female onslaught, had failed to uphold, or had willingly relinquished, the scepter that was theirs to wield. This shift in tone and target reflects the campaign's attainment of a more moderate, inclusive appeal; though most Americans had repudiated the excesses of the New Right, the profather petition achieved broad consensus throughout the culture. It would be a mistake, however, to view the two phases of the campaign as neatly separable; not only did they overlap in time but, as is evident from the following passage, profather forces typically traced dad's ominous eclipse to mom's obnoxious rise:

> Women . . . posted warning signals that, essentially, forced men to discard traditional male behavior or remain outside. . . . The hostility toward men, and their symbolic castration, became acceptable blood sport. . . . Some women came to believe that men were useful

only for impregnation, after which they should be discarded. . . . Men came to accept their exiled status. In some instances, those who hadn't already deserted their families left eagerly, believing they held no valued position in their households or in their relationships. (Barras 46)

In the book of family values, the overthrow of a gendered division of labor, both economic and reproductive—men as breadwinners and authority figures, women as bearers and rearers of children—was the source, original and ongoing, of social dissolution. At bottom, then, whether assailing emancipated women or bewailing emasculated men, family values pinned the culture's woes on its loss or rejection of the father.

The consistency of this message throughout the 1980s and 1990s is little short of astonishing, the rhetoric of rapacious women and faltering fathers insinuating itself into virtually every niche of the era's discourse. It comes as no surprise, of course, that some of the most strident words of denunciation were those issued by the fundamentalist ideologues who had risen to national renown by hoisting the family-values standard. Their convictions that "radical feminists" wanted to "end the institution of marriage" (Lutzer 84), that "men have been feminized" while "women have been masculinized," corrupting the biblical charge for wifely submission without which "a family will not work" (Whitehead 201), were in keeping with an agenda that sought, in Carol Flake's words, to "restore America to the golden age of patriarchy" (85).[6] Similarly, it is unremarkable that so many mass-market publications—from newsweeklies to best-sellers—should piggyback on and profit from the gender-mending trend. For instance, Toni Grant's *Being a Woman* (1988) warns that contemporary America is headed in the direction of the legendary Amazon culture, which exploited men "as a means of procreation, after which they were discarded in black widow spider fashion" (11); in a society in which woman has become a "devouring, consuming monster" (49), Grant muses, it is no wonder that so few men are willing to settle down, for to do so is to take up residence in the very lair of the beast. Similarly, in David Blankenhorn's *Fatherless America* (1995), the calamity of fathers having been reduced, effectively, to sperm donors is expressed in unmistakably genocidal terms:

For the culture, the rise of the Sperm Father constitutes nothing less than father killing, the witting enactment of cultural patricide. For the individual man, being a Sperm Father is not a style of fatherhood but a means of paternal suicide: the collaboration of the male in the eradication of his fatherhood. Toward the end of the fatherless society, the Sperm Father represents the final solution. (184)

If, however, the discourse of female unruliness and male enfeeblement is to be expected in such sources, its presence and prominence might appear unaccountable in Allan Bloom's *The Closing of the American Mind* (1987), a book outwardly about the waning of philosophical inquiry in the nation's colleges. Here, Bloom indicts feminism for its defiance of "nature" and its use of "force" (100), reprehends the idea that "the souls of men—their ambitious, warlike, protective, possessive character—must be dismantled in order to liberate women" (129), and petulantly invokes the days when the father was seen as "the symbol of the divine on earth, the unquestioned bearer of authority" (114); the days when, in keeping with its owner's political prowess, the man's penis was "admired" by women for the "wonderful" thing it is, rather than being "compared and judged, which is daunting" (124). What all this has to do with Kant and Kierkegaard is unclear. Yet Bloom's text indicates how malleable were the terms of the dysfunctional family drama, with its image of unnatural, forceful women lording it over dismantled, daunted men and its argument—explicit or not—that only when men regained the ascendancy would sanity and security return to the land.

These accumulated dirges leave no question, as Faludi writes, that "if the 'pro-family' movement was 'pro' anything, it was paternal power" (263); what was perceived to be in peril was not merely the domestic ideal but the reproduction (or dissemination) of a system of male authority dependent in large part on traditional domestic roles but not limited to them. This slippage between family and social power reveals itself in a variety of ways, as in the tendency of family-values engineers to theorize the state itself as a maternal monster, a secondary, suffocating mechanism violating the naturally occurring organism of the father-headed family—what Allan Carlson terms the "displacement of the patriarchal family by the matriarchal state" (234). It may be fruitless to ask in what sense the state can be characterized as "matriarchal"; though the widely held view that a gluttonous liberal government provided a haven for feminist harridans may provide one answer, it is probably best to say that because family-values theorists believed the family was inherently the first and last preserve of masculinity, any preemption or infiltration of its power *must* constitute an assault by female forces. As such, just as the colonization of the paternal sanctum had shattered the harmony of the family, so did it forebode, as George Gilder warned in *Men and Marriage* (1986), the downfall of civilization itself: "When people lose the power of sexual polarity, they also lose their procreative energy and faith in themselves and their prospects" (x–xi). Gilder elaborates:

> With the breakdown of families, the economy also declines, as the long term efforts of male providers give way to short term and predatory economic behavior. An emasculated state neither can defend

itself against male outlaws and exploiters, muggers and terrorists, hijackers and assassins, nor can achieve the economic growth to finance the welfare programs and police efforts required by a culture in chaos. (111)

Gilder's conclusion is at once sprawling and devastatingly direct:

> The [emasculated] society will pay the costs one way or another: not only through tremendous outlays for day care but also through economic declines, population loss, juvenile delinquency, crime, mental illness, alcoholism, addiction, and divorce. . . . The alternative to traditional family roles is not a unisex family; it is sexual suicide. (154)

Moving fluidly from the smallest unit of society to the largest, from the confidential to the apocalyptic, the rabid logic of family values construes women's excessive and unreasonable grasping for power, and men's inability or unwillingness to rein them in, as inseparable from the ghastly prospect of a grand patriarchal edifice in rapid, headlong decline.

Coupled with gender in such Judgment Day auguries, moreover, was an equally protean and potent ally: race. Predictions such as Gilder's, that is, relied not only on conjuring a feminist menace but on identifying an even more awful bogey at the far end of the social spectrum: that of a fatherless African American subculture breeding (as critics such as Blankenhorn were fond of putting it) "fourteen-year-old girls with babies and fourteen-year-old boys with guns" (184), the former threatening the broader society's economic and moral underpinnings, the latter its physical and economic safety. The motivations behind this foregrounding of race, which became an incessant refrain of the profather movement, are clear: the collapsing of gender and race further mobilized support for the family-values campaign by seeding fear of a minority threat, an operation persuasively conducted under the guise of benevolent concern for the underclass. (The nearly unanimous ovations for the punitive welfare reform legislation of 1994 are only one indication of how playing the race card served the campaign in its pursuit of popular and bipartisan favor.) More subtly, the specter of ghetto tribes on the dole supplied the perfect prototype of matriarchy's supposedly baneful effects. As Gilder describes the disorder, "the black family [is] breaking down because female jobs and welfare payments usurped the man's role as provider" (80). From that, he observes, "It should be clear to any sentient observer . . . that the worst parts of the ghetto present a rather typical pattern of female dominance" (84). The African American man, he concludes, "driven to the wall, threatened with emasculation, surrounded everywhere by formidable women" (85), has not surprisingly struck back against the culture that, in depriving him of a socially sanctioned role, has unleashed his antisocial instincts. That the family-values campaign offered the complementary stereotype of the wanton "welfare mother" as a spectacularly fertile teenaged incubator—of poverty, crime, addiction, and AIDS as well as of whelps—is in keeping with both the narrowly family-oriented and more broadly sociopolitical bent of family-values rhetoric, for in both senses these wayward girls were evidently committed to the reproduction of offspring hostile to paternal or paternalistic authority, oversight, and control.[7]

Taken as a whole, then, family-values discourse formed a unit whose power derived not from empirical validity but from metonymic imposture: in place of hard fact, what the campaign achieved was the creation of a web of signifiers so impenetrable as to appear irrefutable. On the one hand, the penchant to identify the most intimate site of heterosexual contact as the ultimate battleground can be seen as little better than a deception and a dodge, with the call for a defense of the family serving a larger crusade to curtail if not abolish the welfare state. Cloaking an extremist political agenda under the mantle of biology, that is, the mom-and-pop business is at once emotionally resonant, ideologically tidy in its dichotomizing of devoted and deviant, and—since it appears neutral—difficult to contest without seeming fanatical or perverse. Yet on the other hand, it would be equally fair to say that the prognostications of wholesale cultural collapse run interference for a program of institutionalized sexism; nightmare images of welfare-induced crack babies and gun-toting street hoodlums provide justification for dismantling not only welfare but the matriarchy that supposedly sustained and was sustained by it. In the end, the effect of this rhetorical morass was to disguise the ideological nature of the family-values campaign's pleas for the father: to sanctify gender roles by presenting them as purely biological imperatives, while emptying patriarchy of any taint by rendering it natural to the point of invisibility. The campaign, to the extent it was successful, thus had the effect of severing the family from the social and ideological nexus within which it exists; in the fantastic plot of family values, the multiple menaces of the social unconscious—mother-monster, smother-state, other-race—fused into a many-headed hydra, venomously attacking the elemental law of the father-family.

Two issues must be clarified at this point. First, to present the family-values campaign in such an unsparing light is not to say that there was no basis in reality for the alarms it sounded. Though scholars have shown that the "traditional" family widely believed to have fallen prey to the depredations of unruly women and unsteady men was "an ahistorical amalgam of structures, values, and behaviors that never coexisted in the same time and place" (Coontz 9)—not even in the 1950s, the decade that most family-values pundits denominated the period of the patriarchal unit's fullest and final flowering—no responsible commentator would deny that many of the issues the campaign cited, particularly those having to do with poverty, are worthy of serious attention. Yet this being the case, it is important to reiterate that family-values rhetoric functions precisely to *deflect* serious attention from these issues. Representing, in Stacey's astute phrase, "a politics of displacement," the campaign not only lumps many arguably unrelated issues under the shadowy, catch-all category of father-loss but offers apparent solutions that are actually mere "proxy rhetoric for antifeminist, antigay, xenophobic, and antiwelfare sentiments, which themselves displace direct engagement with the most fraught social divisions and anxieties in our nation" (73).[8] The second point I would make, however, is that one must distinguish between a feint and a conspiracy, a backroom cabal; though family values was surely the former, it was probably not the latter. Its spark may well have been genuine concern over trends that many saw as deeply damaging to American life; its tactics, even at the highest levels, were fitful, uncoordinated, and inconsistent; its operatives were far-flung, loosely united, and in all likelihood convinced of both their reactive posture and their unsullied concern for the public good—indeed, save for its shock troops, such as the Million Men marchers or the Operation Rescue thugs, a majority of its "operatives" may have had no conscious sense that they were such. Inasmuch as family-values ideology proliferated throughout every cultural and social stratum—the home, the office, the pulpit, the assembly, the bench, the clinic, the silver screen—my summary has necessarily been selective; focusing on what I consider to be the campaign's principal thrust, I have ignored inconsistencies within this element, not to mention the ways in which family-values discourse was adopted, and adapted, by those throughout the ideological spectrum, even by those who questioned its tenets. Ultimately, a balanced assessment of the family-values campaign would likely be forced to admit that it was less a campaign than a clearinghouse, one in which the myriad anxieties, cravings, and stalemates of the time could be displayed (or displaced) for all, though unraveled by none.

At the same time, however, to question the integrity of this campaign is not to imply that the movement's dominant camp was so diffuse as to be unrecognizable, nor that it was rudderless, irresolute, or inconsequential. Quite the contrary. The barrage of rhetoric attacking women and exalting men, coupled with the systemic (if not wholly systematic) efforts to shore up what were believed to be the sagging organs of male authority, wrought many significant outcomes: draconian welfare reforms, abortion gag rules and parental consent laws, prohibitions on adoption by homosexual couples, and apathy in the face of the putatively "gay disease," AIDS, represent the merest fraction of the family-values fallout. Moreover, though the original defenders of family values witnessed political setbacks and defeats during these decades, it was the conservative vanguard's vision of family values that continued to shape debate, to place alternatives on the defensive, throughout the period. Therefore, though this vision was not all-determining, it did vital service in nurturing the places where public conviction and cultural representation are jointly forged—as in the cinema. And in this project, the *as if* world of fantasy film played a particularly significant role, becoming one of the most open and well-lit arenas for the rehearsal and renewal of the family-values master-narrative: the saga of the knight-errant clad in tarnished mail (or male), tilting to wrest kingdom and kids from the clutches of the dragon lady.

The Other Woman

At first glance, the relationship between film and the family-values campaign appears an antagonistic one; few during this period saw film as a friend to family values, while many considered the entertainment media—film, television, and popular music—an unholy trinity ranged against tradition, religion, and decency. In 1980, when Falwell sought to prove the existence of a "vicious assault upon the American family," exhibit number one came from the small screen: "More television programs depict homes of divorced or of single parents than depict the traditional family. Nearly every major family-theme TV program openly justifies divorce, homosexuality, and adultery" (121). The tune had not changed much by 1990, when conservative analysts charged that the "invasion of moral turf [from the entertainment media] inflicts serious harm on the family" and that "as the mass media's power to influence family life has become stronger and stronger, the family's power to influence the mass media has become weaker and weaker" (Cofer and Jacobvitz 196). In 1992, the year before the release of *Jurassic Park* (and during the ostensible Year of the Woman), movie critic Michael Medved's *Hollywood vs. America* characterized the film industry as "an all-powerful enemy, an alien force that assaults our most cherished values and corrupts our children" (3). More famously, it was in that same year that Vice President Dan Quayle, seeking to spell out the moral difference between Republicans and Democrats during a tight presidential race, targeted sitcom icon (and single mother) Murphy Brown as an example of how the liberal elites running the show had profaned the nation's ideals.[9] As typically presented by family-values fans, film was less an outgrowth of the culture than a degenerate graft onto it; underlying their attacks was the assumption, when not the assertion, that Hollywood, having foisted its amoral visions on a spellbound citizenry since at least the decadent 1970s, had both undermined public morality and left the upright too shell-shocked to protest.

This tidy parable, however, reveals a willful misunderstanding not only of the ideological work of much film of the 1980s and 1990s but, more generally, of the role of film in culture. Typical of the family-values advocates' inclination toward us-versus-them thinking—as in the title of Medved's book—the claim that there is something called "Hollywood" that is alien to something called "America" offers a textbook case of the strategies by which dominant cultural ideologies seek convenient scapegoats. Indeed, Medved goes so far as to charge that national anxiety over the collapse of the family can be traced to "the influence of the popular culture, with its clearly demonstrated and uncompromising contempt for conventional family values" (96). If there is a crisis in the family, he argues, this is attributable to "the huge chasm between our own view of the world and Hollywood's," whose "antifamily images have become so deeply ingrained in our national consciousness that few Americans can summon the courage or the strength to dismiss them as the destructive distortions that they are" (96). Even bypassing the illogic of this review—Medved wishes to argue both that Hollywood has blemished family values and that it has slighted their stainless purity—the reductive nature of his rhetoric is apparent. For if, as is undeniable, a great many Hollywood films deal with families other than the traditional kind, families that are fragmenting, families that are less than perfect, this does not mean that "they"— Hollywood—oppose what "we"—Americans—cherish, but that like the very forces Medved champions, film is involved in the project of presenting "the family" as contested terrain, a tantalizing, fascinating object of desire and attack. In her study of 1980s films that center on family issues, Sarah Harwood nicely summarizes the relationship between such films and their cultural contexts: "These films intersected in very specific and complex ways with broader cultural discourses to interrogate both the actuality and the rhetoric of the nuclear family, producing representations which reverberated with the anxieties of a fracturing social unconscious and polarising political project" (71). Thus it is not, as Medved has it, that film *lacks* "values," the filmmakers' alibi being that it is not "appropriate to impose values at all on the creation or evaluation of entertainment" (23), but that film provides a space in which values that are imposed and created by a variety of forces within the culture—including its cinema—can be tested and contested, compromised and reinforced.

What this means, furthermore, is that like the culture that begot them, family-values films tend to be more fluent in demonizing their adversaries than in defining their own vision, more able to finger that which threatens the family than to point toward some putatively ideal condition that preexists or survives the threat. To cite the most obvious example, consider a film that a great many critics find central to the family-values campaign: 1987's *Fatal Attraction*.[10] As

Faludi sees it, *Fatal Attraction* is the most extreme—and as such, the most popu-lar—of a series of "late-1980s pro-family films [that] are larded with male anger over female demands and male anxiety over women's progress" (137). In the story of a single, psychotic home-wrecker who nearly shatters a philanderer's comfort-able existence before succumbing to a bullet fired by his stay-at-home wife, the film focuses many of the dire admonitions and moral precepts that suffused the era. Yet accordingly, much of the "male anger" in *Fatal Attraction* and its ugly sisterhood—the parade of cookie-cutter offerings like *The Hand That Rocks the Cradle* (1992) and *The Crush* (1993)—is directed against men, and in particular against fathers, who have themselves transgressed the dictates of family values. The plot of *Fatal Attraction*, it is important to remember, unfolds from husband Dan's act of infidelity; that he justifies his affair on the grounds of his waning sex life at home strikes one as the flimsiest, most clichéd of motivations. It is important to recall here too that in attempting to kill the other woman, Alex, Dan becomes, effectively, an abortionist; for so far as the viewer knows, from Alex's report, she is pregnant with his child, and thus from her perspective, her pursuit of the father represents an attempt to fulfill the biological and sociologi-cal directives that family values dictated for women. In this respect, oddly enough, the respectable Dan might be said to merit the reproach that the former secre-tary of education and drug czar and ongoing family-values eminence, William Bennett, directs at (mostly African American) fathers: "It is these absent men, above all, who deserve our censure and disesteem. Abandoning alike those whom they have taken as sexual partners and those whose lives they have created, they strike at the heart of the marital ideal, traduce generations yet to come, and dis-grace their very manhood" (93–94).

If, then, *Fatal Attraction* satisfies both the murderous and the moralistic im-pulses of the period in its elimination of the predatory woman and its reassertion of the value of family, it cannot entirely still the demons it has summoned. In-deed, as Harwood points out, the film's closing image, which figures the "resti-tution of a nuclear family and the mythical serenity of a domestic space," is it-self "so shot through with contradiction" as to be "unconvincing" (73): the photograph of the restored family on which the film's final frames linger "throw[s] into question" the very "closure" it seeks to achieve (1), for this snapshot was taken *before* the events of the film transpired and thus is restorative only in nos-talgic retrospect. These factors suggest that if, as Faludi argues, *Fatal Attraction* provided viewers a forum in which "to express deep-seated resentments and fears about women" (113), those feelings remain unresolved by the film (a fact that may account for its apparently prodigious repeat business): the orgiastic vio-lence of its conclusion succeeds in hiding, not in healing, the rifts in the family, failing to fix—restore or cement—the "values" that presumably render such violence necessary.

To a certain extent, fantasy films prove more adept at stabilizing, or at least appearing to stabilize, family values; these films' existence, one might even argue, owes much to their ability to employ strategies of containment denied their mainstream kin. Most obviously, fantasy films' freedom from tests of everyday validity enables them to embody the monstrous apparitions conjured by family-values rhetoric in their most naked, terrifying forms, forms at once overwhelmingly menacing in pursuit and keenly gratifying in defeat. At the same time, fantasy films enjoy a nearly perfect impunity in their exercise of violence against the monstrous woman. Though the seductress of *Fatal Attraction* might have been designed by her director, Adrian Lyne, as "a raging beast underneath" (qtd. in Faludi 120), on the surface she is demonstrably human, and thus her demise can be acceptable only to the extent that her motivations are damnable. In fantasy film, by contrast, motivation need not be an issue, nor retribution a source of qualm; motivation, such as it is, collapses into physiology, with the monstrous woman "motivated" solely by her reproductive cycle. As Dr. Alan Grant in *Jurassic Park* puts it, the female monsters "just do what they do." Biology thus becomes destiny with a vengeance; the monstrous woman's procreative capacity is possessed of such gale-force magnitude that no familial or social restraints can lasso it, and no end be put to it, short of its utter extirpation. Concurrently, the moral failures of men, their passivity in the face of female misrule or their participation in encouraging it, can reach their most awful conclusion in the fantasy film: the total erasure of men from reproductive significance, their reduction (at best) to midwives for the monstrous woman's delivery or (at worst) to incubators of her offspring once the birthing process has spiraled beyond their control. What this means is that the heroes' labors assume an epidemic gravity and urgency. No longer at stake is the mere survival of one human family, but the survival of the human family itself. And in turn, if under these heightened risks any loose ends might be glaringly evident, the sheer enormousness of the undertaking works to disguise defects in the victory, producing an apparently secure resolution (though even this resolution, as the sequels to *Alien*, *Species*, and *Jurassic Park* or the revelation of surviving monstrous babies in the closing shots of *Little Shop of Horrors* and *Godzilla* attest, is not seamless).

The monstrous-woman film that most epitomizes these features and functions is, as I said before, *Species*, the tale of a genetically engineered alien hybrid who metamorphoses into a reptilian terror during attempts to breed with human males.[11] What distinguishes *Species* from its kindred is its calculated, utterly self-conscious employment of family-values ideology; remarkably unsubtle—and ultimately unsatisfying in its cobbled-together, retread feel—*Species* is nonetheless a useful film in that it highlights elements that operate less obtrusively and doggedly in its sister films.

The plot of *Species* perfectly integrates the twin heads of family-values discourse: bred by government geneticists who have been duped by instructions they received from outer space, the alien, Sil, must be hunted down by a mostly male team (a bounty hunter, an "empath," and a sociologist) before her potential to reproduce overwhelms the human race. "When a predatory species is introduced into a closed ecological system," the sociologist explains, "the extinction of the weaker species is inevitable." During the hunt, the film misses no opportunity to mark Sil as a liberated, sexually aggressive woman; for example, when the project's head scientist notes that "We decided to make [the hybrid] female so that it would be more docile and controllable," the bounty hunter snorts: "Docile and controllable? I guess you guys don't get out much." (As if this line were not ham-handed enough, it is repeated verbatim later in the film.) Visually, *Species* piles on a surfeit of fertility imagery: the womblike cocoon from which the adult Sil emerges; the lapping water of the pools and hot tubs that back her sex scenes; the damp, cramped subterranean passages in which she gives birth. Sil herself is an incarnation of reproductive energy: she grows to adulthood in mere weeks, conceives on her first completed act of intercourse, and delivers a baby that achieves maturity in minutes. Her killing acts, moreover, are expressed in patently sexualized terms: one man whom she deems "unacceptable" is dispatched by her tongue ramming through his mouth and into his brain, while another, balking at how "fast" she moves from foreplay to intercourse, is drowned in his hot tub while one of her tentacles stuffs his mouth in a parodic reversal of oral sex. Furthermore, the fact that Sil is driven by biological mandates so deeply woven into her being that even she does not understand their origin or purpose—recurrent nightmares of her monstrous lineage haunt her sleep—emphasizes the unconscious, instinctual power of women's reproduction and thus the need for those in authority to patrol and control its expression.

In this respect, though the focus of the film's horror is the monstrous woman, the focus of its judgment is the men around her, without whose discretion (or lack thereof) her rampaging hormones would never have found release. Not only, of course, was she initially bred by scientists whose hubris led them to believe that they could control her, but at critical moments, the hunters are either deceived or distracted from their quest. For instance, it emerges that the chief scientist has been unwittingly aiding Sil under the influence of her telepathic powers. More blatantly, though the team is far from certain that Sil has died in an accident she staged, instead of staying on the alert, the boys get drunk in their hotel bar, numbing the empath's misgivings sufficiently for Sil to spring her final trap. Entering the room of the sociologist—who despite knowing her methods is completely unsuspicious when a beautiful stranger seduces him in his hotel room, and who is too irresponsible to wait for her answer to his question "What about protection?"—she makes the man pay for his recklessness when she disposes of him after securing his seed. Even the character who at first seems the film's moral center—the empath, who cannot fathom killing another being, for he feels too deeply their pain—is ultimately revealed as an accomplice in the monstrous woman's designs precisely because he *has* sympathized with her, slowing the course of vengeance by raising moral scruples about the justice of killing a "threatened" creature. In this respect, the empath might be said to stand in for the audience: seeing Sil at first as a frightened preteen girl who, for reasons yet unknown, is caged by white-robed government technicians who attempt to gas her to death, the audience, like the empath, will learn to overcome initial feelings of sympathy once it becomes apparent what Sil "really" is, once she has matured into the sexual predator that the seemingly innocent girl was destined to become. In the film's climactic sequence, when Sil is revealed as a full-figure, computer-generated character, the conversion from woman to monster is complete: no longer does there remain any trace of the human actor who plays Sil but rather, in her place, is a Medusa-like horror, her movements those of a spider, her eyes those of a feral cat, her hair and breasts erupting with tentacles. Thus the bounty hunter's words before firing the shot that brings Sil down at last are fitting: "Let go, you motherfucker." Having been "mothered" by irresponsible men with whom she has attempted, with their own abetting, to copulate, Sil produces offspring that will become a terrible blight unless the man who most fulfills the ideal of traditional male authority, the man who gets the (human) girl in the end, does not "get" the monstrous girl as well.

Its title character notwithstanding, then, *Species* is very much a man's film: it is men who catalyze and resolve the crisis, men who possess choices, and men who can be judged on the basis of their actions. In this drama, the monstrous woman herself is little more than gruesome window dressing; lacking the ability to determine (or even understand) her fate, she is simply a brute fact that must be dealt with by men. That women are not always shoved to the sidelines of family-values fantasy film is obvious from *Aliens*, *Species*'s predecessor by a decade, as well as its model in both core plot elements and (thanks to H. R. Giger's creatures) visual design. A number of critics have read *Aliens* as a commentary on feminism, and from this perspective, the film has yielded diametrically opposed readings: while Robin Roberts construes the film as a liberationist manifesto, Susan Jeffords finds its feminist proclivities outweighed by its extreme gynophobia

("'Battle'"). I would suggest, however, that the film's apparent inconsistencies can profitably be read—if not entirely reconciled—by placing *Aliens* within the broader context of family-values ideology, which helps to account not only for the film's representation of women but for its concomitant meditation on men, children, and the family.

Consider, in this light, the film's critical, when not condemnatory, treatment of its male characters, who are almost without exception stooges, suckers, or pushovers for the monstrous woman (as the alien monarch will turn out to be). If feminism is seen as the film's determining context, such treatment might seem a strategy to set off its strong, capable heroine, Sergeant Ellen Ripley. Seen in terms of family-values discourse, however, it becomes evident that what unites these men is their mishandling or profanation of the father role. Most patently violating the father's charge to foster and protect is the Company man, Burke, who not only seeks to impregnate the prepubescent foundling Newt with the alien seed but who sends families with young children, unwarned and unarmed, in search of the deadly life-form to whose presence Ripley has alerted him. Footage deleted from the film's theatrical run but restored in its DVD release[12] emphasizes the devastation wrought by reckless fathers: scenes of the colonists before they are overrun by the "xenomorphs" reveal that it was Newt's father, in company with his wife and children, who discovered the derelict spacecraft in which the dormant alien eggs are housed. Inspired by the prospect of gain—"We have scored big this time!" he exults—and suggesting that they "take a look inside," it is the father who returns infected by the first face-hugger. With its intimation of illicit sexuality, the father anticipating a "score" within an ominous locale outside the home, this sequence parallels that of *Fatal Attraction*, suggesting that fathers who dally with other women carry contagion to their families, communities, nation, and race.

If, moreover, some of the men in *Aliens* are directly engaged with monsters in the destruction of the family, others are inadequately vigilant, poised, or pragmatic to control the monstrous threat once it has been unleashed. The marines sent to rescue the colonists comprise a posse of arrested adolescents whose pettish need to assert their masculinity is expressed by their pronged ship, massive rifles protruding from waist level, and prefight badinage about the "juicy colonists' daughters we have to rescue from their virginity." The standout representative of such hypertrophied male sexuality is Hudson, for whom militarism and machismo are inextricably entwined and for whom, accordingly, gunslinger vainglory turns to whimpering imbecility when his piece sputters and gutters out within the hot, moist, narrow tunnel in which the scary things lurk.[13] In this respect, Vasquez, the tough female marine whom some critics see as furthering a feminist reading of the film, might better be seen as yet another curiosity in a long parade of paltry surrogates who have rushed in to fill the vacuum of legitimate paternal authority; the question she is asked as she pursues her fanatical program to out-macho the boys—"Have you ever been mistaken for a man?"—is apt not only for her but for the corps as a whole.[14] Even the film's two sympathetic male characters, the cyborg Bishop and the grunt Hicks, prove ineffectual. Though he possesses a gentleness and courage that contrast starkly with the rapacity of the film's "real" men, Bishop, a mere mock-up of a man, cannot measure up when met by the alien queen, who cuts him down to size in the final confrontation. Hicks, meanwhile, though he does not actually betray Newt, does fail her three times: when he cannot cut through a grate fast enough to pluck her from an advancing alien drone; when injuries prevent him from tracking her to the queen's nest; and when he is out of commission during the queen's final attack. Heavily sedated, this would-be dad sleeps blissfully through the child's dream of monsters.

Thus it falls to Ripley to save the child; and in this respect too the film adheres in significant respects to family-values orthodoxy. For Ripley is defined largely, if not solely, as a mother; from the start of the film, when a shot of her profile dissolves to the curve of a planet's surface, she appears as earth-mother, nurturer of children. Footage excised from the theatrical version of the film, moreover, identifies her as a biological mother whose guilt over the death of her daughter, who died older than she due to Ripley's protracted hypersleep, underlies her ferocious defense of Newt: "I promised her that I would be home for her birthday," Ripley moans, a working woman who has abandoned her child to die alone. Commenting on the transformation in Ripley's character from the first film in the series to the second, Constance Penley suggests that "Ripley is . . . marked [in *Aliens*] by a difference that is automatically taken to be a sign of femininity. . . . What we finally get is a conservative moral lesson about maternity, futuristic or otherwise: mothers will be mothers, and they will *always* be women" (73).

As in *Fatal Attraction*, moreover, mothers will always fight to ensure their offspring's survival. Thus in the climactic war between Ripley and the alien queen, "good" and "bad" mothers square off to determine the future of their races. The queen, the "bad-ass mama" who "runs the whole show"—as she is identified in dialogue restored to the DVD version—embodies a monstrous exaggeration of the maternal instinct; her sole function is reproduction, which explains both her spectacular success and her hysteria when Ripley torches her eggs and ovipositor. The queen is thus at once Ripley's double and her rival, a "bitch"—as Ripley snarls at her in the film's most famous line—both in her incalculable fecundity and in the threat this power poses to the human family. To be sure, there are ambiguities here: if the unforgettably horrific depiction of the alien queen fully satisfies, indeed gluts, the family-values stereotype of the female fiend, the replacement of the male action hero with the mother subverts both the stereotype of the monstrous woman's supposed opposite—the sweet, decorous, or decorative, chastely lovely angel in the house—and the reconstitution of the nuclear family. In the film's final shot, showing Newt's face in the foreground and Ripley's just behind as the two settle into hypersleep, the father remains an absence. One might think of this twist, however, in terms of *Aliens'* temporal setting. Whereas the other films I have listed take place in the present or the past and thus allow for the possibility of the world's remaining fathers halting the spread of the monstrous woman's seed, *Aliens* represents the ruinous consummation divined by family-values doomsayers: a world in which "the children are to be had on the female's terms, with or without fathers" (Bloom 105); in which "science will allow women to dispense with male assistance even in the business of getting pregnant," thus reducing men to "drones in the new matriarchy" (Berger and Berger 189); and in which women will have the power "to either deprive a man of his right to become a parent or force him to become one against his will" (Parke and Brott 166). With none but fake fathers left—and with those who came before having slept with the enemy—biological and social reproduction have become the exclusive province of women, leaving men as mere receptacles to be callously consumed and gorily discarded.

Nonetheless, if *Aliens* projects a future world, its depiction of the queen simultaneously locates the film within a specific context of contemporary family-values discourse: that of race. As Amy Taubin notes,

> The misogyny of the [final] scene has often been analysed on a psychosexual level as the refusal of the "monstrous feminine," of the archaic, devouring mother. But it also has a historically specific, political meaning. If Ripley is the prototypical, upper-middle-class WASP, the alien queen bears a suspicious resemblance to a favourite scapegoat of the Reagan/Bush era—the black welfare mother, that parasite on the economy whose uncurbed reproductive drive reduced hard-working taxpayers to bankruptcy. (8)[15]

Indeed, the queen's nest, a bleak cavity in the city's bowels guarded by the fecund mother's dark-skinned, lethal gang, visually suggests the racist stereotype of the black inner city, a squalid place of proliferating violence and illegitimacy. It may be no more than coincidence that *Aliens* appeared in the same year as a report issued by the Reagan White House titled *The Family: Preserving America's Future*, which acclaimed the nuclear family, imagined with *"horror"* the calamitous consequences of a *"welfare culture"* reducing families to *"fragments, households headed by a mother dependent upon public charity"* (Bauer 15; emphasis in original), and characterized the African American family as "a disaster story," a sinkhole of "social pathologies" (16). Nonetheless, both the report and the film developed from, and helped to nurture, the same nascent ideology, the same emerging conviction that the future could be preserved only if a monstrous, female, nonwhite threat to the middle-class, white, father-headed family could be surmounted.

By the time of *Jurassic Park*, that ideology had matured considerably, cutting its teeth on the lessons of successive Republican presidencies, finding its legs—and its voice—during the election of 1992, and weathering the first apparent affront to its invincibility during that same contest. The fact that family-values discourse, or at least its torchbearers, lost in 1992 suggests the possibility of reading *Jurassic Park* as part of a program to defend a putatively threatened ideological consensus: not only to restore a supposedly venerable moral ideal but to redeem a much more timely, specific political legacy. Concurrently, developments in 1990s Hollywood make it possible to see *Jurassic Park* as part of an effort to redress woman troubles still closer to home. As Dawn Sova writes, whereas "women in the 1980s had reason to feel that the only way to assume an element of control was to create a whole new enterprise, their own production company, . . . women in the 1990s chose to invade already existing enterprises" (181). While I would not want to insist on an immediate causal relationship between a particular film and the political fortunes or corporate power-shifts of its time, Sova's suggestive image of women "invading" male-dominated companies of (re)production provides a useful model for thinking about the role *Jurassic Park* played within the political, cultural, and industrial contexts of the early 1990s. What *Jurassic Park* exhibits is both the confidence of family-values discourse as it strides into the mainstream—a surety indicated by the ease with which the discourse inhabits a film-world that offers itself as apolitical, concerned only with crowd-pleasing special effects and neutral ("natural") biology lessons—and, not coincidentally, the intensification of family-values discourse under perceived conditions of attack. Vivian Sobchack writes that during the last two decades of the twentieth century, the genres of "horror, family melodrama, and science fiction . . . exchanged and expended their representational energy dynamically and urgently—with the 'politically unconscious' aim of seeking re-solution, or at least ab-solution, for a threatened patriarchy and its besieged structure of perpetuation: the bourgeois family" ("Child" 27). A mélange of all three genres that Sobchack names, *Jurassic Park* represents the patriarchal family as threatened and besieged by monstrous women, while at the same time seeking to resolve the threat and absolve the father by collapsing ideology into biology.

One of the most remarkable constants in the three *Jurassic Park* films released by the year 2001 is that, though they are all about dinosaur attacks and hairbreadth escapes in one respect, they are all about the creation or restoration of father-centered families in another: In the first film, kid-hating curmudgeon Alan Grant comes to embrace the role of family nabob, sage, and guide. In the second, much-divorced wastrel Ian Malcolm learns to commit to his daughter and girlfriend. In the third, soon-to-be-divorced Milquetoast Paul Kirby manages to repossess his lost son, estranged wife, and dormant machismo through feats of courage, in one scene actually under fire. Such an orientation toward father-friendly plots is characteristic not only of the era's films generally but specifically of those of Steven Spielberg, who directed the first two *Jurassic Park* films and served as executive producer of the third; many of his films, including *E. T.* (1982), *Hook* (1991), and *Schindler's List* (1993), focus on children whose literal or symbolic fatherlessness is amended by film's end. Noting Spielberg's "emphasis on the family as an embattled sphere of empathy and care, threatened by external forces," Michael Ryan and Douglas Kellner argue that the director's oeuvre represents a countertradition to the corporate conservatism that dominates contemporary film (259). I would argue, to the contrary, that the preoccupation of the *Jurassic Park* series with *father-headed* families that are threatened by, indeed that come into existence through their battles with, *maternal* forces places these films squarely in the dominant family-values camp.[16]

From its first scene, in which a male worker is mauled by a raptor while his boss yells, in extreme close-up and with creepy reverberation, "Shoot her!," *Jurassic Park* reiterates the family-values cycle of crime and punishment: the abdication of the paternal role, men's trifling in reproduction outside the nuclear unit, has loosed a band of screeching harpies who rend and tear those foolish enough to court them. In the world of Jurassic Park, gender has been divided across species, and thus reproduction between fathers and mothers has been eliminated: human males may create, but they cannot procreate with, saurian females. The film thus highlights the absence of human females in the park enclave; as in the opening sequence, in which an all-male crew headed by a male game warden unloads a cage containing an unseen creature, women are largely invisible from and insignificant to the events that brought Jurassic Park into existence. In the amber mine, at the archaeological dig, in the control room, in the dinosaur birthing-chamber, women have, at best, walk-through roles, while men are in command—though not, as was apparent when the worker was slain by the caged creature, in control. The film-within-a-film that the team of experts watch when they arrive at park headquarters epitomizes the almost complete exclusion of women as makers of Jurassic Park: not only is it men whom the film shows extracting the dinosaur blood, operating the virtual-reality displays, and laying the fertilized eggs in cribs, but even the cartoon character who narrates the story, the character who represents the fundamental building-blocks of life, is *Mister* DNA.

To recognize the ways in which *Jurassic Park* wields the family-values masternarrative, however, it is necessary to add that the park constitutes not merely a male world but an unmarried and childless male world. There are no tangible signs of marriage in Jurassic Park, no wedding rings, no photographs of spouses, children, or significant others; only Hammond, who might be a widower—or who might be divorced, the fate that has befallen his daughter—possesses visual proof of paternity (his grandchildren). Indeed, at the only moment in the film in which marriage is overtly addressed, one of the male characters turns the subject into a joke: asked whether he is married, chaos theoretician Ian Malcolm, pulling on his hip flask like a barroom braggart, responds, "occasionally." This cavalier attitude toward the institution of marriage defines Malcolm as surely as do his avant-garde theories. Though he has fathered—and professes to love—children, he feels no need to provide them with a stable home; a cad "always on the lookout for a future ex-Mrs. Malcolm," he has the gall to inquire about paleobotanist Dr. Sattler's "availability" despite the obvious fact that she is Dr. Grant's main squeeze. In *Jurassic Park*, clearly, it is not the dinosaurs alone that are predators. And equally clearly, the helpless prey of raptors and rapscallions alike is the traditional family unit.

The film's moral calculus is thus disarmingly simple: the measure of a man is his fidelity to fatherhood, and the punishments meted out to the male characters bear a direct relationship to that factor. Thus Malcolm, despite his unpromising start, does redeem himself in some measure; attempting to rescue the children from the tyrannosaur at considerable risk to himself, he suffers only a crippling leg wound, enough to lay him up for a while and, perhaps, afford him time to atone for past indiscretions. Next to the film's villains, however, Malcolm appears a paragon of paternal guardianship. The lawyer Gennaro most patently personifies the scoundrel of family-values sermons; not only is he a miserly father, denying Tim a toy on the grounds that it is "expensive," but his abandonment of the children before the tyrannosaur attack so plainly recalls the iconography of absentee fatherhood that the film need hardly reinforce it with the girl Lex's panicked shriek, "He left us! He left us!" As such, Gennaro's punishment is particularly cruel (not to mention crude): caught with his pants down, sitting on a toilet seat to which he has fled in bowel-loosening terror, he is snatched from his porcelain throne when the angel of death in the form of the tyrannosaur comes calling. Meanwhile, Dennis Nedry, who initiates the dinosaur attacks when he shuts down the park's defensive systems, is presented as an overgrown teenager, guzzling junk food, posting dirty pictures on his screensaver, and sulkily addressing Hammond as "Dad" when the latter refuses to, as it were, raise his allowance. In one shot of Nedry's workstation, plainly visible as the camera pans across the image, the viewer sees a photograph of Robert Oppenheimer (looking 1950s fatherly with pipe and crewcut) and two Post-it notes: one depicting a mushroom cloud, the other with the words "Beginning of baby boom." The implication is clear: Nedry, like the other men in the park, is in the business of fathering not nuclear families but nuclear nightmares. Thus his fate, while attempting to smuggle dinosaur embryos off the island in the masculine vessel of a Barbasol shaving cream can, parallels Gennaro's: in an enactment of the teenage boy's wet dream and worst fear, he meets his end at the hands and mouth of a coy, frilly creature that turns into a terror in the front seat of a car parked on a ledge evocative of a 1950s-era lover's lane.

In light of these representations of failed or feckless fatherhood, it is inadequate to read *Jurassic Park* as some critics have: as a cautionary tale of science trespassing on, and tampering with, the secrets of life.[17] To be sure, the film itself supplies this reading in the sonorous pronouncements of Malcolm, who as a chaos theorist makes an improbable, but for this reason effective, altar boy of divine nature: staggered by the "lack of humility before nature" displayed by the engineers of Jurassic Park, he terms scientific discovery a "violent, penetrative act," nothing less than the "rape of the natural world," and warns that "Life will not be contained. . . . Life finds a way." To focus on such speeches in isolation, however, is to overlook the ways in which Malcolm's discourse supports the film's consideration of the human family as a microcosm of the same natural order. Indeed, these sentences from Malcolm illustrate the connection, and the deception, linking nature to nurture, as they liken scientific processes to illicit sexuality and offer what is, in the context of family-values discourse, a suggestive abstract of evolutionary processes: "Life finds a way." (Think here of the Arthur S. DeMoss Foundation's antiabortion spots: "Life. What a beautiful choice.") That the "way" life finds involves the transformation of female dinosaurs into male ones furthers the film's equation of legitimate reproduction with father-headed families; despite the scientists' pains to, as they put it, "deny" the dinosaurs the ingredient that makes embryos male, Mother Nature ensures the survival of Father Family. This is what makes the line spoken by the park's chief geneticist— "There is no unauthorized breeding in Jurassic Park"—so painfully funny; for there is nothing *but* unauthorized breeding until the dinosaurs begin to breed on their own, driven by nature's unerring crusade to restore fathers to their families despite the scientists' best efforts to deny and deter them.

The movement of *Jurassic Park*, then, is one in which the human nuclear family, though threatened with extinction, will come into existence as "naturally" as the saurian; just as the dinosaurs will evolve toward paternity, Grant will (as he himself puts it) "evolve" to take his rightful position as patriarch. There is thus another impulse in *Jurassic Park* at variance with Malcolm's tendentious sermons: if on the one hand, the film presents men as prideful violators of the natural order, on the other, it celebrates the right of patriarchy to rule a female world depicted as chaotic and unpredictable. Even before the crucial scenes in which Grant saves the children from the raging tyrannosaur, the film labors to identify him as a man who needs only to channel his energy into family commitment to bring order to chaos: when, for example, his lap-belt buckle in the helicopter turns out to consist of two "female" members, he masters these recalcitrant sisters by, literally, tying the knot with them. Throughout, Grant is the one who takes matters into his own hands: it is he who figures out how to disable the restraining device when the park's first ride fails to satisfy his curiosity, who attempts to study the egg from which the baby velociraptor has hatched (and who cradles the newborn), and who jumps out of the moving car to locate the sick triceratops. When, therefore, he is at last moved to come to the children's aid, he misses nary a step: not only does he fly to their rescue during the tyrannosaur attack but he effortlessly adopts the tones and tactics of the father who knows best, directing the panic-stricken Lex to "stay right here and wait for me" and assuring her that he will not leave her. During the sequences in which Grant leads the children back to home base through a hostile landscape, he confirms his position as the ideal father: nestling in the homemade tree house with the kids, chuckling indulgently at their awful jokes, reassuring them that he will stay awake all night in case the "monsters come back"—and dutifully informing them that the monsters of their dreams are really only animals—Grant represents the power of the father to negotiate and tame a wild, feminized nature.

More subtly yet insistently, the film promotes the ideal of fatherhood not only by privileging Grant's superior activity and know-how but by conceding the power and propriety of his active, expansive gaze. In keeping with Laura Mulvey's well-known dictum that "in a world ordered by sexual imbalance, pleasure in looking has been split between active/male and passive/female" (19), the film champions Grant's vision—his scientific theories *and* his visual standpoint—as a means of asserting the patriarch's authority over female objects and systems, both biological and social, extended and intimate. The first sighting of a full-figure dinosaur, for example, is insistently, even aggressively, "granted" to him; having first spotted the brachiosaur, he rises from the jeep, removing his sunglasses, while Sattler, too busy fussing over a plant to notice that there is something much bigger happening in the field, needs to have her head turned by the force of her partner's hand before she catches on. As the scene unfolds, the act of discovery is aligned even more closely with Grant: as Hammond announces, "Welcome to Jurassic Park," a point-of-view shot of dinosaur herds confirms both Grant's hypothesis—"They do move in herds," he breathes—and his perspective. This pivotal scene thus functions in the manner Mulvey suggests: "As the spectator identifies with the main male protagonist, he projects his look onto that of his like, his screen surrogate, so that the power of the male protagonist as he controls events coincides with the active power of the [male] look, both giving a satisfying sense of omnipotence" (20).

It is also notable that as this sequence concludes, Sattler appears (slightly out of focus) behind Grant, snuggling up to him and confirming his authority of vision, in the reflected glow of which she can only bask. For the necessary complement to the empowerment of the male visionary is, of course, the disempowerment of the female gaze, its circumscription within a narrow, domestic sphere. Thus Sattler—whose last name I use for consistency's sake, though she is the only adult identified in the end credits by her first name (and a diminutive form at that)—is allied not with the farsighted but with the miniature, the dainty, the modest. Indeed, as an object of desire rather than a desiring subject, she not only permits on-the-make Malcolm to treat her like a dim-witted schoolgirl during the flirtatious scene in which he explains chaos theory to her, but she actually ducks her head and averts her eyes when he offers her a tactless compliment. Throughout the film, Sattler acts less like a scientist than a blushing bride-to-be. Content to follow the female (pre)occupation with plants and flowers, she is likewise content to limit herself to visions of maternity: She has, apparently, been nagging Grant for some time about children, for he seems thoroughly exasperated when he asks her in their first scene, "You want to have one of those?" She shares a private look with Grant when Hammond's grandchildren arrive and later tries to engineer their riding in Grant's car on the grounds that their presence will be "good for him." She nurses the sick triceratops, croons, "Oh, God," when the baby raptor is born, and in the film's final scene, watches approvingly as a nuclear family is born. That the film created the romance between Grant and Sattler to begin with is instructive (in the novel they are colleagues, nothing more); that having created this romance, the film permits Grant considerable autonomy of vision but pens Sattler within the bonds of matrimony and maternity reveals much about *Jurassic Park*'s commitment to family-values orthodoxy.

Along these lines, it is important to note that the dichotomy in vision between Grant and Sattler cannot be dismissed as merely individual or idiosyncratic, for the film provides another pair who match them precisely in this gendered division: the children, Lex and Tim. On the one hand, Tim's desire to see is not only presented as a natural outgrowth of his maleness but is encouraged and rewarded.

For example, he forges ahead with Grant to find the sick "Trike," while Sattler and Lex, failing to hold him back, end up simply following, tagging along once again via a trail blazed by males. Similarly, when Grant and the children encounter the Gallimimus herd, it is Tim whom Grant signals to come forward to identify the animals; Tim thus becomes both a stand-in for the audience, who can now name the dinosaurs as well, and an Adam-like figure, who has been granted leave by the Father to name the beasts of the field. Lex, meanwhile, stands to the side, nervously asking whether the dinosaurs are plant-eaters or meat-eaters. Moments later, when the roving tyrannosaur snatches one of the herd, the scene repeats: while Lex pleads, "Go now. Go now," Tim lingers, marveling, "Look at all the blood!" On the few occasions in which Lex does express a desire to look, she suffers punishment, or at least indignity, for doing so. For instance, just before the tyrannosaur's attack, when she asks, "Where's the goat?" she is answered by a bloody leg flung against the roof of the jeep. Likewise, the one time she marshals the courage to approach a dinosaur, her reward is the animal's sneezing all over her, which makes her look—in both senses of the phrase—ridiculous.[18]

For women, moreover, the only alternative to looking ridiculous is looking monstrous: if not Lex, then Rex. In a film in which family-values discourse is translated into the terms of visual difference, the female dinosaurs are not merely spectacles, objects of voyeuristic male pleasure, but *spectators*, for whom men are objects of visual (and gustatory) desire. In her influential essay on vision in the horror film, "When the Woman Looks," Linda Williams hypothesizes that "in the rare instance when the cinema permits the woman's look, she not only sees a monster, she sees a monster that offers a distorted reflection of her own image" (88). In *Jurassic Park*, this visual identification of woman and monster is at once affirmed and transcended: the woman who looks and the monster she sees are not reflections of one another but a single entity. It is remarkable how regularly the film identifies the dinosaurs' power with vision; if their appearance—their size, speed, and ferocity—is simply on display, an automatic source of wonder, their ability *to see* forms a recurring, explicitly stated theme. From the start, Grant invokes the power of dinosaur vision to frighten an obnoxious child with his raptor story: "You keep still because you think his visual acuity is like T. Rex—he'll lose you if you don't move. But no. Not velociraptor. You stare at him, and he just stares right back. . . . Then the attack comes. Not from the front, but from the side, from the two you didn't even know were there." And from that point on, the film distills the dinosaur threat to teeth and eyes: if they can see you—even if you think you can see them—they can get you. Indeed, before Grant tells his tale, it is visualized in the prologue sequence; though the viewer cannot see into the raptor cage, two point-of-view shots showing the workers from the monster's perspective reveal that it (she) *can* see out. The only part of the dinosaur's anatomy the audience sees at this point, notably, is her reptilian eye, lit by sparks from the weapons the workers vainly use against her. Each dinosaur attack staged by the film involves a man losing the battle of vision: the Dilophosaurus, having first disarmed Nedry by playing peekaboo around the trunk of a tree with him, next blinds him by spitting poison in his eyes, while the velociraptors decoy Muldoon, who is busy lining up a kill when a second raptor blindsides him. This sense of dinosaur vision as paralyzing, bedazzling, may also explain the otherwise incongruous shot that follows Muldoon's death: a close-up of the raptor's eye with a serpent sliding past it (suggestive, perhaps, of the serpent that similarly bewitched, bothered, and bewildered the first Parent). Likewise, the sequence in the kitchen in which Lex and Tim evade the raptors—a sequence that begins, predictably, with a shot of a raptor eye pressed against the circular window in the entrance door—identifies power with vision: it is Lex's accidental discovery that the raptor will hunt her reflection in a metal cabinet that provides the children breathing room to escape.

It is during the tyrannosaur attack, however, that the monstrous woman's power of vision is most emphasized; suitably, the biggest, deadliest of the dinosaurs is the most visually oriented. The sequence begins with Tim testing the infrared goggles but quickly shifts from the meager, viewfinder authority this technology provides him to the overwhelming vision commanded by the queen of dinosaurs. Before tearing down the fence, the tyrannosaur turns to look directly at the car (and, given the camera's position, at the audience); after she has cleared the cables, a shot widely aired during the commercial buildup to the film's release—that of her eye framed outside the jeep window, her pupil contracting from the beam of Lex's flashlight—maintains the sequence's focus on the eye. Numerous shots during this sequence constitute the monster's point of view: it is from her perspective that the audience sees the children after she smashes through the roof of the jeep, while a shot/reverse-shot clip of her inspecting Gennaro on the toilet immediately precedes his death. (Later, in the tyrannosaur chase, even the shot of her maw looming in the side-view mirror calls attention to vision: it is, in the truest sense of the term, a sight gag.) When Grant fools the dinosaur with the flare, sending her after the pinprick of light like a dog fetching a stick, it becomes apparent how vital his warnings were about the danger of being seen: "Keep absolutely still. . . . It can't see us if we don't move." His advice is, of course, not only highly speculative but wholly preposterous: with her face practically pressed against him and Lex at one point, the tyrannosaur would surely be able to *smell* them. Yet this lapse from the film's otherwise fanatical quest for dino-verisimilitude underscores the significance of the visual theme: though there is no way of knowing with certainty how dinosaurs saw—or, for that matter, how they looked—the film so strongly identifies power with seeing that it must reduce its centerpiece dinosaur, during its showstopper sequence, to a fearsome, fatal eye.

The tyrannosaur, queen of dinosaurs, peers into Jurassic Park safari vehicle, eyeing her next meal. From *Jurassic Park* (Universal, 1993). Courtesy of Photofest.

The trajectory that *Jurassic Park* traces, then, is one in which the transference of male vision from its proper object of desire—procreation within the sanctioned nuclear unit—to an illicit object of desire—the other woman—results in the empowerment of the monstrous woman's gaze. As in *King Kong*, however, ultimately the gaze in *Jurassic Park* is transferred back to its proper object and reinstated in its proper bearer. This restoration is posited by the two resonant, pregnant images that close the film: as Grant watches pelicans cruising over the ocean, Sattler smiles at the sight of her mate cuddling Lex and Tim, a vision mirroring that of the trio in their treetop nest. These concluding shots function to naturalize patriarchal authority in two principal ways. On the one hand, as Cynthia Freeland notes, the pelicans, silhouetted against the water, bear a striking resemblance to pterodactyls; and accordingly, their presence affirms "the 'heroic' male scientist's creative vision and theoretical achievement in hypothesizing correctly about the bird-like nature of dinosaurs" ("Feminist" 211). On the other hand, the juxtaposition of these *National Geographic* images with the tableau of a newly born nuclear family strongly identifies patriarchy with natural processes; just as the presence of the pelicans reflects the beneficence of natural selection, which in decreeing that dinosaurs evolve into birds has made the world safe for humanity, so does Grant's acceptance of his role at the head of the family reflect the wisdom of human evolution, which in decreeing that men adopt positions of authority has made the world safe for women and children. In a characteristic gesture of family-values rhetoric, then, the film's closing shots disguise the ideological contexts of patriarchy, lifting the father-headed family from the realm of the social to that of the biological. Moreover, since the shot of Grant and the children is one of the few presented as constituting Sattler's point of view, this sequence reiterates at the film's close its gendered hierarchy of vision: the male look is self-affirming, while the woman's is rewarded, indeed permitted, only because it embraces the patriarchal unit to which she willingly subordinates herself. When the woman looks, she sees a family. When the man looks, he sees himself: warrior, hero, savior.

It must be said, however, that the reclamation of patriarchy at the close of *Jurassic Park* is considerably less than convincing; as with the final photograph of *Fatal Attraction*, the family portrait that wraps Spielberg's film is rhetorically masterful but logically moth-eaten. Indeed, *Jurassic Park* does not need me to point this out; in its chaotic final act, from the raptors' hunt to the reappearance of the tyrannosaur, the film makes a merry hash of its own values, in large part by aping them mercilessly: Lex, briefly empowered within the kitchen like the mother in *Gremlins* (1984), fights off the monsters, her weapons of choice a soup ladle and a dumbwaiter. Grant and Sattler, ineffectively barring the front door against a leering intruder, are upstaged by a preteen playing video games. And finally, just before the family group's escape from the island, the patriarch's protective shield is spitefully exposed as tissue-thin: as the raptors in the rotunda coil for the kill, Grant stations himself in front of Sattler and the children—a position that at best prepares him as a sacrificial lamb—only to be rescued by, of all things, a single woman in the shape of the cruising tyrannosaur. The failure of the very ideology that guides the film is likewise expressed when Lex reboots the computers in the control room, replacing Nedry's girlie wallpaper with a blueprint of the park complex—home base—and the words "System secured": this restorative message flashes on the screen for but a split second, and it is illusory in any event, for moments later the raptors shatter the control-room window and the fantasy of its defensive value. The family system is not secured in *Jurassic Park*; the "domestic scene" that concludes the film cannot veil the fact that loose women remain on the prowl, their "matriarchal ability" to shake "the controls of patriarchy" (Harwood 189) hatching sequels to try the marrow and sinews of fresh fathers.

There is, at that, another reason to doubt the stability, or even the sincerity, of *Jurassic Park*'s stance as a bulwark against the assault on family values: the film itself participates with perverse relish in that assault. As W. J. T. Mitchell writes, "a family cannot be brought together by a film that is too violent for the children in it to see" (225). The violence of the film—much of which is directed against children—makes *Jurassic Park* an unlikely candidate for the family-values pantheon. For the children in the film are threatened, debased, and humiliated with a gusto that passes well beyond the gratuitous into the gleeful: Products of a failed marriage to begin with, they are ignored by Grant, dangled as bait by Sattler, and abandoned by Gennaro. They have goat's legs flung at them, jeeps aimed at them, and rib cages dropped on them. They are ground into mud, shoved over cliffs, hung from ceilings, electrocuted, and sneezed on. In short, if they are meant to be, as Hammond puts it, the "target audience," they end up being simply targets for an adult audience to watch—and, one suspects, enjoy—being tormented. However the jeopardizing of the children may be meant to highlight the obstacles that surround the nuclear family and thus the triumph of its ultimate formation, the result is to permit adults to luxuriate in whatever feelings of resentment and hostility they may bear toward children. No more telling indication of the hypocrisy of *Jurassic Park*—or of the family-values discourse it both defends and defames—can be mustered than this: in its righteous zeal to hunt down the dragon lady, it ends up treating the supposed beneficiaries of that hunt, the children, like little monsters.

5

MONSTROUS MINDS Fantasy Film and Mental Illness

The principal problem in psychiatry has always been, and still is, violence: the threatened and feared violence of the "madman," and the actual counter-violence of society and the psychiatrist against him. The result is the dehumanization, oppression, and persecution of the citizen branded "mentally ill."—Thomas Szasz, *The Manufacture of Madness* (1970)

*F*antasy film is insane. By this, I mean to suggest two distinct, but interrelated, qualities. On the one hand, fantasy film is concerned—one might say morbidly obsessed—with the representation of mentally unstable characters. The most prominent of such figures, prominent enough to have provided the name for a venerable fantasy tradition, is the "mad scientist"; from vintage films, such as *The Cabinet of Dr. Caligari* (1921), *Dr. Jekyll and Mr. Hyde* (1931), and *Forbidden Planet* (1956), to modern works, such as the remake of *The Fly* (1986) and the comic-book adaptations *Spider-Man* (2002) and *Spider-Man II* (2004), the saga of scientists whose perilous experiments have splintered their personality (or physical self) has remained remarkably consistent. In a related vein, the late-twentieth-century parade of "slasher" films has revived the story line of such classic works as *Psycho* (1960). In the *Texas Chainsaw Massacre, Halloween,* and *Friday the Thirteenth* series, as well as in countless less popular or long-lived imitators, mental illness is the motivating cause for the gruesome slaughters that constitute such films' principal, if perplexing, allure.[1] Another tradition, though it has yet to receive formal recognition *as* a tradition, comprises what might be termed the "possession" film: from horror stories such as *The Exorcist* (1973) to space sagas such as *Star Wars* (1977) to sci-fi spoofs such as *The Adventures of Buckaroo Banzai* (1984), bodies and minds have been overrun by a host of malevolent intruders, including demons, aliens, and the Dark Side of the Force. Fantasy film, it is apparent, has an insatiable appetite for states of thought that transcend the bounds of the everyday.

To put it this way, of course, is to anticipate the second sense in which fantasy film is insane: if so many fantasy film *narratives* are devoted to issues of mental illness, this may be because the *form* of fantasy film is related to the condition of mental illness. In their survey of insanity in the motion pictures, Michael Fleming and Roger Manvell note that film itself claims an affinity to interior, mental processes:

> Film, even from its silent days[,] . . . has proven to be a medium peculiarly suitable for handling intimate psychological subjects. It is a medium of observation, the almost clinical recording of human behavior. . . . As a medium involving the highly controlled flow of images, film is uniquely able to reflect the flux of mental-emotional experience with an impact similar to that undergone by a human being during a period of psychological deterioration. Through the subtleties of editing and the juxtaposition of sound and image, the film can dovetail the sensations and observations arising out of a character's relationship to illusions, hallucinations, dreams, and nightmares. Reality and fantasy as two forms of experience can be subtly, almost indistinguishably, interwoven. (18–19)

In fantasy films, such "interweaving" of the real and the unreal is at once heightened and, to a degree, abolished: unreal figures, actions, and events assume the vivid appearance of the real. In this respect, fantasy films might be termed public hallucinations (imagined sensory stimuli) or delusions (irrational but fixed ideas). It is not much to the point to protest that the audiences of fantasy films do not "really" think that what they are seeing is true; though this may be the case for the majority of viewers, the fact that the quest for the convincing illusion, the completely believable deception, has been the holy grail of fantasy film from the get-go suggests that fantasy film strives to leave its audience doubtful not only as to *how* its effects were achieved but as to *what* was real and what wasn't. (One modest example should support my point: In the scene in *Jurassic Park III* in which the spinosaur sends the fuselage of the downed aircraft tumbling through the jungle, the shot of Alan Grant's face glimpsed briefly through the plane's window was digitally composited. Though mature audiences surely know that the creature itself is "fake," few would doubt that they were "really" seeing actor Sam Neill.) To a greater or at least more evident degree than in other film genres, fantasy film functions through the tacit understanding that for the two hours of the film's running time—and perhaps afterward—the viewer's ability to discriminate between real and unreal will be suspended or transgressed.

To understand the significance of fantasy film's assault on the reality principle, however, one must recall the larger thesis of this book: if fantasy films lend unreal *visual* propositions the appearance of the real, in so doing they validate unreal *social* propositions. As indicated by the summary with which this chapter began, one of the most tenacious of such propositions concerns people with mental illnesses, who have almost universally been represented in fantasy film as fearsome, alien threats to the "normal." And while it would be possible to devote this chapter to dissecting "madness" films of the fantasy genre's majority tradition, it is my hope that, at this late point in the analysis, the processes of alienation in such films are so overt as to require no explication. Instead, I have chosen to focus on a minority tradition of fantasy madness films: ones that not only *represent* mental illness but that derange audience members' own perceptions and in so doing cultivate a hesitation as regards their audiences' relation *to* the insane. Such films have grown in popularity, due in part to the ability of computer-generated images to simulate mental phantasms with the apparent solidity of the real. At the same time, that such a tradition exists at all is a function of the nature of mental illness: though a white person cannot become black, or a man become a woman (at least not inadvertently), a sane person can, without volition, acquiescence, or even awareness, become insane. It would seem to be the case, then, that fantasy films not only *about* mental illness but *of* mental illness could constitute a self-critical exception to the mainstream; by plunging viewers into the minds of the mentally ill, such films might nullify the fantasy tradition's us-versus-them mentality by expressing "profound uncertainty about the question of how 'other' the Other really is" (Schneider 50).

Such a hopeful prognosis, however, captures only part of the truth. The whole truth is that, if such films sustain an attack on ideologies of alienation, they nonetheless participate in the project of demonizing and ostracizing the monstrous "outsider." That this is so may not be the paradox it appears; the anxiety attending the tenuous nature of sanity, the very anxiety that permits certain fantasy madness films to destabilize categories of normality, necessitates that such films shore up these categories as well. The hesitancy of these films does, indeed, make them more challenging than the general run of fantasy madness films, the bulk of which are so slavishly devoted to processes of alienation that any anxiety the films may express about the failure of those processes is devoured by mayhem and gore. It should not be forgotten, though, that in this chapter I am being considerably more selective than in the foregoing chapters; I am isolating from a great trove of hateful representations only those few that I see as posing potential alternatives to the dominant tradition. And yet in doing so, in showing that even the most self-conscious of such films cannot overcome the fear of monstrous outsiders, I am also reiterating the larger point that fantasy film partakes of its culture's self-delusive belief that its insane convictions are sane.

Madness as Metaphor and Monster

In her germinal work *Illness as Metaphor* (1977), Susan Sontag describes the process by which a real condition becomes an unreal thing:

> Illness is the night-side of life, a more onerous citizenship. Everyone who is born holds dual citizenship, in the kingdom of the well and in the kingdom of the sick. Although we all prefer to use only the good passport, sooner or later each of us is obliged, at least for a spell, to identify ourselves as citizens of that other place. . . . Yet it is hardly possible to take up one's residence in the kingdom of the ill unprejudiced by the lurid metaphors with which it has been landscaped. (3–4)

Sontag's elegant thesis—that the "punitive or sentimental fantasies" (4) societies and individuals contrive about physical illness shield us from the unendurable fact that no one is immune from becoming ill—may be applied with even greater force to mental illness. For the very nature (or lack of one) of mental illness lends itself to metaphor; the very vacancy of the concept reinforces the need for it to be given a tangible shape.[2] Accustomed—or habituated—as the culture is to understanding mental illness as a discrete entity, the absence or opposite of sanity, it is instructive to note that among critics (and providers) of mental health services there is enormous disagreement in regard to identifying, categorizing, or even conceptualizing mental illnesses. Few, to be sure, still subscribe to the ideas propounded by dissenters such as Thomas Szasz, whose book *The Myth of Mental Illness*, first published in 1961, advanced the following tenets:

1. Strictly speaking, disease or illness can affect only the body; hence, there can be no mental illness.

2. "Mental illness" is a metaphor. Minds can be "sick" only in the sense that jokes are "sick" or economies are "sick."

3. Psychiatric diagnoses are stigmatizing labels, phrased to resemble medical diagnoses and applied to persons whose behavior annoys or offends others. (267)

If, however, psychiatric medications and mental imaging techniques developed in the decades since the publication of Szasz's book have cast doubt on his claim that mental illnesses have no physiological basis whatsoever, the core of his argument—that mental illness inheres not in the simple presence of a "defective" mind but in the complex negotiation among psychic processes, cultural values, and clinical norms—remains influential. Thus, for example, in his work with residents of homeless shelters, anthropologist Robert Desjarlais suggests that "the roots of any lifelong debility might lie less in an individual's brain or mind than in culturally systemic ways of meaning and knowing: those cast by others or themselves as being in essence 'psychotic,' 'schizophrenic,' or durably 'sick' can become the direct casualties of what Roland Barthes once called the 'disease of thinking in essences'" (117). Similarly, in his examination of clinical practices undertaken with incarcerated persons, Stephen Pfohl argues that *"diagnostic decisions are inherently bound to and thus dependent upon a variety of ongoing social or social psychological processes that may have little to do with the psychiatric troubles or emotional disturbances of patients"* (217; emphasis in the original). That Desjarlais and Pfohl reached these conclusions based on their work with populations already marginalized by the larger culture—homeless people and prisoners—is instructive, and I will return to the implications of this coincidence presently. For the moment, I wish to point out that however tempting it may be to sequester mental illness within the confines of the individual mind, current theory insists that mental illness, like all human performances, must be viewed within the context of cultural and historical pressures.

If, however, mental illness is anything but an essential state, the field of representation within which madness acquires cultural significance *has* been essentialized, limited to a particularly narrow, paltry, and invariable range. According to Sander Gilman, this strict circumscribing of mental illness within the bounds of a culture's representational or signifying practices is due to the psychological anxiety such protean disorders occasion:

> It is the fear of collapse, the sense of dissolution, that contaminates the Western image of all diseases, including elusive ones such as schizophrenia. But the fear we have of our own collapse does not remain internalized. Rather, we project this fear onto the world in order to localize it and, indeed, to domesticate it. For once we locate it, the fear of our own dissolution is removed. Then it is not we who totter on the brink of collapse, but rather the Other. And it is an-Other who has already shown his or her vulnerability by having collapsed. (*Disease* 1)

"The construction of the image of the [psychiatric] patient," Gilman writes, "is thus always a playing out of this desire for a demarcation between ourselves and the chaos represented in culture by disease" (4). In Gilman's view, mental illnesses are particularly apt to be projected outward as fixed essences precisely because they are such intensely inward, and unsettling, diseases: they are "elusive" both in the sense that they often do not manifest the distinctive symptoms of physical illnesses and in the sense that, by causing the "collapse" or "dissolution" of the sufferer's own cognitive and perceptual apparatuses, they may prevent detection even by the individual they afflict. As Gilman writes, "The banality of real mental illness comes into conflict with our need to have the mad be identifiable, different from ourselves. Our shock is always that they are really just like us. . . . We want—no, we need—the 'mad' to be different, so we create out of the stuff of their reality myths that make them different" (13). Gilman identifies visual representations of the mentally ill as one of the most powerful forces in casting these internal phenomena outside the realm of the "normal": "The images themselves become the space in which the anxieties are controlled. Their finitude, their boundedness, their inherent limitation provide a distance analogous to the distance the observer desires from the 'reality' of the illness portrayed" (*Picturing* 34). No matter how idiosyncratic or unrepresentative such images may be—and those from the eighteenth and nineteenth centuries, when the practice of classifying mental illnesses burgeoned, strike one today as laughable[3]—each culture develops, against a background of generally accepted depictions, historically unique schemas of the mentally ill with the potent authority of cultural consensus. Indeed, in significant respects, the more outlandish the stereotype the better, for this exaggeration of difference facilitates the act of exorcizing madness from the individual and social body/mind. To employ Sontag's terminology, then, one might say that in the case of mental illness the mad individual becomes the metaphor, the inflexible and consolatory substitute for the mutable, terrifying thing itself.

If this is so, then it is unsurprising that representations of the mad are so typically terrifying; it is little wonder that the commonest form the metaphor of madness takes is that of the inhuman, feral berserk. This image is curiously comforting: not only does it externalize the threat of one's own mind becoming a monster, turning in violent insurrection against itself, but it makes identifying the mad a stunningly simple matter. As Gilman notes, under the hypnotic trance of such representations, "one does not even have to wait for the insane to speak" for their madness to announce itself (*Disease* 48). In modern times, the image of the violent mad person is supported not only by a lengthy history of (mis)treatment of those defined as having mental illnesses but by current practices in the legal definition of the mentally ill.[4] Following the depopulation of state psychiatric hospitals in the 1960s and 1970s, the criterion of "dangerousness to self or others" has evolved as the generally applied rule for involuntary commitment, thus suggesting a natural link between rampant mental illness and "danger." Whether people who suffer from mental illnesses truly are more prone to violence than the general population is a complex question, tied as it is to the issue of defining mental illness to begin with; at the same time, a host of contextual factors render the answer anything but certain. (To cite only one complicating factor, the positive correlation between mental illness and poverty, regardless of the cause-and-effect relationship, may lead to increased criminality among some mentally ill individuals.) Given the fact, however, that the seriously mentally ill, by any definition, represent a small minority of the population, and that according to most studies only a fractional minority of that already limited sample are violent, it is clear, as John Monahan writes, that "mental health status makes at best a trivial contribution to the overall level of violence in society" (519). Moreover, because "psychiatric professionals," as Pfohl notes, "have little ability to predict validly who will act in [a] violent or dangerous manner" (18), invariably overpredicting rather than underpredicting its likelihood among those classified as mentally ill, it may be that "dangerousness" itself has become little more than code for mental illness.[5] Yet in defiance of sociological evidence and mitigating factors, the stigmatizing figure of the "raving mad person" (according to which mental illness forms the sole, necessary, and inevitable source of violence) persists, giving birth in our time to the twin stereotypes of "wackos" committing random acts of street violence and crazed serial killers leaving a trail of butchered bodies in their wake.[6]

The principal means by which such images of murder and rapine are disseminated are, of course, the mass media: newspapers and magazines, television and radio, the Internet, and the movies. In 1961, Jum Nunnally reported that media presentations strongly contributed to the mentally ill being "regarded as all things bad" (51); though much has changed (if not necessarily for the better) in terms of the clinical treatment of people with mental illnesses, little has changed in terms of media caricatures. E. Fuller Torrey, a supporter of the involuntary hospitalization of the chronically and seriously mentally ill, contends that "since 1961 [just before deinstitutionalization began] it has become evident that the number of violent acts committed by mental patients has increased dramatically" (*Nowhere* 17). Yet as another of Torrey's works reveals, his allegation rests at least in part on highly questionable data:

> What is the evidence for this [increase]? For the nonscientist, the evidence consists of an increasing number of news stories, describing senseless violent acts by individuals identified as former mental patients. . . . Recent reductions in crime notwithstanding, New Yorkers still live with the fear that, as one local columnist put it,

"from out of the chaos some maniac will emerge to . . . cast you into oblivion." ("Some" 151).

Even granting that Torrey has an agenda to pursue, the illogic of his thoughts is stunning. Not only is the relationship between *former* hospitalization and violence negligible (*active* psychosis, scholars such as Monahan have established, is the only factor that has any bearing on violence) but the fact that news stories in increasing numbers are reporting such acts and identifying those who commit them as having received treatment for mental illness may mean only that "the media are highlighting a tiny minority of cases relative to the very large number of people with mental health problems, and that in doing so media accounts are distorting public perceptions of the whole area of mental health" (Philo xii).[7] Indeed, if a purported advocate such as Torrey can resort to such sensationalist scare tactics, it can hardly come as a surprise, as Otto Wahl comments in his study of media depictions of mental illness, that "the 'mad murderer' is as persistent, pervasive, and powerful a media stereotype as one can find anywhere. It occurs repeatedly within our most popular media and consistently across virtually all forms of mass media" (56). Wahl identifies a great number of falsifying facets to this stereotype: that *most* mentally ill people are violent; that mental illness in itself *causes* violence; that mentally ill people are *extremely* violent; that the violence of people with mental illness is *indiscriminate*; that the violent mentally ill person is *incurable*; and that the violence of the mentally ill person has *moral* implications—that it is not just violence but active evil. And as Wahl eloquently concludes, the usefulness of such a stereotype lies in its capacity for individual and social denial, inaction, and alienation:

> Without madness as a simple cause, violence requires more difficult explanations. . . . The media tendency to associate mental illness with violence and murder and to assume or imply mental illness when violence occurs thus serves to meet the needs of the public for relief from "blame". . . . People with mental illness, we are reassured in media depictions, are different and dangerous. They are not like us and their plight is not relevant to us. It is not in the best interest of ourselves and our families to deplete our emotional resources caring about a group of deviant and undeserving strangers. . . . They are evil and deserving of punishment, and we have no reason to feel bad if they are treated harshly. (127–28)

Not only, then, do reductive portraits of mental illness serve the need for psychological distancing that scholars such as Gilman have identified, but perhaps more important, *personal* distancing has far-reaching *political* implications.

Indeed, one might argue that the tendency to individualize mental illness is itself a principal indicator of the stereotype's political function. As Pfohl argues, "individual theories of deviance . . . affix the blame for violent, harmful, or dangerous behavior on the psychiatric realities or 'individual pathos' of patients" (226), thereby denying "potentially plausible cultural, class, and political accounts" of violent behavior (227). As is evident from the fact that homeless persons and prisoners are disproportionately depicted as dangerously mentally ill, such individuating strategies maintain, if they do not actually create, prevailing systems of inequality. It is this socially alienating power within the diagnosing of mental illness that leads critics such as Szasz to argue that "the problem of the differential incidence of (hospitalized) mental patients among various social classes in the modern West . . . disappears if we regard mental illness as a stigmatized status imposed on citizens by their oppressors, instead of as a condition or disease exhibited by or contained in suffering patients" (*Manufacture* 106). Szasz likens the persecution of the mentally ill in modern times to the persecution of accused witches during the Inquisition; even if, arguably, such an analogy exaggerates, the effects of personalizing social pathologies are evident today in trends toward incarcerating mentally ill persons, placing severe limits on the insanity plea, reducing health care benefits for mental illness, criminalizing the acts (or the mere presence) of the homeless mentally ill, and so on.[8] In a final paradox of mental illness, a condition that ostensibly involves purely interior dramas is, by virtue of that very definition, played out in public pageants of disciplinary power; metaphors of madness, swollen to violent spectacles, turn that violence against its supposed agents.

For the most part, films of the late twentieth century participate with consummate relish in this project of calcifying, ostracizing, and victimizing mental illness. In particular, the slew of films featuring homicidal maniacs—whether mainstream thrillers such as *The Silence of the Lambs* (1991) and *Seven* (1995) or fantasy screamers such as *A Nightmare on Elm Street* (1984)—feed the public perception of mentally ill individuals as violent monsters who must be eliminated to restore order to the social world and thereby deny the alternative possibility: that the social world may be the breeding ground for monsters. In the end, perhaps it is less the fear of psychological instability than of social alienation that such films mollify; convincing their audiences that the tables could never be turned, that the viewers themselves could never become the victims of persecution, these films support the culture's conviction that social outsiderhood and degradation are fated by individual flaws rather than formed by cultural forces. In a few instances, however, films emerging from this tradition undertake to complicate its central, interlocking truisms: that it is the mind alone, not the milieu, that makes someone mad; that the normal and the mad are inherently unlike; that the latter are characterized by inhuman, inexplicable violence; and that the sole sane response to such creatures is their isolation, detestation, and immolation. The two films I will consider, *The Cell* (2000) and *12 Monkeys* (1996), concern themselves with problematizing the very basis of such convictions: audience members' ability to identify themselves and their society *as* sane and thus to pronounce individual or communal judgment on the insane. That both films are thrown back, though to greatly varying degrees, on the judgments they have shown to be the true insanity is thus a measure of how powerfully the energies of social victimization shape even the few self-critical entrants within the fantasy film tradition.

In the Mind of Madness

The Cell is of two minds. Literally: the film's action takes place largely within the minds of its two principal characters. One of the minds belongs to the protagonist, Catherine Deane, a social worker who, thanks to an experimental technology, has been given the ability to enter the minds of the mentally ill in an attempt to effect an intimate, internalized talking cure. The other is that of Carl Stargher, a vicious, psychotic serial murderer who abducts young women, toys with them by confining them in an isolation cubicle, and then drowns them and turns them into actual toys, human dolls to satisfy his perverse sexual fantasies. When Carl lapses into a coma related to his mental deterioration, Catherine must enter his mind in an effort to locate the last woman he abducted, a woman who will die if Catherine's search proves unsuccessful.

But *The Cell* is of two minds in another sense, and it is this second sense that makes the film such a disquieting production. On the one hand, the film manages in some degree to humanize its depraved killer, whose illness and behavior, it is suggested, bear some relationship to the severe physical and emotional abuse he suffered as a child. Simultaneously, the film manages to involve its audience to such a degree in Stargher's mind that identification with him, in the sense of sharing his perceptions and even his failure to differentiate reality from fantasy, complicates the audience's ability to distance themselves from this apparent monster. Yet on the other hand, *The Cell* employs a variety of devices to reinvigorate the categories of difference it appears to enervate: not only does it insist on the equation of mental illness with violence and villainy but it asserts the opposition between "normal" and "abnormal" minds as strenuously as it denies that opposition. In this respect, it might be said of *The Cell* that it flirts with identification in order to achieve a more perfect alienation: sympathy for the monster actually alleviates the audience from any guilt that might arise from the monster's destruction, or (more precisely) from the audience's desire for and approval of it.

The Cell's opening sequence betokens the film's strategy of disorienting viewers, leading them to question their perceptions and thereby sensitizing them to the possibility of accepting another's perceptions. The first shot has the character of a nonrepresentational artwork: a white horizontal line, pink backdrop, and blurred, white moving shape are unidentifiable as any "real" setting or objects, though the shape does appear to be heat distorted, thus locating it in some relation to the physical world. Later shots establish the referential nature of these abstractions—sand dunes, a white-robed rider on a horse—yet still allow for a certain abstract quality, as the sharp curves of the dunes against a brilliant blue sky appear to be flat, geometric shapes more than three-dimensional objects. A moving camera, quick cutting among elements that seem not to occupy the same physical space, and a cacophonous sound track add to the difficulty in digesting this introduction. Gradually, however, the narrative begins to take on the familiar generic conventions of the dream sequence: the horse becomes a two-dimensional cutout, voices ring with a hollow reverberation, dialogue is sibylline, objects (such as a child's sailboat) inexplicably appear, and a boy's face is contorted into leonine rage. When, therefore, it turns out that this was indeed a dream—or at least, that it represented the mental landscape of Edward, a child in a schizophrenia-induced catatonic state—viewer expectations are for the moment confirmed.

Yet it is characteristic of this film that such ready confirmation will in turn be tested, and the boundaries of the real and the fantastic, the sane and the insane, thereby threatened. For after Catherine's "trip" into Edward ceases, the film cuts to a landscape remarkably similar to that of Edward's mind: a desert field, across which a large tortoise creeps. Images of a snow-white dog and a pale-blue pickup truck against a stark blue sky, as well as the return to helicopter camerawork and the failure to show diverse elements of the mise-en-scène in relation to one another, arouse expectations that the film has returned to Edward's mind. When a shadowy figure enters a dark room and stands before the apparently incongruous image of a fully clothed woman floating in what seems an enormous, topaz-blue fish tank, the viewer's suspicion seems confirmed. Yet this time, the scene is not fantasy—it is all too real, the consummation (as the viewer will learn) of Carl Stargher's horrid fantasies. These early scenes, then, initiate a process that will become both more pronounced and more urgent as *The Cell* progresses, a process whereby the film challenges its audience's fundamental ability to distinguish fantasy from fact.

That this inability is, according to Catherine, the hallmark of the insane mind—"for severe schizophrenics," she asserts, "there's no discerning between fantasy and reality"—makes this manipulation of viewers' reality a significant element of the film's discourse on the mentally ill. Not only, that is, does the film plunge viewers into Carl's twisted universe, where reality is a nightmare of hideous, stomach-turning images and unendurable, extravagant violence, but even more significantly, it disrupts the conventional relationship of viewer to viewed, subject to object: if Carl is, quite literally, subjected to the experimental mind-probing technology, the viewer is similarly subjected to an experiment in mental distress. Indeed, it is one of the paradoxes of *The Cell* that the fevered fantasy of Carl's mind, a carnivalesque cascade of blood-soaked images from Hieronymus Bosch, Salvador Dali, Edvard Munch, and other surrealists, comes to seem the most unthreatening space in the film; here at least one can be sure that, as the FBI agent who follows Catherine into Carl's mind keeps reminding himself, "it's not real." Elsewhere, what is real and what is not are considerably less certain. For instance, when Catherine, dreamily watching cartoon aliens on television, drifts (apparently) to sleep—the camera tracking from her point of view over bedcovers that imperceptibly turn to dunes—there is a momentary hesitation concerning not only the continuity effect but the return to Edward's mind: does the scene represent a dream, a flashback, a memory, a dissolve to a new session, or (inasmuch as Catherine was smoking pot shortly before) a hallucination? More tellingly, on Catherine's second "trip" into Carl's mind, the process seems to have gone awry: she awakens within the experimental chamber, her colleagues telling her that the machine has malfunctioned—but when she rises to fix the mechanism, she realizes that she is already "in," as she views her own body and Carl's from afar. Later, when Peter, the FBI agent, enters Carl's mind in pursuit of Catherine, a similar shot of the three bodies in the chamber leads one to believe that another trick has been played—but this time, the shot turns out to be an objective rather than a subjective one, a "real" shot of the chamber and thus, however paradoxically, a deceit. In this sense, if one of the principal functions of the cultural conceit of the "mad killer" is to mitigate the intolerable precariousness of individual and cultural sanity, the film's formal instability seems to encourage rather than allay the fear that the slayer may not be so distant from the norm as it might appear.

Even more jarring than these acute episodes of confusion are the many ways in which *The Cell* closes the gap between its heroes and villain; whereas the technical devices may seem but eye-catching tricks, the suggestions of identity between protagonist and monster are harder to shake. For instance, in an early segment before Catherine's acquaintance with Carl, crosscutting between shots of her at home and of him preparing his human doll creates not only contrast between the cozy domestic retreat and the repulsive private party but, uncannily and uncomfortably, a sense of kinship between the two: both are single individuals disturbed by failings in their lives and acting out intimate, isolated dramas, a similarity on which the film tastelessly insists when it cuts from Catherine asking her cat, "Want some milk?" to a shot of Carl's dead victim's face floating in a tub of milky liquid. Likewise, Carl's masturbatory ritual, in which he hangs like a marionette above the dead woman's body, suspended by hooks and chains, forms an inverted, and perverted, parallel to the therapeutic procedure in the lab, in which those undergoing the mind-merging operation hang face-up from the ceiling in visceral, muscle-sheathed rubber suits.

Indeed, if this visual connection between dismemberment and treatment appears grotesque, it is in keeping with the film's suggestion that psychotherapy may share features with the acts of the criminally insane. Both, the film implies, transform another human being into a thing, a toy; both depend on an absolute dichotomy of observer and observed; both construct a relation of power of one person over another. Thus if Carl's practice of filming his victims' deaths so as to view the tapes during masturbation seems the epitome of inhumanity, the fact that the scientists who supervise the mind merge are positioned in front of a screenlike window, avidly watching the inanimate bodies of the experimental subjects in the chamber, draws a correlation between his deadly acts and their kindly arts. Inside Carl's mind, hearing him tell the tale of his childhood abuse at the hands of his father, Catherine responds, "What your father did is evil. He treated you like a thing. No one should be treated like that." That psychiatrists may indeed treat their patients like things—that they may consider people, in Szasz's words, "mere objects or things to be classified and manipulated" (*Myth* 19)— is suggested by one doctor's claim that the psychologists who first tested the machine wanted only to "observe and report" on their mental guinea pigs and in another doctor's gleeful, hand-rubbing exclamation, "round two," before he sends Catherine into Carl for another go. Carl's monstrosity, the film suggests in a further assault on comfortable categories of difference, may have at least a partial parallel in the abusive (but licensed) behavior of the professionals who are dedicated to saving the likes of him; indeed, it may be precisely the cultural narrative that turns the mad into brute things that reveals the monstrosity of the norm.[9]

What distinguishes Catherine as an exception to her culture's mad narrative is her ability to sympathize, or empathize, with Carl—not only to run the risk of granting his fantasies the power of the real but also to welcome him into her own mind, to accept him as, literally, a part of her despite (or because of) his monstrous acts. In this respect, Catherine will trace a process akin to that which the viewer undergoes: at first seeing Carl as a stereotyped lunatic, a "twisted" thing whose mind, she protests after she panics and aborts her first venture inside his world, she cannot possibly grasp, she will come to see him as a suffering child and herself not as a clinician but as a ministering spirit, a layer-on of hands who soothes and heals a tormented soul. Thus on her second voyage into Carl's mind, Catherine finds herself not in the ghoulish fantasy arcade where his victims are displayed as life-size, captive puppets but in a "real" space: his childhood home, where she witnesses his father's verbal and physical abuse, branding Carl a "faggot" for playing with dolls and burning the child with a hot iron. When she next encounters the adult Carl, bent over a bloody bathtub in which his first victim lies—a shot that visually recalls that of Carl just before his arrest, as he lounged in his tub innocently singing "Mares eat oats"—the shock of this image, unlike that of the earlier shot, is tempered by the dawning of an unwanted yet irresistible fellow feeling. Whereas previously the audience, lacking any context by which to comprehend the killer, could only gag at the profanity of a mass murderer babbling nursery rhymes, now the links between childhood trauma and adulthood terror, particularly in the adult Carl's recitation of his horrifying baptismal experience, begin to cohere. The most wrenching transformation *The Cell* effects in the viewer's perception of reality, then, has little to do with drawing the viewer into the computer-generated fantasia of Carl's mind; rather, it has to do with a projection outward, a discomfiting of the social orthodoxy that turns madness into a brute outrage, utterly beyond the understanding or experience of the norm.

Yet if, on the one hand, *The Cell* struggles to bring the viewer into the mind of madness, to implicate the viewer in that mind and thereby inculcate a sense that madness is *not* beyond the human ken, a countervailing force is at work as well, one that restores the culture's comfortable fiction of the mentally ill as absolutely alien and of violence as absolutely the province of the mentally ill. The most obvious emblem of this force lies in the rendering of the adult Carl, who—both in reality and in his fantasized self-images—is so thoroughly loathsome that it beggars belief that any degree of abuse could have turned a spotless child into such a heinous killer. Peter, who registers resistance to this environmentalist etiology on numerous occasions, thus stands in for a similarly skeptical audience. Moreover, when Peter says, with absolute conviction and penetrating emphasis, that "a child can experience a hundred times worse the abuse" than a serial killer "and still grow up to be somebody who would never, ever, ever hurt another living thing," the obvious implication is that he himself underwent such abuse, but that far from serving as a pretext for him to damage innocents, the trauma catalyzed his desire to protect them. Too, the film repeatedly reminds viewers that Carl's victims are themselves, in the largest sense, vulnerable and blameless children; not only does he live across the street from a school (one assumes the better to hunt his future prey) but in a gruesome video clip of one of his drowning victims calling for "Mommy" and comforting herself as she dies by repeating "Daddy's girl," *The Cell* thwarts identification with the ruined child Carl may in fact be.[10]

At the same time, the film refuses to credit the environmental explanation unreservedly; indeed, it ultimately renders that explanation so tenuous as to appear nonsensical. Against images of abnormal CT scans, a doctor addressing the offscreen agents (and thus the film audience) explains that Carl suffers from "Whalen's infraction" (infarction?), a rare, severe form of schizophrenia that does not respond to "normal psychotropics," since it is "caused by a virus that infects the neurological system in utero" and that "lies dormant until it's triggered by some trauma," typically involving "water." There is no need to belabor the idiocy of this trumped-up malady, a hodgepodge of neurological, congenital, virological, environmental, and (given Carl's penchant for water) developmental precipitants. The significance of this alternative diagnosis is that, in its very impenetrability, it casts doubt on Catherine's understanding of Carl, undermining her belief that preadolescent psychic affliction translates into adult psychosis. And in any event, the film drives home the point that "understanding" Carl (a word at which Peter scoffs) is less significant than picking his mind. Repeated cuts to the young woman in the isolation chamber as her death draws near serve as reminders both of Carl's depravity and of the urgency of Peter's investigation, which ends thanks not to Catherine's gentle probing but to Peter's chance discovery of the one piece of stable data within Carl's wretched mind that enables him to track the monster's victim to his lair.

Just as Catherine serves as the principal vehicle for audience identification with the mentally ill, however, so does she serve as the principal means by which *The Cell* refuses such identification, revealing it to be dangerous, if not deadly. For it is immediately after the scene within Carl's mind of the killer preparing his first victim, the scene in which Catherine seemingly begins to unlock the riddle of his mind, that she becomes ensnared in that mind: failing or declining to terminate the mission in time, she succumbs to Carl in his most bestial form, as a white-faced, leprous goat-man, who clamps an iron collar around her neck. The manner in which Catherine separates herself from Carl, moreover, restores difference, conflict, and indeed violence as the proper, or only, response to the mentally ill: when she is freed from her delusion that she is the evil queen of Carl's kingdom, Catherine's first act is to skewer the mad king. The very sign of sanity, then, is striking out against the insane, treating them like the monsters they are. In a realization of the film's ability to hold two mutually contradictory ideas at the same time, it appears that though "no one should be treated that way," the insane should.

Or perhaps, on reflection, this is not a contradiction: the "no one" of Catherine's pronouncement comprehends only humans, not things. And though the young Carl is still human, thus vindicating Catherine's promise to him, after she stabs his adult manifestation, that "I would never hurt you," the adult Carl has forfeited his claim to humanity, has become, essentially and inveterately, what Catherine calls him: "this horrible thing."

I say *inveterately* because, despite Catherine's conviction that the child Carl is still salvageable, the film strongly suggests that the only resolution to his conflict, the only hope for his salvation, lies in his death. In the film's climactic sequence, Catherine, having escaped from Carl's mind, makes the decision to introduce him into her own. Within Catherine's mind, the monstrosity of Carl's becomes clear; whereas his was characterized by bizarre images, unmotivated cuts, and dizzying angles, hers, though dreamlike, is distinguished by order (stately marble pillars), light (including the halo that surrounds her), peace (a gentle snowfall), beauty (the ornamental border that scrolls across the frame), spirituality (the costume she wears being that of a nun, a saint, or even the Madonna), and all the conventions of narrative unity: continuity editing, mood-setting classical music, and so forth. As soon as the monstrous Carl enters, however, the devices of his world return: the border vanishes, the music turns dark, tarantulas and millipedes propagate, the light fades, and sudden shifts from shot to shot recommence. Against the monstrous Carl, Catherine becomes a warrior princess, garbed in black; with the bolts of a crossbow, she pins his limbs to the floor and then stabs him through the chest with her sword. Once again, it seems, the only recourse when confronted by the insane is violent defense; the only law or reason they honor is the animal rule of bloody conflict.

And yet, in one more turn of the screw that holds *The Cell* together—or tears it apart—Catherine's violence is unavailing; Carl will not die. Instead, repeating to her the words she must have brought into his mind when she sojourned there— "it's not real"—he remains pinned to the floor like a prisoner stretched on the rack, or like a suffering Christ, his bloody wrists and ankles pierced by arrows. In this context, his words take on a new thrust: what is "not real" is both her violence against him (it is not the real answer) and her commitment to him (it is not the real thing). What Catherine is called to do, then, is to reject the unreal visions of her society, and her profession, according to which Carl is a monstrous symbol to be sacrificed in the mad attempt to hold madness at bay; she is called, instead, to "save" him, the word the boy-Carl pronounces before she, having resumed her religious garb, holds him beneath the water in a baptism of death. This is a disturbing scene in many respects, not least because the shot of the habit-and-wimple-clad Catherine cradling the drowned child unmistakably invokes the tableau of the Pietà, thereby reinforcing the crucifixion imagery of her assault on the adult Carl. It is troubling also to recognize that in the film's terms, for Catherine to purify the child in holy waters, thereby renouncing both the hypocritical piety of Carl's father and the sanctimonious charity of the psychiatric cult, she too must become a killer: when she croons to the dying child, "You're gonna stay here with me," her words suggest both her acceptance of the other and her realization that murder has become her birthright. What makes this mercy killing even harder to read is the fact that, as it unfolds, parallel action shows Peter discovering the trapped young woman, freeing her from what seconds later would have been her watery grave, and embracing her in a shot that mirrors that of Catherine and Carl, even to the detail of both rescuers hushing, "You're okay" to the children they have "saved."

To adopt the culture's (and the cinema's) most widespread misconception of mental illness, then, *The Cell* is schizophrenic, exhibiting two separate personalities. Or, to adopt the clinical nomenclature, *The Cell* is delusional; it is nonsensical to see the mentally ill as twin, diametrically opposed persons—innocent children and mad monsters—but the film tenaciously maintains both images, and neither can shake the other. The film's conclusion does nothing to resolve this fixation. Though Catherine, cautioned at the start not to "take [her work] home" with her, has come to reject this advice and has admitted the mad into her home—both by adopting Carl's dog and by opening her mind to Edward—Peter remains a spokesperson for alienation, questioning her decision to let Edward in on the grounds that it might pose a "danger" to her. If, then, Carl's sacrificial death liberated one soul from its mortal fear of the Other, its effect passed another by. The final shot shows Edward within Catherine's mind; whereas in the opening sequence she aborted her mission at the first sign of the child's recalcitrance, one has reason to hope that this time she will tough it out and effect his recovery. Is the implication, then, that early intervention may prevent children from becoming monsters? Or is the film, by establishing empathy as the hallmark of humanity, reinscribing the line between the normal Catherine, who feels others' pain, and the abnormal Carl, who inflicts it? And if the latter, is the film not allowing the audience's having identified this once with the mentally ill to relieve any future need to identify with the mentally ill?[11] That *The Cell* raises such questions is a testament to its weird power to upset categories of difference; but it is also an indication of the film's compulsive need to set those categories aright.

There is, at that, another and significant sense in which *The Cell* supports the very oppositions it seems to abrogate: by confining the principal action and conflict quite literally to the warped mind of the mentally ill, the film supports the alienating process by which mental illness is torn from its social context. To be sure, there are some indications in *The Cell* that Carl's actions possess broader social determinants: the indictment of the psychiatric profession, the critique of institutional Christianity, and even the implication that law enforcement remains blind to the torment of mental illness may suggest that it is not Carl alone who is mad in this world. Nonetheless, these sociological markers are perfunctory at best; the drama of descent into the maelstrom of Carl's mind crowds out the social setting in which that mind exists and by which it is defined. If, then, one might view the manic intensity and gratuitous goriness of *The Cell* as representative of anxiety about not only mental but social chaos, it is still difficult to discover any sense in which *The Cell* holds up the social construction of madness to meaningful scrutiny.

The same cannot be said for *12 Monkeys*, which takes the social nature and function of madness as axiomatic. This film is, of course, about physical illness, about plague: the annihilation of human life on earth through the race's own arrogant experimentation and exploitation. If one were to summarize the film's story, it would go something like this: A young boy watches a man being shot in the airport. Shortly thereafter, a supervirus destroys nearly all human life on earth, driving the few survivors underground. Years later, a man named James Cole is sent back into the past to discover a pure strain of the virus, which the scientists of the future have assured him will enable them to devise an antidote to the still-active plague that prevents the human race from reclaiming the planet's surface. Though institutionalized as psychotic upon his arrival in the past (the viewer's present), Cole is ultimately able to convince his psychiatrist of the truth of his story. But in a vain attempt to prevent the man who apparently holds the supervirus from releasing it, Cole is shot in the airport as a young boy watches. It seems, then, as if the boy and the adult Cole were the same person, separated across the bar of time but reunited only to witness the consummation of a fate that cannot be averted or altered.

The trouble with this plot summary, however, is that it achieves a definitiveness that the film itself will not allow—and not only because time-loop tales are by their nature destabilizing. Rather, what makes the film so difficult to follow—by which I mean both to understand and to accept—is that all of the events I have enumerated are quite possibly fantastic (or fantasized) figments of the (possibly) psychotic consciousness of James Cole. As David Lashmet writes in a keenly perceptive reading of the film, "it might be best to imagine its apocalypse as a psychological phenomenon, a 'plague of madness,' as much as a biological epidemic" (58). And in exploring the "plague of madness," *12 Monkeys* extends the arguments of critics such as Szasz that insanity is socially defined, propagated, and enforced, a construct that disempowers the visibly deviant outsider, while loosing the true agents of mad destruction to work their murderous will.

The film *12 Monkeys* cites two principal settings in which the culture seeks to isolate and identify mental illness: the ward and the street. Its protagonist, the possibly time-traveling, possibly insane Cole, spends the majority of the film bouncing between these twin locales. Initially seen sleeping in what appears to be garbage, dressed in tattered clothes and with a chain-link fence behind him, he is committed to a psychiatric hospital for the film's first half before taking to the streets again, foul smelling by his own account and wearing the stereotypical costume of the homeless mentally ill vagrant: a fur-lined coat, a hooded sweatshirt, rags binding his hands. According to the public discourse of the 1980s and the 1990s, these two high-profile settings were, indeed, interrelated, each representing for the mentally ill the sole alternative to the other: the growth of the homeless population during this period was typically linked to the emptying of psychiatric wards during the preceding decades.[12] As with the broader question of what mental illness is, however, such discourse radically simplifies the relationship between homelessness and mental illness; numerous contextual factors make an explanation—or even an accurate count—of mental illness among the homeless tremendously difficult (which suggests why estimates have ranged from as low as 15 percent of the total homeless population to as high as 85 percent). At the simplest, such variation reflects the fact that the condition of homelessness thwarts accurate assessment; not only is a transient population, by definition, difficult to pin down but, as Leona Bachrach writes, there is great difficulty in establishing "the presence of psychopathology in an individual who is suffering extreme physical deprivation" (16). Indeed, some scholars argue that such deprivation may be a cause, not an effect, of mental illness; as Paul Koegel and M. Audrey Burnam point out, "Chronic malnutrition, sleep deprivation, hypothermia, and many other consequences of extreme privation are known to induce delirium, memory impairment, apathy, dementia, personality disorganization, and even paranoid psychosis" (79). Moreover, the authors note, behaviors that appear deranged in other social settings may be necessary or "adaptive" on the streets; persons eating from garbage cans when other sources of food are unavailable or women wearing multiple layers of malodorous clothes to dispel potential attackers are behaving in ways that are rational for their circumstances (80). As Thomas Kuhlman concludes, it is likely that "homelessness and mental impairment interact upon and within the individual in ways that defy reduction to simple cause-and-effect notions" (33). The homeless mentally ill, then, provide a particularly compelling illustration of the significance of social context and definition on the phenomenon of mental illness: it is impossible to isolate the insane mind from the pressures of homeless existence and the images devised by the dominant, nonhomeless population.

At the same time, however, the construction of the homeless mentally ill provides a perfect illustration of the ways in which mental illness, ripped from its social context, can serve as a means of distancing, alienating, and denying. For in the popular mind, craziness and homelessness are virtually synonymous; as Koegel and Burnam write, "in spite of the marked diversity characteristic of today's homeless population, a single image—that of the floridly psychotic street person—has eclipsed all others and mistakenly has come to represent the population as a whole" (78). What this mistaken attribution has meant, Jonathan Kozol argues in a cogent analysis, is that *social* explanations of homelessness are minimized, if not neglected outright: "The label of mental illness places the destitute outside the sphere of ordinary life. It personalizes an anguish that is public in its genesis; it individualizes a misery that is both general in cause and general in application" (158). Confirmation of Kozol's insight appears throughout popular discussions of homelessness; for example, in a classic case of victim blaming parading as sympathetic concern, C. J. Carnacchio writes of the homeless, "While clearly [mental illness] is not the result of bad individual choices, it is still a problem confined to the individual and not in any way society's fault" (26–27). More honestly, but even less humanely, when David Brooks advocates the arrest of the "hardcore homeless" to rid public places of "evil, dangerous people" (138) and shortly thereafter defines the "hardcore homeless" as "mentally ill, often schizophrenic" (139), the brief ellipsis cannot mask the connection: the "mentally ill" are "evil" and "dangerous" and need to be swept from the streets.[13] These examples typify how the "medicalization" of homelessness, to use Arline Mathieu's term, has been used to "delegitimate the plight of homeless people as victims of national political and economic shifts," to "divert attention from the structural causes of growing poverty," and to "justify the removal of homeless people from public spaces" (170), thereby both ideologically and physically denying the link between the putatively private (mental illness) and the public realm.[14]

There is, at that, a further sense in which this model serves the functions of alienation, a sense that is critical for a reading of *12 Monkeys*: the medical model constructs the homeless as a plague, a hostile, foreign entity acting upon the social body as illness acts upon the physical. Thus Myron Magnet, deriding those who see in the "numbers and degradation [of the homeless] the rising injustice and inequality of the social order," writes:

> Anyone who goes home by train or subway and trusts the evidence of his senses knows this just isn't so. What you see, if you stop to look, is craziness, drunkenness, dope and danger. Far from being the index of the nation's turpitude, the homeless are an encyclopedia of social pathology and mental disorder. . . . A society that feels that . . .

madness might be an acceptable "alternative life style" to sanity . . . has so lost confidence in its shared values that its sense of the meaningfulness and coherence of life has grown confused. . . . The reassertion of order in public places . . . will improve the health of the body politic and will help stop the social disintegration that has landed so many of the homeless in their deplorable plight. (A31)

Here Magnet not only identifies the homeless as a disease, an external agent that threatens an originally healthy body with "disintegration," but also employs the language of the visual to assert the axiomatic difference between the sane and the insane: anyone who "trusts the evidence of his senses" can "see" the craziness of the homeless, and anyone who doubts what he sees has, as it were, become so infected with this creeping blight of craziness as to lose "coherence" and grow "confused." According to this model, the mentally ill lie beyond the realm of the social (or even the human), their insanity fingering them as monstrous organisms that must be kept, violently if need be, from contaminating the social body.[15]

This is, of course, precisely the argument advanced in *12 Monkeys* by Jeffrey Goines, institutionalized (or incarcerated) son of the distinguished researcher who has fathered as well a virus with the potential to terminate the great majority of human life on earth. As Jeffrey explains to fellow inmate Cole, there is a reason that psychiatric patients are denied access to the "outside world" until their doctors so decree: "If all of these nuts could just make phone calls, you could spread insanity, oozing through telephone cables, oozing into the ears of all those poor sane people, infecting them. Wackos everywhere, plague of madness!" Yet it is characteristic of the strategy of *12 Monkeys* that, in opposition to arguments that seek at once to visualize and to depoliticize insanity—to make it, that is, a purely individual condition that manifests itself in readily legible stigmatic figures—the film will reveal mental illness to be both inherently social and, for that reason, supremely difficult to spot. As Jeffrey puts it, "You know what crazy is? Majority rules. . . . There's no right; there's no wrong; there's only majority opinion." The example Jeffrey offers to substantiate this relativist position is telling: belief in invisible agents of destruction—germs—was, until Semmelweis's hypothesis was accepted within the clinical and popular community, considered insane. And in the creepy climactic scene in which Dr. Peters, the "apocalypse nut" who apparently bears the virological superweapon, opens his vials for inspection by airport security, Jeffrey's theory is realized: completely undetectable by the viewers on-screen and those in the movie house, its presence indicated only by Dr. Peters's rapt, aghast reaction as he "watches" the disease organisms infiltrating the atmosphere, the presumed virus represents the fallacy of projecting plague onto visible scapegoats. For if Dr. Peters *is* a nut, he is also a member of Dr. Goines's research team; invisible as the virus itself, he cannot be seen as a menace or a madman because of his intimate relationship to the scientific knowledge and power that his society most values.

What *12 Monkeys* attempts to do, then, is to inculcate not only a distrust of the authorities, scientific or otherwise, but, more profoundly, a distrust of the visual and cultural authority by which judgments of sanity and insanity are rendered. In this respect, the film adopts a scheme similar to, but more all-embracing than, that of *The Cell*: whereas *The Cell* stops short of collapsing the viewer's vision with that of its madman, *12 Monkeys*, by aligning viewers from start to finish with the mind of the troubled and possibly unstable James Cole, produces a dizzying and unrelenting sense of disorientation regarding the nature of the real. Most obviously, the repeated "flashback" sequences (I call them that for lack of a better word) involving the shooting of the man in the airport place one in Cole's position of uncertainty; not only does one not know whether these are memories, hallucinations, dreams, or something else but one does not discover their significance, their role within the narrative, until that narrative has ended. (And even then, one is not entirely certain whether the flashbacks represent the young James's foreknowledge of witnessing his adult self's death, another of the film's many bizarre coincidences, or a function of the adult Cole's delusional beliefs.)

At the same time, numerous shots that are presumably consistent with the film's narrative nonetheless confound audience expectations and perceptions. When, for example, Cole is accidentally sent by the engineers of the future to a World War I battlefield, the initial shot of running figures in futuristic gas masks raises doubts as to whether he has remained in postapocalyptic time or perhaps arrived at the moment of the plague's outbreak. Likewise, shots of lions, giraffes, and elephants stampeding in the streets past signs reading "We Did It" lead one to believe that the Army of the 12 Monkeys has unleashed its plague, returning the film to the postapocalyptic nightmare with which it began, where lions and bears prowled the winter wasteland of the abandoned earth's surface; it turns out, however, that the innocent idealists have simply staged a bit of harmless "gorilla" theater, releasing animals from the zoo. Even in minor, seemingly incongruous moments, the film keeps viewers off balance (a fact signaled visually by the low-angle, canted framings characteristic of the film as a whole). During his abortive attempt to escape from the psychiatric institution, for instance, Cole sees an elderly security guard unaccountably change into a young man. Similarly, while in the department store with his onetime psychiatrist and later (possibly) insane accomplice, Dr. Catherine Railly, who purchases disguises for the two, Cole's upward glance at the ceiling is interrupted by a blue-tinged shot of the same space, now gutted and empty, with pigeons flying through a broken skylight. Whether these shots represent flash-forwards, memories of the future, or ephemeral visual blips is never resolved, and it is the accumulation of such unenlightening images that produces the chronic perceptual instability that infuses the film.

What these and other elements point toward, moreover, is an even more fundamental sense in which *12 Monkeys* disturbs and distorts the capacity to trust the evidence of one's senses: the question of who its protagonist is, whether James Cole is an emissary from the future or a delusional drifter—or both—remains open to interpretation. At the film's beginning, before the opening credits, an apocalyptic prediction starkly typed across the screen is credited to a "clinically diagnosed paranoid schizophrenic"; but whether Cole *is* what he is "clinically diagnosed" to be, the film refuses to answer. According to director Terry Gilliam, the question of whether Cole was simply "one more apocalyptic nut" is an unsettled one: "I wanted to keep it vague enough that it could just be a product of his deranged mind. To me the trick was to try and make it feel like he was mad" (qtd. in McCabe 167).[16] Nor need one rely on the director's word alone to be convinced that *12 Monkeys* profoundly troubles its protagonist's identity and authority. One of the patients in the psychiatric hospital, clearly echoing the mystical mantra for recovery that Dr. Railly has implanted in him, characterizes insanity as follows: although his imagined world represents "a totally convincing reality for me in every way, nevertheless [it] is actually a construct of my psyche. I am mentally divergent in that I am escaping certain ugly realities that plague my life here. When I stop going there, I will be well." If this definition is to be believed, then the viewer too is "plagued" by Cole's possibly delusional belief in the "totally convincing reality" of his life in the future (or, conversely, of his return to the present), for the film revels in appearing to confirm, then denying, the reality of its time-travel narrative.

For instance, when Cole escapes from solitary confinement, it seems clear that he must have received assistance from some force outside the present world. Yet immediately following this escape there occurs an overhead shot, virtually identical to that taken in the isolation chamber, of Cole lying on a table in a tall, narrow room, where a voice seeming to issue from a speaker in the wall hisses, "Maybe I'm not even here. Maybe I'm just in your head. No way to confirm anything." Sharing Cole's point of view here, as in much of the action involving him, the audience necessarily suffers in its ability to determine what is real and what is unreal. Later (or is it earlier?) in Philadelphia, when Cole is approached by a homeless man whose voice resembles that from the speaker and who seems to know about his mission, the reality of his time traveling seems confirmed again; yet after Cole's second disappearance and Dr. Railly's discovering the apparently unassailable evidence of the World War I bullet she extracted from Cole's leg, when she accosts (it seems) the same homeless man, he appears baffled by her (insane?) questions. And indeed, when Cole "returns" this time, already cloudy about whether he did, as Jeffrey claims, plant the idea of the killer virus in the younger madman's mind, Cole is convinced that he *is* insane, that the postplague future is but a delusion—a judgment that seems confirmed when Dr. Railly calls the phone number supposedly being monitored by the overlords of the future, only to reach a carpet-cleaning company. Yet a moment later, when Cole repeats the crank message that Dr. Railly left on the company's answering machine, it seems once more that the time-traveling narrative *is* real and that Cole, far from being insane, is the only person in the present sane enough to grasp the events that are about to unfold. In short, the film creates sufficient disequilibrium for one to believe, even at the end, that Cole's story may be all in his mind. When in the next-to-last scene Dr. Peters settles down for his round-the-world flight next to Jones, one of the scientists from Cole's future, her unexpected reappearance and ambiguous line, "I'm in insurance," fail to resolve the question of whether Cole accurately predicted the future because he had indeed lived in it—or, inasmuch as the film ends before one sees the supposed plague begin, whether he *did* accurately predict it at all.

In this respect, if *12 Monkeys* resembles *The Cell* in its tendency to complicate the viewer's relationship toward its principal mentally ill character, it differs from *The Cell* in its tendency to question the very basis on which one can determine whether that character—or anyone—is mentally ill or not. To Dr. Railly's supervisor, as to the psychiatric profession and the social system as a whole, making such a determination is inherent in the very essence of psychiatry: "You're a rational person; you're a trained psychiatrist. You know the difference between what's real and what's not." But as Dr. Railly responds, her words "irrationally" echoing those of one of her "insane" patients, Jeffrey Goines, "What we say is the truth is what everybody accepts, right? I mean, psychiatry, it's the latest religion. We decide what's right and wrong; we decide who's crazy or not." That she is, as she says, "losing [her] faith" in this positivist religion shifts the locus of madness from the mind to the medium; if, like Dr. Railly, a psychiatrist can adopt one mad person's quest and another's quotes, then perhaps madness *is* contagious, inhering not in the individual but rather in the individual's loss of faith in society's unquestioned truisms. In raising the possibility that madness may be purely a matter of social, clinical, or consensus judgment, then, *12 Monkeys* complicates the viewer's confidence as to the nature and function not of individual but of *social* reality; if there is no stable basis for determining who is mad and who is not, then the conventions or constructs of insanity, deprived of their necessary or obvious character, are revealed as tools in the maintenance of social power, alienation, and injustice.

In accordance with this critique, *12 Monkeys* emphasizes the continuities between the disciplinary mechanisms of the authoritarian scientific state of the (possible) future and the treatment of the clinically insane in the present, the ways in which "medical intervention against deviance," as Peter Conrad and Joseph Schneider write, becomes a "de facto agent of dominant social and political interests" (250). The film's first sequence in the future, in which Cole's apparently homeless roost turns out to be one unit in an endless series of wire-grated cages or cells, and in which a shot of a huge grappling hook descending from the structure's cavernous ceiling yields to a shot of Cole clothing himself in sterile latex gloves and suit, links the mechanisms of criminal justice and medicine; in both, the film suggests, individuals branded as different serve the totalitarian state's need *for* difference. Mirroring shots in the future and in the present reinforce these links: for instance, during Cole's examinations before the boards of engineers and psychiatrists—both of them constituting "dangerousness" hearings, the point at which psychiatry and criminal law converge—Cole is flanked, respectively, by two guards and two orderlies; in both instances, the examiners sit behind a long table in white lab jackets, and in both cases, they insist on his being inoculated and scrubbed vigorously in a disinfectant bath before his interrogation. In the future, he is manacled into a chair and physically distanced from the review board both by the elevation of the seat and by the video monitor through which they speak to him; in the present, both the orderlies and the psychiatrists react with alarm when he rises from his chair and closes the distance between himself and his judges. Likewise, when Cole is picked up by the police in the present, numerous devices link present and future incarcerations: Cole is held—along with a motley assortment of similarly "mad" vagrants—in a block of cells strongly reminiscent of those of the future. When Dr. Railly first views him, it is through a wire-mesh grating identical to that which composed the cages of the future prison, and his "restraints" (as she calls them) are identical to those of the future examining chair. Too, when the officer who briefs Dr. Railly on Cole's condition describes him as "totally irrational, totally disoriented, doesn't know where he is, doesn't know what day of the week it is, all that stuff," it is evident that, though deviance has not actually been bar-coded as in the future, it *has* been routinized, reduced to a readily identifiable schema: "all that stuff." And when Dr. Railly asks him—or tells him—"You've been in an institution before, haven't you?" the word *institution* (not to mention *before*) gains added resonance: deviants such as Cole have indeed been placed in institutions before and will be placed in institutions again, to safeguard what counts as normal to the powers that be.

Detainee and psychiatric patient James Cole (Bruce Willis) is examined by scientists of the future. From *12 Monkeys* (Universal, 1996). Courtesy of Photofest.

In short, *12 Monkeys* exposes both the characteristic power and the characteristic infirmity of social reality: those who subscribe to the majority opinion of what constitutes the real—in particular, an opinion that decrees the mentally ill as deadly threats to social order—are prevented from questioning or even detecting the actual violence perpetrated by the "legitimate" agents of society, a violence that is neither aberrant nor exceptional but inherent in the discourse of normalcy and abnormality itself. In this respect, the fact that the film leads the viewer to suspect Jeffrey, the "fruitcake," of the plot to unleash the killer virus places the viewer in the ultimately impotent position of Cole and Dr. Railly: seduced into tracking the most obvious carrier of plague, they overlook the invisible bearer until it is too late. What *12 Monkeys* seems to critique, finally, is the compelling power of social fantasy to shape (or misshape) the real: hunting monsters of its own making, society fails to see what a monster it has made of itself.

This is, without question, a significant position of social critique—one with the potential to turn the tables on the fantasy film tradition of social alienation. Yet this being the case, it is particularly suggestive of the grip this tradition holds that even as *12 Monkeys* implicitly points the finger away from the supposedly mad individuals within society's midst, at the same time its depiction of the mentally ill returns to a language of overt, visible evidences of madness. In the psychiatric ward, most noticeably, all of the patients are cardboard caricatures of madness, straight out of the news and entertainment media: inmates talking to themselves gesticulating violently, a man blowing soap bubbles, and the wildly excitable Jeffrey Goines are all recognizable types. Indeed, the film seems to go out of its way to spotlight the eccentricities of its collected crazies; for instance, after the African American inmate calmly explains to Cole the nature of his condition, the film cuts to a low-angle shot of the two men's feet, whereupon one can see that the man, though dressed in formal attire, is wearing bunny slippers. This minor swipe seems innocuous enough; yet its incongruous, and gratuitous, placement in the film makes one suspect that it serves not only to provoke a laugh but, more troublingly, to assert a visible sign of difference in the "crazy" juxtaposition of formal wear and child's slippers. The presence of this monstrous asylum midway might, it is true, serve the very point I made above, illustrating that, in one's focus on the visible sign of madness, one easily overlooks the covert madness of society itself. Indeed, it may be that the film, by coaxing viewers to react to the accustomed image of madness made manifest, is once more illuminating the lethal discourse of convention and conformity; if, that is, one sees Jeffrey and his flock as insane, this is because members of a medicalizing society cannot see otherwise. I think, however, that this suggestion grants the film a greater indulgence than it merits, and in any event, the suggestion can be turned back on the film itself: for all its critique of institutional madness, *12 Monkeys* cannot envision the institutionalized mad save through the very stereotypes of the institutions it critiques.

There is, in this regard, another reason to doubt how deep the critique of madness in *12 Monkeys* goes: though the film insists that madness is an institutional matter, a social construct, it nonetheless adheres in significant respects to the institutional fictions that tear mental illness from its social context. Consider, in particular, the film's representation of homelessness: the legion of the street consists entirely of adult, unmarried, unstable males, a cluster of traits that distinguishes not only Cole but the men who attempt to rob him and rape Dr. Railly, the old man who may or may not be a fellow time-traveler, and the street preacher who likewise may come from another time. Violence too seems to be endemic to the streets: the savagery of the men who attack Cole and Dr. Railly is matched by the fury of Cole himself, who responds to their assault with excessive and deadly force. Such representations, as I have indicated, are wholly in keeping with the dominant tenor of contemporary discourse on the homeless mentally ill; indeed, when conservative commentators such as Charles Krauthammer term these social castoffs an "army" (103), the connection to the mad Army of the 12 Monkeys unleashing chaos on the city—and to street warriors such as Cole dealing out death in the thoroughfares—suggests the ways in which *12 Monkeys* reinforces its culture's anxieties about the threat of hostile, alien forces massing within its breast. Too, as I have insisted, the most significant sense in which such representations support ideologies of alienation may be the way in which they disguise the social forces that shape both madness and homelessness, the forces that not only foster, define, and stigmatize these conditions but, having done so, deny that they have done so. As Linda Fuller points out, this strategy of denial, offering "easy allowance for keeping our distance from both the [homeless] people and their problems" ("From Tramps" 170), is characteristic of the many films in the 1980s and 1990s that deal with homelessness; indeed, it is characteristic of Gilliam's *The Fisher King* (1992), which fleshes out to an even greater extent than *12 Monkeys* a homeless subculture composed of adult male schizophrenics whose fall from grace is wholly due to personal tragedy.[17] In this sense, *12 Monkeys* cloaks the very thing it exposes: the exercise of social injustice in the alienation of the mentally ill. If the society—or societies—in this film are plagued by a madness of their own invention, the film itself constructs an image of madness so powerful, so tantalizing, that it is at once impossible to avoid and impossible to see.

One of the principal cultural forces that makes insanity impossible to see, of course, is the deluge of media images that likewise make it impossible to avoid. In this respect, it is intriguing how frequently *12 Monkeys* suggests the links between popular culture and alienation as it creates a world awash in media images: throughout the film, events are mediated by, and alternative realities represented within, televisions, high-tech video screens, tabloid periodicals, and perhaps most important, in the scene in which Cole and Dr. Railly don their traveling disguises in a movie house, theatrical films. In the next chapter, I will consider at length the role of such self-referential devices in fantasy film; for the moment, I will simply say that in *12 Monkeys* these devices suggest a self-critical awareness of how alienating images of mental illness—including perhaps its own—are fashioned by the cinematic medium. If, that is, *12 Monkeys* critiques the ways in which authorities manipulate audiences into accepting as real the alienating fantasies that cannot objectively be proven, one of the central authorities the film appears to hold up for inspection is the authority of film itself. The true plague in *12 Monkeys*, as in our own time, may thus be film itself, that most visible of media that paradoxically possesses the power to render itself invisible and in so doing to lend fantasized images of the marginalized and oppressed the appearance of reality. In this sense, if in *12 Monkeys* "the future is history," the sign, the science, and the cinema of madness are absolutely present.

On the other hand, the shot functions to emphasize conventions of seeing, in the double sense that it cites the spectatorial quality of the sideshow and implicates the film's viewers in a similar prurient voyeurism. Indeed, in an important sense, the shot structures *Freaks* as a whole; returning to the frame with which the film began, in which the barker beckons his audience to peer into Cleopatra's pen with the words "You are about to witness the most amazing, the most astounding living monstrosity of all time," the climactic shot fulfills the desires not of the viewers on-screen (for they have already looked into the pen) but of the viewers in the movie house. In both of these respects, then, the scene hinges on exposing the constructed nature of social rules and roles, ways of seeing and being: it not only emphasizes the arbitrary and self-interested character of relations of power grounded in physical difference but uncovers the cooperation of film and its audience in the illusion that the social fantasy of insider/outsider is necessary and real.

Throughout this study, I have explored the ways in which fantasy films participate in constructing the dichotomy of insider/outsider. Yet as Browning's film (which appeared the year before *King Kong*) suggests, the dominant fantasy film tradition of social alienation may have been contested from the start by another tradition, one capable of performing alternative, even potentially liberatory social functions. In the previous chapter, I broached the potential of that counter-tradition in fantasy madness films. In this final chapter, I wish to argue that certain fantasy films centering on the freak may work to challenge processes of social alienation by bringing those processes to the surface, holding them up for inspection, indeed reflecting on film's culpability in promoting them. As my discussion of Browning's film indicates, I believe that such films accomplish their inspection (and introspection) both through narrative means—inversion and subversion of the self/other divide—and through practices of cinematic self-reference or self-reflexivity, through identifying and interrogating their viewers' habits of seeing and their own habits of representation. These films, I will argue, are distinguished by what is typically termed *metacinema*: processes by which a film calls attention to its audience's viewing or its own signifying practices and thereby fosters a break in the audience's taken-for-granted acceptance of what it sees on the screen.[3] In metacinema, the audience potentially becomes aware of cinema's artifice, or of the cinema itself as artificial: a frame, a way of seeing. Likewise, the audience—rather than being encouraged in acts of alienating others—may be alienated from its own preconceptions. Finally, film itself may be alienated, exposed as a social construct, both product and producer of its social context rather than (as film is generally portrayed) an objective slice of reality or a fantastic escape from it. And if it seems that *fantasy* film might be unable to mount enough realism to rupture that realism, the singular relationship I have shown the genre to bear toward the real—a relationship that lends not only visionary scenarios but patently unreal *social* propositions the appearance of the real—may make fantasy film especially suited for an exposé of social alienation and of its own role in sustaining it.

Toward that end, it is worth noting that it is not solely a handful of freak films that deploy metacinema; rather, one might consider such self-referencing moves one of the salient features of the fantasy genre. I have remarked, for instance, on the keenly visual orientation of a number of films in this study: *King Kong, Jurassic Park,* and *12 Monkeys* are all concerned with ways of seeing, with the function of the gaze as an instrument of power and oppression. At the same time, I have demonstrated that some films, such as *The Wizard of Oz,* possess distinctly self-referential leanings; thanks in particular to its Emerald City sequences, *Oz,* I have suggested, may be treated as 1930s Hollywood's half-serious autoanalysis. And given *Kong's* film-within-a-film plot, it is not surprising that critics have called attention to the self-reflexive elements in it. Bruce Kawin, for example, analyzes how one of the film's most famous scenes, the "scream test" aboard ship, (con)fuses the filming *of* the movie with the filming *in* the movie: as the audience watches from the perspective of Denham's camera, the director's voice provides Darrow with instructions similar to those Cooper must have offered Wray, who often was reacting to something she could not see (247–53).[4] Along the same lines, *Kong's* lavish use of rear-screen projection is suggestive: many of the film's "monster" shots were achieved through the rear-screen technique, which O'Brien first employed in the test reel by which Cooper sold *Kong* to RKO. As Jeff Rovin points out, "beyond its comparative simplicity, the rear-screen process has an advantage over the matte in allowing the player to *see* the menace to which he or she is reacting" (33); by the same token, it has the effect of allowing the viewer to view the film's filming, to watch on a screen the actors watching things on a screen. It thus seems fitting that Kong attacks the photographers whom Denham, votary of the visual image that he is, has lined up for his monster premiere; for in so doing, one might argue, Kong attacks the processes by which fantasy film packages the monstrous, fabricating and blowing it up to gigantic proportions to justify ideologies and practices of social alienation.[5]

In metacinematic moments such as these, then, one glimpses the potential of fantasy film to reframe its own vision(s), to turn its sights into insights: as the film genre most deeply, one might say indistinguishably, affiliated with the spectacular qualities of the medium, fantasy films may be particularly suited to reminding audiences that their monstrous beings are not visually or socially real but are sophisticated, orchestrated illusions. In this respect, as Garrett Stewart contends, metacinema in fantasy film may serve to "talk us out of the truisms of ready identification by which we are lured to these films in the first place" and may thereby provoke "reflection on the ideologies by which we see and so lead our lives" ("'Videology'" 207).[6] And if this is true, then perhaps the self-critical current in fantasy film is not a "minority" tradition after all; perhaps applying metacinematic readings to all of the films I have engaged thus far might be a means of challenging, or even overturning, the paradigm I have thus far pursued.

Before one takes such a radical step, however, several complicating factors must be considered. To begin with, if metacinema *is* as pervasive as all that, it may be that it is no more than a convention, a pitch—even a means of enhancing rather than attenuating processes of dominant-group identification and minority-group alienation.[7] At the same time, even if one admits the revisionary *potential* of metacinema, it may be that the strategy expresses itself variably throughout the genre, sometimes being no more than tomfoolery, while at other times being a significant element of self-critique. And in fact, I would argue that this is the case; though it may be true that metacinema exists in many fantasy films, the freak films I will consider in this chapter utilize its techniques to such an extent and in such distinctive ways as to cast doubt on its inherently transformative power. But to add a final complication: even in such films, metacinematic techniques prove inadequate to cancel out processes of alienation; even at its most self-conscious and self-consuming, metacinema cannot overthrow traditions of alienation that pervade fantasy cinema and its social milieu. Indeed, one might even contend that like all the films in this study, metacinematic freak films are engaged not in short-circuiting but in supercharging hallucinatory propositions about social outsiders—or that, like the madness films I examined in the previous chapter, the anxiety attending their radical potential makes such films particularly active in shoring up the categories of difference they transgress.

At the same time, however, I believe there is value in concluding a study on alienation in fantasy film by considering films that, more productively than any other I have explored in these pages, attempt to take a critical standpoint on the tradition of which they are a part. This chapter thus differs from the previous one largely in emphasis: whereas in the previous chapter I insisted on the films' alienating processes notwithstanding their progressive intimations, here I acknowledge the films' alienating work while striving to discover their power to frame more progressive visions. In this sense, though I continue to believe that no fantasy film succeeds fully in neutralizing the insider/outsider dichotomy, I advance the hopeful proposition that, by making that dichotomy visible, some few fantasy films may offer viewers the opportunity to conceptualize, and perhaps even realize, a world in which social equality would no longer be a fantasy.

Showing Freaks

The history of the freak is a history of visual exploitation. Or, to put this another way, it is the fact of visual exploitation that accounts for the history of the freak; the latter is inconceivable without the former. To a certain extent, of course, all social "monsters" are defined, or designed, in terms of supposedly unimpeachable marks of visual difference; as this book has illustrated in the particular case of the cinema, visualization is a particularly potent tool in processes of alienation. Too, it is not the freak alone whose monstrous otherness has been showcased within lavish public ceremonials: the racial "others" of *Kong*'s decade, for example, have the grotesque history of minstrel shows and lynching bees (not to mention photographic and cinematic exhibitions) to attest to the centrality of public spectacle in the making of monsters. Nor, for that matter, should one forget that other categories of difference may be intertwined with, indeed constitutive of, the category of the freak: racial and sexual differences, in particular, are fundamental to "freak shows," sometimes to such an extent that these differences alone may make the freak.[8] Visual exploitation, it seems evident, is fundamental to the process of framing monsters.

Still, if the case of the freak is not wholly unique, it is nonetheless special. For it is the freak alone that is constituted principally—one might say wholly—through public exhibitions of seeing; it is the freak alone that needs not only to be seen to be believed but to be seen to *be*. In her study of disability discourse, Rosemarie Garland Thomson argues that the body of the freak is "a cultural text that is interpreted, inscribed with meaning—indeed *made*—within social relations" of power expressed through the differential equation of seeing/being seen, a visual disequilibrium that Thomson finds most plainly but by no means singularly evident in the antebellum American freak show (*Extraordinary* 22). Particularly malleable thanks to the significant potential for variation in the human form and the far greater potential for variation in cultural norms, the freak operates as a sort of monster of convenience, a visual representation suitable for framing in any number of contexts. In two respects, then, the exhibition of the freak exemplifies Donna Haraway's dictum that "bodies are maps of power and identity" (99). On the one hand, the very act of exhibiting "abnormal" bodies signifies relations of inequality between the freak and the viewers who are, through this transaction, enabled to identify themselves as physically normal. On the other hand, the exhibition of those designated freaks extends beyond considerations of bodily difference, narrowly defined, to act as a compressed, dramatic spectacle of the ideal social order, with the condition of the "deformed" or "diseased" body producing, by contrast, the constitution of the sound, healthy "body" politic. The freak show thus highlights the special but crucial sense in which, as I have argued throughout this book, works of fantasy achieve the illusion that "seeing is believing": seeing the monstrous freak facilitates not only belief in this abominable wonder but the far more wonderful (and abominable) belief that the alienating ideologies constructed through the freak show are not constructed but real.

From classical times to the present, the freak has functioned in this way in the imagination of the West: as a figure through which ideologies of physical-cultural soundness versus depravity, order versus chaos, have been defined and demonstrated. During the medieval period, and at least through the Renaissance, the dominant tradition of freak-viewing construed the freak as "a divine hieroglyphic" (Davidson 39), a visible symbol through which the Almighty exhibited his will, and wrath, for all to see. A particularly striking, though to modern eyes preposterous, demonstration of the visible freak's role in enforcing social orthodoxy appears in an anonymous 1647 broadside concerning the birth of

> a Child, or rather a Monster, . . . with two heads, growing severally, somewhat distant one from the other, bearing the similitude of man and woman. . . . [T]he Eyes standing in the middest of the Forehead (they having but one a piece) cannot unfitly be paralelled with that horned Monster *Polyphemus*. . . . The Armes had their growthes from severall places, being of great dimensions, but very small, having annexed to their wrists great Tallons, like to a Griffins. From the Secret parts (which shewed it to bee both Male and Female) downewards, all hairie, like your Satyres. . . . In short, all the parts about it were monstrous and ill-shapen; insomuch, that it shooke into a quaking terrour all those that were eye-witnesses of this horned production. . . . [T]he Monster (with a hoarse, but lowd voyce) was heard to speake these words, being ever after silent, *I am thus deformed for the sinnes of my Parents.* (*Strange Newes* 1–3)

Contrived though this hodgepodge of pagan parts clearly is, its presence signifies the cultural function of the freak in early modern times: the sight of the perverted body—along with, in this case, its carefully scripted line—was purposed to invoke holy "terrour" and, presumably, repentance in all "eye-witnesses" to the "production" (a word as tellingly ambidextrous as the monster itself, with its suggestion of both natural gestation and theatrical exhibition). That the conjuring of visibly terrifying freaks as a means of regulating social behavior was not confined to the popular broadside tradition is evidenced by one of the earliest attempts to systematize the study of congenital abnormalities, French physician Ambroise Paré's *On Monsters and Marvels* (1573): the bestial acts of "atheists," Paré announces, are responsible for the birth of "hideous monsters that bring great shame to those who look at them" (67). Consistent with this querulous conviction that viewing the freak could threaten the onlooker with a sort of deformity-by-proxy, Paré begged his reader's indulgence: "Now I shall refrain from writing here about several other monsters engendered from such grist, together with their portraits, which are so hideous and abominable, not only to see but also to hear tell of, that, due to their great loathsomeness I have neither wanted to relate them nor to have them portrayed" (73). It is worth noting, however, not only that the doctor's disclaimer titillates as much as it abstains but that his text is littered with all manner of spectacular freaks; clearly enough, the injunction against disclosure was at war with the monitory and voyeuristic imperatives of revelation. For folk as well as clinical observers, the freak was a being able to attract, and to repel, the curious gaze and in so doing to exhibit (or to extort) social power relations of which bodily difference was both a prominent category and a general prefiguration.

At the same time, if the role of the freak was to exhibit the sanctity of physical and cultural relations of power, it is no marvel that the body of the freak moved beyond the printed page to appear in exhibitions of another sort: the public displays that predated the more elaborate spectacles of the late-nineteenth- and early-twentieth-century sideshow. Such exhibitions were common enough in the fairs, pubs, and byways of Shakespeare's time to rate a reference in *The Tempest* (1611): when Trinculo muses of Caliban that in London "would this monster make a man; any strange beast there makes a man" (2.2.30–31), the pun on "make a man" not only suggests the profitability of early modern freak shows but the fact that the figure of the freak was meant to "make," by contrast, the figure of the normal or natural man.[9] During the eighteenth and nineteenth centuries, the fascination with the freak continued unabated in both Europe and the United States; indeed, discourses and practices of freak exhibition burgeoned during this period, disseminating throughout all levels, sites, and sanctums of modern culture. Thus it was not only in the popular productions of the midway but also in the cabinets of curiosities patronized by polite society and the examining rooms of the doctors who carved out the new science of "teratology" that the body of the freak was collected, inspected, and dissected for the purposes of cultural stimulation, identification, and stratification.[10] Nor can these diverse practices of freak-gazing among "high" and "low" culture be so easily distinguished; as Stephen Pender argues, "the marvelous and the scientific coexisted in the reception and study of monsters and continued to do so long after the monster's absorption by 'legitimate' scientific discourses in the eighteenth century" ("'No Monsters'" 150). The modern freak show thus exhibits not only the deformed body but, more significantly, a capacious social architecture in which every body is implicated—and inspected—according to dominant cultural ideals and practice.

One revealing instance of the overlap and reinforcement among the various discourses of freak watching in the nineteenth century appears in the autobiographical reminiscences of Frederick Treves, the Victorian doctor whose fame today rests largely on his having been the deliverer and confidante of Joseph Merrick, the Elephant Man.[11] Whereas Treves contemns the prying, lower-class "porter" or "wardmaid" in the London hospital who would periodically "open [Merrick's] door to let curious friends have a peep at the Elephant Man" (19), he misses the irony of Merrick's captivation of (or by) the cream of high society: "Merrick's case attracted much attention in the papers, with the result that he had a constant succession of visitors. Everybody wanted to see him" (22). This continued desire of every "body" in London society to see the celebrity freak—and in so doing to confirm their distance and difference from him—underscores the argument of the Elephant Man's modern-day interpreters that Merrick has long served as "a shape-shifting curiosity whose different guises variously suit the needs of particular audiences, genres, and interpreters" (Graham and Oehlschlaeger 2). In particularly spectacular ways, due to his flagrant symptoms and equally flagrant popularity, the Elephant Man underscores the social role of all freaks: to make "everybody want to see him" and in the seeing to exhibit, to stage, the grand pageant of social order, deviance, and alienation.

In this respect, it is fitting that the culminating act of this Victorian "superfreak's" life, the final exhibition of his social conformity, according to Treves's memoirs, involved Merrick's attendance at a theatrical performance. Treves's description of the Elephant Man's rapture on watching the pantomime is suggestive: "To him, as to a child with the faculty of make-believe, everything was real; the palace was the home of kings, the princess was of royal blood, the fairies were as undoubted as the children in the street, while the dishes at the banquet were of unquestionable gold. He did not like to discuss it as a play but rather as a vision of some actual world" (32). In this account of the freak spectator viewing a stylized performance of the ideal social order, Treves's memoir suggests the disciplinary imperatives of the freak show: socialization, this passage suggests, is signaled by one's ability to accept social fantasy *as if real*. The apotheosis of this Victorian-era freak thus emphasizes the ways in which the freak show activates institutionalized forms of "structured seeing" (Thomson, "Beauty" 185) to map the extraordinary body within a dominant social protocol: whether in the marketplace, the medical clinic, the museum, or the mediated space of the theater, the freak comes into being through acts of visual definition, differentiation, and discrimination that simultaneously create a "vision of some actual world."

Given this vital cultural function, I would challenge those critics who argue that in contemporary times the freak show has been "killed by the change in public attitudes towards caring for the handicapped" (Wilson 2). True, sideshows and dime museums were largely suppressed in the years following World War II due to changing standards of taste.[12] But freak shows were never reliant on "public attitudes towards caring for the handicapped"—or on the handicapped themselves, for that matter—so much as on public visions of normality and difference. Thus it is telling that, just as the freak show seemed to be decamping from the fairgrounds, the power of film to actualize such visions ensured that these shows would reemerge—with a vengeance—in the mediated space of the movie theater. As Martin Norden writes in his survey of disability imagery in the Hollywood cinema, the bewildering array of freak figures in the movies collectively serves a function identical to that of earlier freak exhibitions: that of encouraging "audience members to perceive the world" from the perspective of the "normal" and in so doing to enhance the freak figures' "isolation and 'Otherness' by reducing them to objectifications of pity, fear, scorn, etc.—in short, objects of spectacle—as a means of pandering to the needs of the able-bodied majority" (1). Paul Longmore refines Norden's argument: noting that representations of the freak in film regularly associate "disability with malevolence," as "physical handicaps are made the emblems of evil" (32), Longmore establishes that the modern cinema owes more than it realizes to the ancient tradition of reading the freak's body as a proclamation of divine displeasure. Too, as Longmore points out, this association of "deformity of body" with "deformity of soul" achieves its summit in fantasy film: "The subtext of many horror films is fear and loathing" of the freak, with many of the cinema's most famous monsters—from the Phantom of the Opera and the creature of Frankenstein in classic Hollywood cinema to the Joker and the Penguin of Tim Burton's *Batman* films—taking the form of hideous outcasts who exact gory retribution from the "normals" (32). Browning's *Freaks*, in fact, provides a case in point: whatever the film's revisionary energies, the culminating act of freak violence transforms the title characters into the monsters their society has always seen them to be. If it is true that the existence of the freak depends on principles of "structured seeing," then it is no wonder that film, a medium that functions precisely by structuring what and how one sees, should have become such a powerful vehicle for the excoriation of the monstrous freak and the exaltation of the norm.[13]

Having returned to the example of *Freaks*, however, it is equally apparent that the history I have sketched thus far has been incompletely attuned to the ambiguity and ambivalence implicit in acts of freak exhibition.[14] Consider, in this respect, the theater passage from Treves: if in one respect the freak's vision suggests an assimilative model of social orthodoxy, by the same token, that theatrical vision opens up the possibility of exposing the production of social reality as pure stagecraft, a prefab performance in which the freak itself plays a formative role. It is this possibility that informs modern critical thinking on the freak; in the words of Robert Bogdan, whose 1988 book *Freak Show* instituted the social-constructionist study of the freak: "'Freak' is a frame of mind, a set of practices, a way of thinking about and presenting people. It is the enactment of a tradition, the performance of a stylized presentation" (3).[15] It is this possibility, perhaps, that accounts for the aspect of *Freaks* most often denounced: casting real sideshow performers, such as conjoined twins Daisy and Violet Hilton, to play themselves, the film dramatizes the theatrical nature of the freak.[16] And it is this unwonted (or unwanted) possibility that dances at the margins of freak discourse all along, surfacing in such places as the over-the-top staginess of the monstrous birth's production or, to cite another example, in the fears of Paré, freak-interpreter-cum-entrepreneur, that the undeserving indigent might be riding the culture's morbid fascination with monsters by counterfeiting the role for a profit (74–84). Intriguingly, as Norden notes, some of the earliest works produced by the American film industry followed Paré in decrying the supposed plague of beggarly freak performances: first appearing in Thomas Edison's 1898 *Fake Beggar*, the image of "beggars, especially those with fake disabilities," visualized the prospect of social (mis)identification (14). In such moments of disclosure, the truism that Thomson articulates peeks through: "What we assume to be a freak of nature [is] instead a freak of culture," a social mantra rather than a divine mandate ("Introduction" 10).

Indeed, however far-flung such revelatory moments may be, the possibility of the freak show's self-exposure is inherent in the nature of the case. For if, as I have maintained, the freak is not a stable, integral entity or identity but a function of social seeing, then the very rituals necessary to produce this figure for mass-cultural consumption invariably teeter on the verge of announcing their own artifice. In this sense, freak shows might be considered examples of *liminal* experience, anthropologist Victor Turner's term for ritual performances that institute "ambiguity and paradox, a confusion of all the customary categories" (97). "This coincidence of opposite processes and notions in a single representation," Turner continues, "characterizes the peculiar unity of the liminal: that which is neither this nor that, and yet is both" (99). In such a threshold site/sight, where customary categories are suspended, transgressed, and unmasked as the contrivances they are, the possibility exists for reevaluation, reformation, indeed revolution of the alienating processes on which the freak show relies. That is, because of the freak's paradoxical genealogy—the incarnate performed, or the performative incarnate—the awareness may always dawn in the freak show that all is spectacle and signification—that instead of seeing *things*, one is really only *seeing* things.

I would not want to push this claim too far: it has proven all too tempting to homogenize and romanticize the liminal,[17] to treat it as always and everywhere a devastating engine of social critique, despite Turner's insistence that the liminal state might be no more than a way-station en route to an affirmation of orthodoxy rendered all the more inexorable by the transitory encounter with chaos. At the same time, however, in my attempt to discover a more liberatory pedigree for fantasy film than I have thus far pursued, I follow the lead of performance scholars in avowing the "*potential* of liminoid activity to provide a site for social and cultural resistance and the exploration of alternative possibilities" (M. Carlson 24, my emphasis). Whatever the case for liminality in general (if there is such a thing), I would agree that certain liminal experiences, in certain contexts, may serve certain purposes of social evaluation, challenge, and reconstruction. Thus when, in *The Tempest*, Prospero (re)claims Caliban, intoning "this thing of darkness I / Acknowledge mine" (5.1.275–76), he performs the move by which "owning" the freak may disarm the freak show's alienating properties: acknowledging that the "thing of darkness" in the theater is "mine," in the sense that this monstrous creature is indeed a projection of his culture's darkest fantasies, Shakespeare's magus and possible dramaturgical stand-in draws back the curtain on the machinery of the freak show. And Shakespeare's stage, as Steven Mullaney reminds us, stood in its physical relationship to the centers of power precisely as the golden-age freak show (and the modern-day movie theater) now stand: "The place of the stage was a marginal one, and in the world of early modern culture such marginality was in itself significant" (9). Mullaney continues:

> When Burbage dislocated theater from the city, he established a social and cultural distance . . . that provided the stage with a culturally and ideologically removed vantage point from which it could reflect upon its own age with more freedom and license than had hitherto been possible. It was a freedom, a range of slightly eccentric or decentered perspectives, that gave the stage an uncanny ability to tease out and represent the contradictions of a culture it both belonged to and was, to a certain extent, alienated from. (30–31)

Situated on the verge of the acceptable, *midway*, as it were, between norm and not, the freak show on film, like the theatrical exhibition in the "Liberties" skirting London or the sideshow's itinerant iteration under Barnum, possesses the potential not only to focus the energies of social alienation but to refocus that alienating lens, to alienate itself (and its audience) from the monstrous social fantasies to which all belong.

One last word before I turn to the films. To emphasize the performative nature of the freak, I must make clear, is not to suggest that the categories of monstrosity I have considered previously are more natural and therefore less open to re-vision; however diehard distinctions such as black/white or male/female may appear, I would insist that these are as much a function of social ways of seeing as they are expressions of biological fact. Social alienation, as I hope I have made clear throughout this book, is inherently performative; if it appears to have a basis in some ultimate reality beyond the values and judgments of a particular historical culture, that is only because social fantasy—including the fantasy on film—sees it so. And this being the case, the reader might wish to view my focusing on freak films in this chapter not as a plea for the radical uniqueness of such films but as a means of advancing a new frame, a new way of seeing, by which to read the signs that have come before.

The "Freak" in the Frame

For the Walt Disney studio, the 1990s was the decade of the freak. In *The Little Mermaid* (1989), the title character, Ariel, is literally a fish out of water. In Tim Burton's Disney-produced *The Nightmare Before Christmas* (1993), the human skeleton who rules the Halloween Town sideshow longs to join the jolly world of Christmas. In *The Hunchback of Notre Dame* (1996), the deformed bell-ringer of Hugo's novel seeks to belong in a society that regards him as a hideous reject. In *Hercules* (1997), the immortal son of Zeus, stranded among mortals, is cursed as a freak because of his unmanageable strength. In *Tarzan* (1999), the hero must adopt the habits of a gorilla troop whose leader insists that he will "never be one of us." Closing out this tradition on the brink of a new millennium, the studio offered the one-legged hero of *Fantasia 2000*'s "Steadfast Tin Soldier" segment—a profreak battle cry compromised somewhat by the fact that the villain, a leering jack-in-the-box, is himself legless. Notably, in many of these films the protagonist's freakishness inheres specifically in bodily disfigurement, dysfunction, or presumed inferiority; even the seemingly perfect physical specimen Hercules, whose hypercorporeality translates into handicap on earth, fits the mold of alienation-through-embodiment. (This in marked contrast to the majority of Disney's classic films, in which the protagonists' able-bodiedness is simply assumed when not, as with the heroines, positively and punitively prescribed.) Though it may be no more than Disney's notoriously formulaic proclivities—particularly when the formula is garnering accolades and Oscar nods—that accounts for the persistence of this pattern, it is nonetheless intriguing how many of the studio's films during this period bring the marginalized freak to the cinema's center.

Developments in the cultural and legal landscape of the United States during the same period were doing their part to recenter, or decenter, discourses of
bodily difference. Climaxing with the 1990 passage of the federal Americans with
Disabilities Act (ADA), subtle yet significant changes in the cultural construction of the abnormal body had begun to vie with the tradition of social alienation. Or perhaps it is best to say that those changes involved a growing awareness that bodily disability—or ability, for that matter—*is* culturally constructed;
as Claire Liachowitz writes in her history of pre-ADA legislation, disability had
increasingly come to be regarded less as "a direct result of personal physical disorder" than as "a complex of constraints that the ablebodied population imposes
on the behavior of physically impaired people" (1), a set of "social constructions
that *force* handicapped individuals into a position of deviance" (5). Disability, in
other words, had come to be construed more as a civil rights issue than a medical problem; as with the discrimination against and disenfranchisement of African Americans in the pre–civil rights era of the South, the "handicaps" of most
if not all disabled Americans could be traced to "society's structural barriers"
(Gostin and Beyer, preface xiii), rather than to innate, private, physiological short-
comings or flaws. (Again, consider Hercules: avatar on Olympus, aberration on
earth.) In its definition of disability, the ADA confirmed this social-constructionist—or, as Bogdan's *Freak Show*, published two years before the passage of the
ADA, would have it, this *performative*—perspective. First, the act asserted that

> individuals with disabilities are a discrete and insular minority who
> have been faced with restrictions and limitations, subjected to a his-
> tory of purposeful unequal treatment, and relegated to a position of
> political powerlessness in our society, based on characteristics that are
> beyond the control of such individuals and resulting from stereotypic
> assumptions not truly indicative of the individual ability of such
> individuals to participate in, and contribute to, society. ("Act" 267)

Then, the act defined *disability* in two principal, and significantly different,
senses: "a physical or mental impairment that substantially limits one or more
of the major life activities of [the] individual," and "being regarded as having such
an impairment" (268). In both the preamble and the definition proper, then,
the ADA removed the idea of disability from a strictly individualized, internalized, or naturalized locus, emphasizing instead the dynamic interaction between
bodily conditions and social discourse ("being regarded as having such an impairment"), representation ("stereotypic assumptions"), and practice ("restrictions
and limitations" indicating "purposeful unequal treatment" and fostering "political powerlessness").

The effect of the ADA and of comparable initiatives on feature film is anything but clear-cut; needless to say, the "freak" monster has not died out even as
of this writing, long after the act's passage. That this is so reinforces the point I
made earlier: the freak show has never been either wholly reliant on, or wholly
synonymous with, cultural attitudes toward persons with disabilities. Rather, it
represents a much more fundamental, systemic, and protean program of social
alienation grounded in discourses of the body. Thus though Longmore believes
that the spate of "positive images" of disabled persons in recent Hollywood cinema "reflect[s] the growing socio-political perception of disabled people as a
minority group and the increasing impact of the disability civil rights movement"
(37), I would be particularly reluctant in this instance to endorse the notion that
any set of films reflects corresponding social changes. Norden suggests judiciously
that it is "simply too early to assess [the ADA's] impact on the Hollywood community" (309); I would add that whether the ADA or any legislative action can
dislodge deeply entrenched cultural and cinematic representations concerning
normalcy and deviance is probably a question larger than that of simple lag time.
All the same, however, even if one avoids assuming some kind of causal relationship between disability law and Disney fantasy, the historical conjunction of the
two developments is suggestive. If nothing else, this conjunction encourages one
to view the Disney freak films not as they are typically seen—as timeless fairy-
tale narratives of an outsider gaining acceptance as the reward for a self-sacrific-
ing act—but as participants in an ongoing cultural debate concerning physical
difference, representation, and alienation.

Beauty and the Beast (1991), perhaps Disney's most celebrated film of the
modern era thanks to its unprecedented Oscar nomination for Best Picture, is
also one of the studio's most notable for its tapping of the revolutionary potential of the freak film.[18] The animated cartoon (and its computer-generated off-
shoot) is perhaps uniquely geared for an examination of cultural representation;
for unlike live action or stop-motion techniques that rely on three-dimensional,
"real-world" referents, drawn animation consists of fixed, flat images whose appearance of mass, dimension, and motion is wholly simulated. Cartoon animation, in other words, is inherently performative, an act of bringing to apparent
life compelling images that bear no necessary relation to the real. In this respect,
animated cartoons may themselves be seen as freak shows, cultural dramas by
which images are invested with bodily presence. Of the films I have listed, it is
Beauty and the Beast that most fully embraces its affinity with the freak show, using
the premise (or pretense) of bodily difference to engage a range of critical, inter-
woven issues: issues of appearance, representation, intolerance, and alienation.

From the film's opening shot, metacinematic effects begin to activate these issues. While voice-over narration sets the tale, the multiplane camera zooms from a distant vantage toward the Beast's castle and then dissolves to a stained-glass window on which prefatory events are depicted. As punishment for being "deceived by appearances," we are told, an arrogant prince was cursed to wear the form of a hideous beast. This introduction provides a framework for thinking about the representational or performative nature of the freak: like the prince himself, and like the townspeople who will similarly prove unable to penetrate surface appearances, the audience at first encounters only a series of stylized, static images captured by the mosaic of the stained glass. Vision at this crucial moment of first acquaintance is, accordingly, constrained, shaped by predetermined ways of seeing: not only are there few art forms more circumscribed within inflexible canons of style than stained glass, but the absence of animation in this sequence—all apparent motion being generated by camera "moves" and dissolves—recapitulates the sense that one's seeing is prefabricated, conventionalized. Following this sequence, the film provides the viewer with yet another representation: a fleeting glimpse of a formal portrait containing the prince's human countenance, across which the agonized Beast's claws rake, ripping the painting to tatters. When, directly after this prologue, the film's main title, *Beauty and the Beast*, appears on the screen, the effect is to call into question what might otherwise have seemed an unproblematic opposition of beauty and bestiality; for the audience has been alerted that to idolize that opposition is, like the prince, to be doomed to live it.

The opposition that *Beauty and the Beast* constructs, conversely, lies between those who accept social appearance as reality and those who delve beneath or beyond this crippling perspective. As such, though the most insistent narrative element in *Beauty and the Beast* may be the romantic triangle of Belle, the Beast, and Gaston, the film delves beyond this superficial plot instrument to explore the social grounds of physical beauty; or to put it more precisely, the film reveals the love story to be but an outgrowth or microcosm of a social conflict over standards of normalcy. Thus the next sequence after the main title, in which Belle roams her provincial village to the accompaniment of the film's first song, "Bonjour," extends the argument of the prologue by emphasizing the *communal* nature of (mis)representation. Of the six songs in the film, four are choral ensemble numbers; and with the exception of "Be Our Guest," performed by the enchanted objects of the Beast's household, all are sung by the narrow-minded community by which bookworm Belle and her addled-inventor father find themselves stifled, misunderstood, and persecuted. Moreover, whereas "Be Our Guest" is a song of welcome to a stranger, the songs of the townsfolk—"Bonjour," "Gaston," and "Kill the Beast"—define the community's obsession with conformity and alienation.

"Look, there she goes / That girl is strange, no question," the people sing behind Belle's back as she strolls through town; reiterating the verse's indication that it is through *looking* that the town forms its deforming opinions, the visual motif of figures framed within the rectangle of a window repeats throughout the song. This motif recurs at the conclusion of the song "Gaston," as the one-dimensional villain and his toady sidekick Le Feu are frozen, and visually flattened, within the window of Gaston's hunting lodge. The song itself, moreover, further witnesses the town's devotion to appearances: "There's no one in town as admired as you," Le Feu sings to the brooding giant after the latter's rejection by Belle. "You're everyone's favorite guy. / Everyone's awed and inspired by you / And it's not very hard to see why." As proof that the man is the community's "paragon," Le Feu points as he sings to the portrait of the physically princely Gaston that hangs in his lodge; this echo of the opening segment, in which the prince's portrait is defaced by the beast he has become, yet again animates the discourse of appearance and representation. Likewise, the fact that the chorus of drunken townsfolk who sing Gaston's praises can summon only physical evidence for their adoration of him—his size, his spitting ability—reveals yet again that Gaston's is a community ruled by the surface, the representation.

Gaston himself is, of course, similarly consumed by appearance. His only interest in Belle is in her beauty—"Here in town there's only she / Who's beautiful as me" he sings in "Bonjour" while studying his reflection in a mirror—and in the effect that such a match would have on his appearance in the community: "Just watch," he sings in the same song, while the people surrounding him do just that, "I'm going to make that girl my wife!" Distressed that Belle's book has "no pictures," limited in "imagination" to a stale domestic vision of himself returning from the hunt while Belle tends to his needs and those of his "strapping" sons, Gaston is the epitome, the paragon—and as such, the icon—of those for whom representation is reality.

It is therefore fitting that the film's climactic scene centers on Gaston's use of a visual representation, an image in a mirror, to inflame the community against the outsider. Throughout the film, mirrors appear in numerous shots: of Gaston worshiping his own visage, of the Beast contemplating his magic mirror, of Belle's reflection multiplied and fragmented by a shattered glass in the Beast's haunted castle. What these images suggest is that mirrors distort in any number of ways: by masking the ugliness beneath a handsome shell; by exaggerating a chance moment into the whole; by corrupting the real. Thus when the townspeople assemble outside Belle's house to ship her father to the lunatic asylum—itself a sign of their intolerance of difference, for even the asylum keeper agrees with Le Feu that the man is, at worst, a "harmless crackpot"—the metacinematic scene that unfolds provides a culminating moment in the film's critique of representation. Seeking to convince the community that her father's apparent ravings about a beast are true, Belle holds aloft the magic mirror, crying, "Show me the Beast!" A brief radiance bursts from the mirror and then, framed within it, the Beast's head appears, his mouth stretched in a roar. In this shot, the magic mirror forms a smaller screen within the movie screen, so that the film's audience watches an audience watching a projected image, an image not physically "there."[19] And what moviegoers subsequently watch is the community "reading" this image, constructing the freak as a deadly threat to their security. Prodded by Gaston, who spins a tissue of fabrications around the figure of the Beast just plausible enough to be taken for the real, and who threatens ostracism with his dictate that "if you're not with us, you're against us," the people join his assault on the Beast's castle, parading first through the village (its presence a reminder that both prejudice and perception are born of community will) as they sing "Kill the Beast." The film's audience, of course, knows that the villagers' reaction is unwarranted; the Beast in the mirror is howling not in rage but in anguish over his loss of Belle. But as the Beast has told Belle, "The mirror will show you anything—anything you wish to see." The hesitation in his statement and the double meaning of the word *wish* are telling: the mirror will not, in fact, show you *anything*; instead, it will show you what you *wish* to see. And what this implies is that the townspeople construct a rapacious beast from the image in the mirror because they wish to believe in external threats. They wish to locate evil on the margins, whereas, the scene makes clear, it resides dead center in the form of conformity, bigotry, and a lynch-mob mentality, which their ringleader Gaston can trigger but which he alone could not effect. This scene, then, utilizes metacinema to bring the film's critique of representation graphically to life, revealing how a community can be led by images of its own devising to commit acts of violence against someone innocent though different.

Yet central to *Beauty and the Beast* as an examination of social fantasy is its insistence that the people's willingness to be deceived makes them, and their most representative product, Gaston, paradoxically the mirror image of the monster they seek to destroy. As Cynthia Erb points out, there is a fundamental correspondence between Gaston and the Beast: his rueful experience notwithstanding, for much of the film the Beast remains, like Gaston, "obsessed with the business of having beauty or not having it" ("Another" 63). This identification between the twin "beasts" is underscored by numerous visual and verbal references: The lovesick trio that pines for Gaston terms him a "brute." The shot of Gaston after he falls into a mud puddle joins his hindquarters with the head of a pig, thus invoking the half-man, half-animal Beast. In the song "Gaston," it is the huntsman's own boasting line, accompanied by a shot of his shaggy chest, that "every last inch of me's covered with hair." Moreover, in their similarly violent tempers and similar acts of malice and domination—most notably, Gaston seeks to have Belle's father committed to the asylum in order to gain access to her, while the Beast, though not intending this outcome, does gain access to Belle by cruelly and needlessly imprisoning her father—the two exhibit analogous traits that deeply complicate the community's faith in appearance as a sure sign of moral or ideological legitimacy.

The Beast, of course, ultimately renounces this faith; he learns that he need not act as his exterior suggests, whereas Gaston remains convinced that he is the man he appears to be. This inversion of the hierarchy of normal and freak—with the freak being the one who reflects on the bestiality of the norm—is brought home by a remarkable reversal during the final fight between hero and villain: as the Beast holds his victim by the throat, the camera cuts to his face while a spark of recognition, one of the few convincing illusions of interiority I have seen in an animated cartoon, transforms his murderous expression to one of terror. A "liminal" moment, where the monster sees the man's bestiality mirrored in himself, this shock of familiarity collapses the distance between normal and freak. And in so doing, it betrays the dichotomy of normal/freak to be a particularly fearful construct, a deadly social performance that is no more inherently meaningful than the physical differences by which the dichotomy is lent the appearance of the real.

Needless to say, this is a fairly reflective point for a supposed children's film. Yet at the same time, there are factors that work against the film's *self*-reflection and that permit the discourse of alienation a certain authority. Most eloquent in this regard is the film's conclusion, in which the Beast reclaims his beauty, wealth, and position at the top of the power structure. As with Treves's account of the Elephant Man's premiere at (or in) the theater, this transformation can be read variously: as another means of emphasizing the performed, inessential nature of appearance or as a restoration of social orthodoxy, with the Beast abdicating the throne for the rightful prince. Lending support to this second reading is the prince's rapturous exclamation at the recovery of his teenybopper prettiness, gleaming castle, and faithful servants: "*Look* at us!" Echoing an earlier line in which the Beast had despaired of earning Belle's love because "she's so beautiful, and—well, *look* at me," this return to the primary, determinative power of *looking* is troubling in a film dedicated to undermining the power of the social(ized) look: not only does the prince's self-approving look seem to cap a conformist educational process hinted at by Belle's dismay at the Beast's "unrefined" habits and table manners, but more fundamentally, it suggests the extent to which the film backtracks on its own revelation of the fellowship between normal and freak. In order for the Beast to have stayed a beast—physically—the studio would have needed to resolve a problem it has failed to work out in any of its films: the problem of difference. Whether by segregating those who differ—as in *Pocahontas* (1995), where, in defiance of the historical Pocahontas's life, the Indian woman is left in the New World, while the white man sails back to the Old—or by insisting that only by renouncing their own culture can immigrants join another world—as in *Tarzan*, where Jane and her father abandon civilization for tree-swinging jungle freedom—Disney films repeatedly enact the exclusionary, us-versus-them politics that *Beauty and the Beast* so powerfully challenges. If, as Erb writes, the mirror scene suggests that "the business of seeing an/other is inextricably bound up with the business of how one sees oneself" ("Another" 65), then perhaps looking in its own magic mirror on the wall, Disney still sees chaos in the prospect of Beauty alienating itself in intimate union with the Beast.[20]

This relapse of vision may derive from, or explain, another sense in which *Beauty and the Beast* is less self-reflective than the freak film I wish to consider next: only by inference can one attribute to the film an awareness of the representational work performed by its own medium. With the possible exception of the magic-mirror scene, whose potential along these lines remains largely undeveloped, the film is content to, as it were, represent the politics of representation rather than to explore the cinema itself as one of the principal sites within which social fantasy is generated and disseminated. The next film I discuss, Tim Burton's 1990 *Edward Scissorhands*, uses metacinematic devices much more extensively and pointedly to implicate film and its audience in the work of constructing the freak. Burton has been devoted throughout his career to making films that challenge the definition and stability of the norm. In his two *Batman* films, for example, the final battles between hero and villain draw out what the comparable battle in *Beauty and the Beast* only insinuates: that, in Burton's words, we are witnessing "the duel of the freaks" (qtd. in Salisbury 80). In *Ed Wood* (1994), the discourse of freakishness is so amplified that the norm all but disappears; from the title character to the cast of misfits he directs, it is hard to find anyone in this film who is *not* a freak. And in *Planet of the Apes* (2001), the simple, tables-turned conceit provides fertile ground for an exposé of contemporary discourses and practices of social alienation. Of all Burton's films, however, it is *Edward Scissorhands* that most powerfully suggests the continuity between freak discourse within and beyond the movie theater. Indeed, perhaps more so than any modern freak film, *Edward* exposes the dependence of what society calls reality on the fantasies it constructs and consumes, and in particular, those it constructs and consumes through film.

One might, in fact, consider *Edward* on the whole a metacinematic commentary on its own medium. Unlike *Beauty and the Beast*, Burton's film relies less on dramatic self-referential moments that break the frame of the film's narrative than on a pervasive texture of artificiality, an abiding sense that the film's narrative—indeed, film narrative as such—is a contrivance, a made-up thing. Most insistent in this regard is the film's setting, a pastel-colored suburbia reminiscent not so much of any real place as of a movie set, a thoroughly designed and engineered construct meant only for show. Within this prefabricated paradise, the kitschy furnishings—particularly the reproductions of natural objects, such as the plastic grapes, floral slip covers, and white plastic Christmas tree of Edward's adoptive household—make not only the neighborhood but the film take on a look of tawdry secondhandedness, as if both are engaged in paltry, transparent attempts to impersonate the real.

Moreover, this stale utopia provides the site for the film to take gleeful liberties not only with the norms of cinematic verisimilitude—as in its unaccountable mixing of 1950s-era homes, hairdos, and rotary phones with 1990s-era references to VCRs and CD players—but with its own illusion-making faculties. For instance, what is amusing about the shot in which Avon Lady Peg Boggs drives toward Edward's roost is not merely the absurdity of a Gothic castle perched at the end of a suburban lane but the preposterously obvious special effect, the tacky abandon with which a real street and a two-dimensional, optically composited backdrop are united. In keeping with this shot, in which two patently disparate pieces of film are forced to share screen space, *Edward* unremittingly broadcasts its representational status through a dense intertextual network, a stream of thematic and visual quotes from other films. Most obvious of these cinematic cross-references are the *Frankenstein* nods, cued not only by the narrative of a manmade man but by industry standbys, such as the scene of the angry mob storming the castle. But with his ashen face and ability to draw blood at a touch, Edward also recalls Browning's *Dracula* and its many heirs (most notably the Freddy Krueger *Nightmare* films), a tie-in that the presence of horror-film luminary Vincent Price reinforces. The casting of Price, moreover, connects *Edward* to Burton's short film *Vincent* (1982), which the actor narrated. Tributes to classic cinema such as *Citizen Kane* (1941)—to which I will return shortly—likewise abound. As Burton himself has insisted, the film is "not a new story. It's *Frankenstein*. It's *Phantom of the Opera*. It's *Hunchback of Notre Dame*, *King Kong*, *Creature from the Black Lagoon*, and countless fairy tales" (qtd. in Smith and Mathews 92). Whether "fairy tale" is any more appropriate a descriptor for *Edward* than for *Beauty and the Beast* is a question I defer for the moment. More pertinent for now is the fact that *Edward* is not merely, as Leonard Heldreth puts it, "adorned with cinematic allusions" (155). Rather, it exists precisely as a vehicle for those allusions; it announces in the clearest possible terms that the world it represents, or of which it is the representative, owes its very being to the machinations of Tinseltown.

This self-conscious artifice serves a number of purposes, the most obvious being its indictment of the "in" film community's artificial, clichéd nature. Unable to generate fresh ideas or challenge timeworn patterns—a trait visually expressed by the first shot of Peg primly and robotically following each zig and zag of the walkway leading to a neighbor's house—the people who will ultimately reject Edward as a freakish threat are, ironically, like him, assemblages of used parts. More profoundly, the artifice of *Edward* is the medium by which the film critiques the very nature of narrative film, the power by which narrative, once activated, seems to organize everything within its orbit, creating a script so captivating that each individual part seems predetermined to take its assigned place. That such a process—the same by which normals are assigned an inside role and freaks are cast out—is *not* predetermined, that there is no single narrative to which the parts must be sutured, is inherent in the nature of film; for the existence of multiple takes, the practice of shooting out of sequence, the cutting of filmed footage, the juggling of scenes, and so on belie any claim of narrative necessity. Most narrative films, of course, seek to disguise the constructed, inessential nature of the final product; they seek, through continuity editing and other means, to convince the audience that what one sees is what was meant to be, what had to be. As Jean-Louis Baudry puts it, the routine "concealment of the technical base" of film (41)—a concealment achieved through the illusion of "narrative continuity" (44) and through other effects of "representation" (46)—is essential to the production of film ideology, to film's power to enforce the discourse and practice of the status quo. By contrast, films that engage in self-referential practices to effect a "revealing of the mechanism," an "inscription of the film-work" (46), will, in Baudry's view, "produce a knowledge effect" and a consequent "denunciation of ideology" (41). If this is so, then one might argue that by revealing itself to be a pastiche of ill-fitting, recycled parts, by highlighting the affront and effrontery by which individual images, each potentially signifying nothing or anything, are stitched together to create the impression of a seamless whole, *Edward* profoundly exposes, and dismembers, the ways in which fantasy films lend the appearance of reality to society's alienating narratives.[21]

To borrow Donna Haraway's ironic—and by her own terms, a bit utopian—formulation, then, the film *Edward Scissorhands* (like the title character) is a "cyborg," not only in the narrow sense of being a coming together of human being and machine but in the larger sense of being composed of "contradictions that do not resolve into larger wholes" (65). The cyborg, Haraway imagines, is a figure that reveals "the tension of holding incompatible things together" (65), with no abiding "belief in 'essential' unity" (72); aware of its own partiality, its own artifice, the cyborg occupies "a self-consciously constructed space that cannot affirm the capacity to act on the basis of natural identification" (73). Indeed, according to Haraway, the cyborg rejects "*all* claims for an organic or natural standpoint" from which cultural taxonomies may be mapped (75), for the cyborg recognizes that any "epistemology and ontology—including their negations—erase or police difference" (77), defining a center against which the alien can likewise be defined. *Edward* thus illustrates James Cherney's argument that the cyborg film seeks to render "distinctions based on bodily ability senseless. . . . As cyborgs, biologically distinct bodies become irrelevant, so socially constructed disability becomes an artificial abstraction" (170). That *Edward* seems finally to wake from its cyborg dreams, that in the end it appears to reinvent the fictions of bodily and social difference it has shown to be "artificial abstractions," bespeaks the truly utopian nature of its aspirations and the real-world difficulty of overcoming the alienating legacy of fantasy film.

As with *Beauty and the Beast*, an opening prologue to *Edward* intimates and activates the film's critique of social alienation. Following the credits, in which a montage of seemingly disconnected, blue-tinted images—a door, a figure cloaked by spider webs, scissors, a snowfall of cutout cookies, hands—spin through a darkened void, the film introduces the image of a tiny house perched atop a hill, with snow falling in the foreground. When I first screened *Edward* in a class on fantasy film, students noted that this shot visually suggests a miniature snow globe; not only does the image fill the screen and thus crowd out elements that might mark its scale but the house itself is unmistakably toylike, lacking depth, like a paper cutout.[22] Shortly, however, the camera's perspective broadens, revealing at first the window from which the house is being viewed and then the aged Kim Boggs, whose first line—"Snuggle in, sweetie"—at once locates the scene in a conventional domestic narrative and suggests the premium her character places on security and shelter. In a variety of ways, this opening shot asks the viewer to doubt, or at least adjust, perceptions. To begin with, the unexpected change in scale suggests the uncertainty of seeing, requiring viewers, literally, to reframe how they see the house. Too, by riffing on, or ripping off, the comparable shot in the prologue to *Citizen Kane*—except that Welles's film works the surprise in reverse, revealing what had seemed a full-scale panorama to be a toy miniature—this optical turn connects questions of vision to questions of how we read others; for *Kane* too is about appearance and interpretation, about the ways in which diverse viewers construct diverse narratives of a single life and, ultimately, about whether any of these narratives can be suitable as a summary of the real.

The suggestiveness of the opening image does not, however, end here. If the dismissal of the viewer's original interpretation destabilizes the act of viewing, it also, and insistently, summons a specific kind of viewing: the viewing of motion pictures. For the audience's initial experience of the house as unreal cannot fully be overcome by the restoration of size and context; indeed, given this initial experience, it becomes evident that the camera movement does not *restore* the house's "proper" size but *constructs* it. The shot thus invokes—even as it exposes as a hoax—the power of film to create a reality beyond belief and yet believable. The *Kane* reference contributes to this discourse; by reproducing a trick from an earlier film, and specifically a film celebrated for its exploration of the possibilities (or trickery) *of* film, the opening shot of *Edward* enhances the viewer's awareness that the shot *is* a shot, a movie device. As such, the shot revises viewer expectations not only to expose the risks of rash judgment but to implicate film in the processes by which what is demonstrably fantasy is presented as the real.

Yet this opening shot performs one more, and a vital, function: at the same time that it fingers film for toying with the viewer's perceptions, it implicates the viewer for acceding to or endorsing the film's skulduggery. For despite the viewer's misgivings, despite the viewer's unshakeable sense that the house on the hill is a miniature prop, the viewer must accept the film's assertion that it is a house on the hill to make narrative sense of the film: though the viewer knows that *Edward* is a fantasy film and that fantasy films take certain liberties with the real, nowhere does *Edward* suggest that life-size people can live in miniature houses. What the opening shot does, then, is make the viewer as much an accomplice in willful misreading as Edward's ghoulish neighbors; it suggests that viewers are trained, willing, even eager to distort the real, to credit the unacceptable, to endorse what they know to be untrue in the interest of maintaining the culture's (and the cinema's) coherent, comfortable fantasies. From the start, then, *Edward* makes the viewer culpable for what Burton terms a "dynamic of misperception" (qtd. in Smith and Mathews 98); the film's open contempt for expectations encourages the viewer to recognize not only cinema's narrative-making capabilities, its ability to pass off the fabricated as the real, but the viewer's part in certifying this illusion.

The visual chicanery with which *Edward* is awash thus serves a far from trivial purpose. A green-and-orange-striped behemoth on the suburban street turns out to be a circus tent. The shadows from an aquarium in Kevin Boggs's room momentarily literalize the expression "life lived in a fish bowl." A sheepdog mutates into a poodle after Edward clips its hair. Distorting lenses in the shot of Edward being "Avoned" by Peg make faces bulge and recede unnaturally. A shaggy, six-foot hedge becomes a flawlessly shaped, twelve-foot topiary tyrannosaur. It is not to much purpose to pass off these and other eccentricities and impossibilities as the trappings of a fairy-tale narrative, as reviewers of the film almost unanimously have done.[23] More accurately, *Edward* is a film that exposes how a community's fairy tales, including those it produces through film, shape its perceptions, beliefs, and behavior. Refusing the opposition by which popular debates over film in society are customarily framed—that film *either* "gives the people what they want" *or* imposes its insidious standards on an unsuspecting public—*Edward* betrays the vital interrelationship between audience desire and film narrative, their mutual work in sustaining social discourse and practice.

Toward this end, it is particularly critical to examine the multitude of instances in which *Edward* examines how film and audience join forces to fashion the figure of the freak. The scene in which Edward is introduced in his castle-top aerie launches this process. The scene begins with Peg perusing Edward's chimney clippings. Though the images are scanned too quickly to register in a theatrical viewing—only DVD frame advance reveals them to be a hodgepodge of diet and home furnishing advertisements, body parts, religious icons, and freak stories—the audience nonetheless perceives these representations as producing a coherent picture of Edward because of their seeming narrative significance: their placement in the film to begin with, and the intensely probing look on Peg's face on which the camera focuses. Similarly, when Edward is revealed hiding in the shadows, though the viewer catches only the briefest glimpse of him at first, visual and musical prompts—Peg's alarmed reaction and the sudden introduction of a "slasher" theme—lead the viewer to form a judgment of Edward based not on anything intrinsic to him but on external factors, one of which (the music) does not originate in the story-world but is wholly a cinematic construct. This introductory scene thus places the viewer on the same level as all the other interpreters and interrogators of Edward within the film: the sex-starved Joyce, for whom Edward is a mere plaything, first of her pleasure and later of her vengeance; the twitchy religious fanatic Esmeralda, who warns the community to "trample down" the creature she sees as a "perversion of nature"; the nameless bank functionary who overlooks the self-reproaching irony in his pronouncement that Edward, lacking a Social Security number, "may as well not exist"; the disabled war vet who at first counsels Edward not to let anyone tell him he's "handicapped" but who later, in a perverse echo of holiday parades, sets up a lawn chair in his driveway to watch his community stalk and capture the renegade "cripple." However ready the viewer may be to censure, mock, or dismiss these cardboard grotesques and their caricatured responses, all are merely doing what the viewer has already done: reading Edward in terms of set, self-confirming narratives. The viewer first perceives Edward as ominous, and later as cuddly; the neighbors first perceive him as a curiosity, and later as an atrocity. In either case, Edward has not changed so much as varying narratives of the freak have been constructed from images that—like the opening montage, like Edward's chimney clippings, like the film's cyborg protagonist, like film itself—have no single or inherent significance.

A more overt and extended exploration of the freak-making activity of film and its audiences occurs in the scene in which Edward appears as a guest on a daytime talk show hosted by real-life TV personality John Davidson. The scene opens with a shot of Edward and Peg seated onstage, flanked by a camera and a monitor in the foreground, so that the viewer sees their image reproduced twice in miniature. "Quite a story, yes?" Davidson asks out of camera range, his voice identifiable even before the camera cuts to shots of him among the studio audience. The questions Davidson solicits, and the responses offered by Edward and Peg, are precisely the sort viewers have come to expect from the popular media: "What's been the best part of your life in town?" Edward is asked, to which he responds (garnering canned applause), "All the friends I've made." One woman's stilted delivery indicates that she has scripted and memorized her question; another, giddy and giggling, asks Edward if he has a girlfriend. Following this question, the film cuts to a shot of Edward framed within a television set, with Kim, her boyfriend Jim, and Kevin watching. This startling reminder that *Edward* (and Edward) is as much a representation as the framed image in the Boggses' living room is followed by a shot/reverse-shot sequence of Edward's and Kim's faces, the camera tightening on each until Edward's face fills not only the television set but the movie screen. With its self-reflexive touches and nods to the viewer's real-world experience—it is ironic, but fitting, that in *Edward* the most determinedly realist settings, characterizations, and techniques are drawn from the unreal world of film—this scene explores the process by which the freak is constructed by the visual media. And if the scene appears to indict television alone, the familiar metacinematic device of Edward's face framed within a screen performs the further function of recalling to viewers that they are not merely witnessing the processes by which the freak is constructed but participating in those processes even as, indeed because, they are witnessing them.

But celebrity freaks, the viewer also knows, do not hold the spotlight for long. Underscoring both the predictability of the failed fairy-tale plot and the source of its familiarity, the scene in which Edward is, in another sense of the word, *framed* by the unscrupulous Jim is shot, edited, and dubbed in ways strongly reminiscent of "reality" shows of its time, such as *Cops*. A handheld camera, alternating shots of the spotlighted criminal and, from behind the criminal's shoulder, of the police cars hidden by the glare of the spotlights, ambient sounds of sirens and of distorted voices filtered through megaphones, and other devices all contribute to the retread, been-there, done-that feel of this screened episode. As in the talk-show scene, this insider's peek at Edward's fall from grace thus reaches beyond the confines of the film screen to make contact with the viewer's real-world experience—an experience, however, defined once again by the representational fantasy of film screens. A complex self-referentiality is thus created, one directed at once inward toward *Edward* and outward toward the experiential basis on which the viewer tests film art. That is to say, as the viewer recognizes in the fantasy world of *Edward* the supposedly real visualizations of another medium, both are revealed to be equally, and interdependently, constructs. There is no "real" here, only a closed loop or hall of mirrors in which each media show acquires the appearance of veracity in light of its audience's ability to recognize one show's representations in the other.

These scenes of Edward's (and *Edward*'s) multiple and conflicting interpretations-through-film serve, then, both to involve the viewer in the construction of the film's narrative and to alert the viewer to the role of film narrative in rendering real the inequitable fantasy of social difference and alienation. There is, however, another and more unsettling sense in which *Edward*, shattering the funhouse hall of mirrors in which the freak is exhibited, reflected, and reproduced, assails the viewer's comfortable participation in the fantasy of insider/outsider, normal/freak. In *Beauty and the Beast*, as I have noted, visual and other references to the freak as an object of the community's gaze are paramount; though looked at, seldom does the freak look back. The line from *Beauty and the Beast* that I quoted previously—"*Look* at us!"—is indicative of this dichotomy; even freaks direct their gaze at themselves, judging themselves through the lens of community judgment. Such references do, of course, permeate *Edward* as well: the dialogue of Peg's neighbors ("Did you get a good look at him?"); the shots of religious kook Esmeralda watching events through her window; the images of Edward's face framed within mirrors; the shot of his face framed within the television set—all of these serve to call attention to the constructed nature of the freak and to challenge viewers' innocence in (mis)taking the constructed for the real. Yet in a notable departure from the Disney film, *Edward* also encourages the audience regularly to adopt the position of the freak, to share his, Edward's, look; indeed, virtually all of the scenes in which Edward appears, including those I have discussed, offer his internal, subjective experience balanced against the outside, subjective experience of the community. As such, *Edward* challenges the viewer's viewing not only by revealing the limitations of communal judgment but by closing the distance and upsetting the difference between the normal (who looks) and the freak (who is looked at). For when the freak looks, the performance of normalcy—including the act of freak gazing—becomes, in and through his eyes, the greatest freak show on earth.

The visual affinity between viewer and freak commences at once; if the frame narrative opens with a shot of Kim looking at Edward's miniaturized castle, it closes with a shot of Edward looking out on what, from his point of view, appears to be her equally miniaturized village. Similarly, the scene of Edward looking at the Boggs family photos is edited in such a way that it precisely matches the scene in which Kim watches Edward on television; increasingly tight close-ups of her framed image are shuffled with shots of his face reacting to her image. Moreover, in addition to the countless instances in which the camera records events as if through Edward's eyes, a number of sequences draw particular attention to his viewing. The flashbacks to Edward's creation, for instance, represent internalized, private reflections that the community cannot share (and that accordingly break the flow, visually and temporally, of the community's narrative). In another instance, the scene in which Peg exerts her dubious makeover skills to cover Edward's scars employs shot/reverse-shot close-ups of their faces; aside from the visual pun of Edward being "made-up" to fit in, a pun reinforced by Peg's monologue—"Blending is the secret. More concealing cream?"—this sequence enables the audience at once to view Edward as a curiosity, purple-faced and pathetic, and to view from his position the befuddled artificer who has made him so. An even more suggestive sequence occurs at the Boggses' dinner table. Edward, invisible except for his scissors (and thus corporeally absent, since these shots were accomplished using robotic talons designed by Stan Winston), occupies the viewer's place, creating uncertainty as to who is staring at whom: the viewer/Edward at the Boggs family, or the Boggs family at the viewer/Edward? Peg's reprimand of Kevin, "Think how it would make you feel if someone were staring at you," directs attention to this paradox, this collapsing of the viewer—the "normal," whose gaze is presumably all-controlling—with the "freak," who is presumably left vulnerable and defenseless before such acts of unsolicited, incontestable vision.

What scenes such as these suggest is the most radical possibility of the freak film, one that extends but ultimately perplexes the critique of insiderhood and outsiderhood: employing metacinematic devices to compromise the critical awareness on which metacinema relies—an awareness of the self *as* viewer—such scenes raise the possibility of the viewer's *self*-alienation in union with the freak. This possibility, I must emphasize, fundamentally differentiates *Edward* from films such as *Jurassic Park*, where the "monster's-eye-view" camera work functions to further alienation, turning the dinosaurs into the equivalent of the villains in

stalker films. To some extent, such self-alienating effects arise within the madness films I considered previously; but in those films, as I have shown, the possibility of the viewer losing a sense of self—or mind—is largely controlled, so
that the viewer maintains a "proper" distance from the mad. In *Edward*, by contrast, such distance is compromised, hobbled, collapsed; the viewer is at once the
one who subjects the freak to an omniscient gaze and the one who, in turn, is
subjected to the penetrating gaze of the freak. The power of the freak's gaze may
best be indicated by the sequence in which Kim watches Edward on television;
when his face fills the screen, such that his questing eyes appear to be focused
on the movie audience, Kim, in a reaction many in the theater might share, drops
her eyes, overcome by whatever uncanny awareness his televised gaze has sparked.
Hers is a reaction perhaps akin to that which Leslie Fiedler describes upon viewing the doubled freak of the sideshow:

> Standing before Siamese Twins, the beholder sees them looking not
> only at each other, but—both at once—at him. And for an instant
> it may seem to him that he is a third brother, bound to the pair be-
> fore him by an invisible bond; so that the distinction between audi-
> ence and exhibit, we and them, normal and Freak, is revealed as an
> illusion, desperately, perhaps even necessarily, defended, but unten-
> able in the end. (36)

Such an awareness effectively annuls the dichotomies inside/outside, us/them,
normal/freak; for it leaves no stable position, no certain identity, from which these
dichotomies can be either refuted or affirmed. It is in this sense that *Edward* wields
the power of the liminal: the power to reveal all social performances and identities—indeed, the social performance of identity itself—as constructed, inessential, the sport of cyborgs. Thus if, as Russell Potter argues, *Edward* manifests the
"realization that in expelling otherness is born self-alienation" (para. 29), it also
heralds a communion in which the other can never be alien to the self.

Needless to say, however, this radical communion embodies an equally radical threat. Perhaps for this reason, *Edward* ultimately retreats to a stable, con-
ventionally alienating position: refusing or failing to join the Boggs family or their
community, Edward is forced into—or, arguably, chooses—banishment. Indeed,
the scene I have just examined, a scene that seems so promising in its revision of
the normal/freak dichotomy, precipitates the restoration of that dichotomy: seduced by what Haraway terms "the fabrication of the heterosexual mate" (67)
but unable to consummate his desire for the golden girl, Edward is left with
nothing but the otherworld of the ostracized social monster. Many of Burton's
films, disconcertingly, fall in the end into this camp, where closure is achieved

through the freak's renunciation or ruin: In *Batman Returns* (1992), when his suspicions are raised by the mutant Penguin's stint as a sideshow attraction, Batman ensures that the freak's scheme to run Gotham City from the inside will end in ignominy and death. And in *The Nightmare before Christmas* (1993), Jack Skellington's comparable plan to usurp Christmas calls forth (for a children's film) a shocking act of military violence, which leads to the penitent Jack's pledge never again to trespass beyond his proper sphere. Critique thus yields to complicity: however justified Edward may be in using his aberrant equipment as a weapon against Jim, Edward's act of murder and his ensuing erasure from all but Kim's consciousness support Longmore's argument that "even when the handicapped character is presented sympathetically as a victim of bigotry, it remains clear that severe disability makes social integration impossible" (33).[24]

And yet, in *Edward*, perhaps this is *not* so clear; there remain intimations that the alienating conclusion is itself subject to critique. For Edward's story, one must recall, is told by Kim, who appears in the frame narrative as a woman who in many ways has failed to tap her potentially radicalizing tale to move beyond conformity: she has lived out her life in the community, has apparently married— though not, one hopes, someone as loathsome as Jim—and has remained both fearful of exceptional experience (as her opening line, "Snuggle in, sweetie," suggests) and faithful to a normative discourse of superficial beauty (as her flimsy excuse for not visiting the castle, lest Edward see her in physical decline, attests). Moreover, the flashback that interrupts Edward's idyll with Kim, a flashback in which he slavishly caresses and kisses the human hands given him as a Christmas gift only to see his dreams shatter at his own touch as his creator slumps to the floor in death, suggests that the film continues to look askance at the deadly narrative of normalcy and alienation. In a film so deeply, one might say essentially, aware of its inessential nature, even the most seemingly resolute gestures of alienation become suffused with an ironic, metacinematic consciousness of their own artifice.

With this in mind, let me offer, in conclusion to this chapter, one additional consideration that further complicates any reading of *Edward* in respect to discourses of social alienation. To this point, I have explored only the ways in which metacinema may function as critique: of seeing, of social attitudes and prejudices, of film effects and narratives. There is in *Edward*, however, a scene that uses metacinema to explore the *positive* potential of the cinema, to suggest that film may be a medium of enlightenment, one in which the all-too-real alienation of the freak may be reenvisioned. I refer to the scene in which Edward, abandoned by the community as Christmas nears, nonetheless brings them the gift of snow. What interests me about this scene, in light of all I've said before, is its unrelieved movieness: the impossible prop of the gigantic ice block from which Edward chisels his snow angel, the choreographed dance into which Kim "spontaneously" glides, the ultra-slow motion and swooping, circling, eye-catching camera maneuvers with which her dance is recorded, the suspension of sounds other than Edward's shears scraping against the ice, the swelling of Danny Elfman's wondrous score, and the partial repetition of the scene near film's end (the only scene in the film to be played more than once) all underline that this scene depicts not what *is* but what film can envision and possibly help to enact: a world in which the freak, no longer subject to the narcissistic gaze of normals, is instead the creator of a beauty so intense that one can, like Kim, lose oneself in it.

Kim Boggs (Winona Ryder) dances in the artificial snowfall created by the artistry of Edward. From *Edward Scissorhands* (Fox, 1990). Courtesy of Photofest.

To be sure, there is much in this scene that counters such a hopeful suggestion. For one thing, the only character who appreciates Edward's artistry is Kim: Bill, blithely oblivious as usual, overlooks the "real" snow as he staples fiberglass snow to the roof. Peg, hopeful that "everything will just go back to normal"— the line that precedes the snow-dancing scene—is too blinded by convention to see that the "abnormal" may be stunningly, rapturously beautiful. And Jim, who interrupts Edward and Kim's reverie, is of course too filled with hatred to see Edward as anything but a "freak" (the word he uses as he thrusts Edward out of the Boggses' yard and into the rampage that ends in his death and Edward's banishment). If, then, as the picture of Madonna and child in his alcove and the ice angel itself suggest, Edward is positioned as something of a Christ figure, who offers himself as a hallowed sacrifice to issue a miraculous dispensation, there is scant indication that his Word is heeded. Indeed, the only character other than Kim who seems at all touched by Edward's story, the African American cop who has, no doubt, been similarly stigmatized by the all-white community he is sworn to protect, proves ineffectual in shielding Edward from the people's wrath.[25] Then, too, Kim herself, as I have suggested, may not be so much transformed by her tale as transfixed by it; the repetition of the snow-dancing scene during the return to her framing narrative may indicate that this propitious moment has become for her merely another stale facsimile, as indeed it may have become for Edward (who, the final shot of him reveals, has frozen Kim as a literal ice princess). At that, it is even possible that the scene's manifest unreality cancels its radical promise, suggesting that such utopian moments are nothing more than movie tricks.

But then again, maybe that's only one way of seeing things.

CONCLUSION Monsters' End?

Cultural performances are not simple reflectors or expressions of culture or even of changing culture but may themselves be active agencies of change.—Victor Turner, *The Anthropology of Performance* (1986)

*F*antasy film, as a genre and an idea, is inseparable from the birth, development, and identity of the cinema. Not only were some of the earliest narrative films works of fantasy, but the history of film more generally is a history of the fantastic, the illusion, the unreal. The earliest theatergoers were attracted by promises of an experience beyond their immediate or imaginable experience; present-day viewers continue to be lured by the cinema's (and its partner the computer's) ability to project dream worlds every bit as undeniable as they are unbelievable. As a single measure of the power of cinematic fantasy, or of the cinema as an essentially fantastic art form, most of the top-grossing films in recent history, including *Star Wars* (1977), *Raiders of the Lost Ark* (1981), *E. T.* (1982), *Jurassic Park* (1993), and *The Lord of the Rings* (2001–2003), have been films of fantasy (and it is at least arguable that such effects-laden blockbusters as *Titanic* [1997], *Gladiator* [2000], and *Pearl Harbor* [2001] might better be termed fantasies than histories). Fantasy films, in short, have defined the cinema's past and dominated its present. And if one thing seems certain, it is that fantasy films will continue to play a substantial and vital role in the cinema's future.

Considerably less certain is whether, on the whole, the fantasy films of coming years will remain vehicles of alienation or whether, building upon the countertradition suggested by films such as *12 Monkeys* and *Edward Scissorhands*, they will advance more progressive visions. Of course, even if this were not an impossible question to answer, it would be beyond the scope of this book, which has aimed to explore fantasy films as they are, not to speculate about things to come. But since the question is one of social consequence more so than of generic curiosity, it is worth offering, if not an answer, then at least some further contemporary examples to suggest the shape that fantasy films may take in the future.

In many respects, the signs are less than promising. I concur, for example, with those who found the first two installments of George Lucas's second *Star Wars* trilogy—*The Phantom Menace* (1999) and *Attack of the Clones* (2002)—stuffed with racial and ethnic slurs: the evil Trade Federation quislings, with their overthe-top Japanese accents and wardrobes; the simpleminded, carefree Gungans, with their minstrel-show stepping and fetching; the ruthless desert slave-dealer Watto, with his stereotyped Semitic stubble and avarice. Similarly, I was disheartened that the sole African American character in *Jurassic Park III* (2001)—a character whose role was so insignificant that anyone could have been cast for it— was also the first to be graphically, horribly killed. And though I was practically first in line for each of the films in Peter Jackson's *Lord of the Rings* trilogy, I was distressed by its presentation of freaks: not only are there outright monsters like the pig-faced, cancerous orc captain who leads the assault on Gondor in the trilogy's final installment, but Gollum, whose wasted frame and gibbous cat eyes identify him as a freak,[1] proves by trilogy's end just how dangerous identifying with the Other can be. As with such classic fantasy films as Disney's *Fantasia* (1940)— much on my mind because my five-year-old daughter has been watching it daily for some time—where the only characters of color are the slave-girl centaurs of the "Pastoral Symphony," many contemporary fantasy films adopt rituals of alienation compulsively, unconsciously, as if such rituals are no less than the real.

And yet, there are indications that the self-critical current in fantasy film, though still no more than a trickle, may be working its way into the mainstream. The films I explored in the last two chapters provide some hope for this transformation; the popular success of more recent works such as Burton's *Planet of the Apes* (2001), which addresses matters of prejudice head-on, may further substantiate this trend. To me, however, the film of the modern era that best expresses both the promise of fantasy film and the problems it has yet to overcome is the millennial *X-Men* (2000), a production that is ambitious, ingenious, and self-contradictory, that flirts with a profound critique of social alienation, but that degenerates into a silly comic-book slugfest that defeats not only the villain's scheme but much of the work that has gone before. I would like, therefore, to conclude with a brief consideration of this fine, flawed film that embodies both the liberalizing direction in which fantasy films may be headed and the alienating tradition from which they derive.[2]

What makes *X-Men* so remarkable in its early movements is its unequivocal anchoring in a contemporary milieu of prejudice and victimization. Where films such as *Edward Scissorhands* merely imply a real-world context for the fantasy, *X-Men* makes clear that its fantasy is but an exaggeration—or, better, an expression—of actual conditions. The film begins in 1944 Poland, where the ten-year-old Jewish boy who will become the mutant supervillain Magneto first manifests his power in a vain attempt to save his parents from the death camp to which they are being driven. This opening, in which the mutant difference is situated within history's most notorious act of genocide, provides not only a context for Magneto's villainy but a signal that "mutants" are stand-ins for any group persecuted for a perceived variation from, and menace to, the norm. Magneto's address to the novice X-Man Rogue crystallizes this connection: "There is no land of tolerance. There is no peace. Not here, and not anywhere else. Women and children, whole families destroyed simply because they were born different from those in power." Seldom has the "monster" in a fantasy film had so sound, indeed in some sense laudable, a motivation for his acts; having witnessed the fate of the social monster, the progression from stigmatization, to discrimination, to dehumanization, and finally to extermination, Magneto can hardly be accused of exaggerating the threat posed by the demagogic Senator Kelley and his projected Mutant Registration Act. In this respect, however scary Magneto's plan to mutate the world's leaders may be—incarnating as it does the threat of chaos captured on a smaller scale by films such as *Freaks*—the viewer is forced to consider not only whether such retributive violence is justified but whether one's sense that it is *not* justified reflects one's own privileged position within the systems of inequity and iniquity Magneto attacks.

For *X-Men* is smart enough to acknowledge, indeed to cultivate, its viewers' own prejudices, to place before its audience not only villains but heroes whose mutant powers are unsettling, if not horrifying. The shape-shifting, viperous Mystique evinces perhaps the most visibly shocking of such powers; her scaly, blue-skinned "natural" appearance is far less menacing than her violation of individual identity (captured most notably in the mind-bending scene in which the viewer witnesses the "real" Storm apparently being skewered by the "fake" Wolverine, only to discover that he is real and she is Mystique in disguise). But Xavier, the high-minded pacifist leader, and Rogue, the forsaken waif-hero, possess powers that are at least as threatening to human integrity as Mystique's: he invades people's minds, taking away, as Kelley bombastically puts it, "our God-given free will," while she steals people's life force, in her first scene alone nearly killing with a kiss. Thus in the metacinematic scene in which the senator addresses colleagues and citizens on the dangers of those who differ, he is addressing (and arousing) the prejudices not only of the Senate audience but of the theatergoers, a point made clear by his speech's persistent coding in terms recognizable from current attacks on homosexuals: "I think the American people deserve the right to decide whether they want their children to be in school with mutants—to be taught by mutants."[3] The world of *X-Men* is not, as the subtitle that introduces the main narrative reads, of the "near future" but of the immediate present—a world in which hallucinatory fears create mutant monsters of the outcast and disempowered.

Given *X-Men's* intensive critique of such irrational prejudices, it says much about the readiness with which fantasy films return to the opposition of us-versus-them that this intelligent film must contrive its own irrational plot twist to make Magneto's revolution appear illegitimate and Magneto himself simply villainous. His mutating machine, it turns out, produces genetic changes that are "unnatural"; the body of any "ordinary human being" subjected to the machine's radiation, we are told, will "reject" this abnormal reaction, leading to the body's breakdown. And *X-Men* produces a body to prove it: specifically, the bloblike body of guinea pig Kelley, which swells, bursts, and disintegrates in a flood of viscous liquid. This flaw in the machine, it is plain, rests on very bad science: it makes no sense that mutants should be unaffected by the machine when ordinary people are, for it is obvious from their physical and mental attributes that in virtually every respect the mutants are genetically identical to ordinary folk. But this lapse of credibility in a film that is otherwise careful to maintain a tight internal logic is emblematic of the lengths to which *X-Men* must go to preserve the timeworn fantasy film plot of normalcy threatened by the abnormal, a plot the film itself has shown to be not merely invalid but, for those branded abnormal, lethally so. As such, by the time the final battle between the X-Men and Magneto's forces is waged, its suggestive backdrop—the Statue of Liberty—comes to seem no more than a prop or a set piece to enhance the spectacular qualities of a conventional, and tidily moralizing, scuffle between normal and freak.

It is futile, perhaps, to expect fantasy films to be any better than the society that spawned them, a society that perpetually fantasizes monstrous threats to its safety and security. Indeed, if my contentions about fantasy film are at all correct, then it is predictable that any film produced by such a society will in some measure reproduce (and in turn help to produce) its vile and violent fantasies. But the part of me that loves fantasy films still hopes for better, not only from the films and their society but from myself. For if fantasy films are in many ways resistant to, even antipathetic to, social justice, at the same time, by projecting our prejudices onto the monsters of our own imagination and magnifying them on a screen ten feet high, these films are capable of making our prejudices visible, inescapable, and, as such, remediable. I remember distinctly that the first time I saw *King Kong*, at age five, I wept so bitterly at the monster's fall that I could not even choke out to my parents why I was crying. One might explain

FILMOGRAPHY

NOTES

WORKS CITED

INDEX

FILMOGRAPHY

Included here are only those films that receive extended treatment in the book. I have listed technical personnel when possible and (where I deemed it particularly important) additional individuals involved in the production.

12 Monkeys. Dir. Terry Gilliam. Perf. Bruce Willis, Madeleine Stowe, Brad Pitt, and Christopher Plummer. Cinematography Roger Pratt. Editing Mick Audsley. Special effects Vincent Montefusco. Universal, 1996.

Aliens. Dir. James Cameron. Perf. Sigourney Weaver, Paul Reiser, Michael Biehn, and Carrie Henn. Creature design H. R. Giger. Special effects John Richardson. Fox, 1986.

Beauty and the Beast. Dir. Gary Trousdale and Kirk Wise. Perf. Robby Benson, Paige O'Hara, David Ogden Stiers, Jerry Orbach, and Angela Lansbury. Supervising animators Glen Keane and James Baxter. Musical score Alan Menken. Lyricist Howard Ashman. Disney, 1991.

The Cell. Dir. Tarsem Singh. Perf. Jennifer Lopez, Vince Vaughan, and Vincent D'Onofrio. Cinematography Paul Laufer. Editing Robert Duffy and Paul Rubell. Special effects Clay Pinney. New Line, 2000.

Edward Scissorhands. Dir. Tim Burton. Perf. Johnny Depp, Winona Ryder, and Vincent Price. Cinematography Stefan Czapsky. Production design Bo Welch. Musical score Danny Elfman. Makeup effects Stan Winston. Special effects Michael Wood. Fox, 1990.

Freaks. Dir. Tod Browning. Perf. Wallace Ford, Harry Earles, Olga Baclanova, Daisy and Violet Hilton, and Johnny Eck. MGM, 1932.

The Golden Voyage of Sinbad. Dir. Gordon Hessler. Perf. John Phillip Law, Tom Baker, and Caroline Munro. Creator of special visual effects Ray Harryhausen. Columbia, 1974.

Jurassic Park. Dir. Steven Spielberg. Perf. Sam Neill, Laura Dern, Jeff Goldblum, and Sir Richard Attenborough. Live action dinosaurs Stan Winston. Full motion dinosaurs Dennis Muren. Dinosaur supervisor Phil Tippett. Special dinosaur effects Michael Lantieri. Universal, 1993.

King Kong. Dir. Merian C. Cooper. Perf. Fay Wray, Robert Armstrong, and Bruce Cabot. Musical score Max Steiner. Sculptor Marcel Delgado. Chief technician Willis H. O'Brien. RKO, 1933.

The Seventh Voyage of Sinbad. Dir. Nathan Juran. Perf. Kerwin Matthews, Kathryn Grant, and Torin Thatcher. Creator of special visual effects Ray Harryhausen. Columbia, 1958.

Sinbad and the Eye of the Tiger. Dir. Sam Wanamaker. Perf. Patrick Wayne and Jane Seymour. Creator of special visual effects Ray Harryhausen. Columbia, 1977.

Species. Dir. Roger Donaldson. Perf. Ben Kingsley, Marg Helgenberger, and Natasha Henstridge. Creature design H. R. Giger. Special effects Richard Edlund. MGM, 1995.

The Wizard of Oz. Dir. Victor Fleming. Perf. Judy Garland, Ray Bolger, Jack Haley, Bert Lahr, Margaret Hamilton, and Frank Morgan. Musical score Harold Arlen. Lyricist E. Y. Harburg. Musical numbers Bobby Connolly. Special effects A. Arnold Gillespie. MGM, 1939.

X-Men. Dir. Bryan Singer. Perf. Hugh Jackman, Patrick Stewart, Anna Paquin, and Sir Ian McKellen. Special effects Michael Fink. Fox, 2000.

NOTES

Introduction

1. For those who enjoy perusing guides to fantasy film, there are many from which to choose. For a sampling, see Annan; Kinnard; Nicholls; Searles; and Von Gunden.

2. For comparable arguments concerning the relevance of sci-fi film to social reality, see the essays in Cartmell et al. For a reading of fantastic literature as social-historicist production, see Monleón.

3. For a fascinating study of *Kong* that describes a "shifting reception dynamic, in which multiple viewing frames became possible, according to both regional and temporal variables present during [its] release" and the years afterward, see Erb, *Tracking*; quote on 50.

4. As if this were not confusing enough, Palumbo admits that some "science fiction and fantasy films . . . occupy a middle ground" where the putative discriminations he draws are undone (212).

5. Attebery's distinction is all the more curious inasmuch as it occurs within the context of a discussion of "science fantasy," a "hybrid form" that "can with equal justice be defined either as a form of fantasy that borrows from science fiction or as a subgenre of science fiction drawing inspiration from fantasy" (*Strategies* 106).

6. For an additional argument concerning the indistinguishability of fantasy from science fiction, see Zgorzelski.

1. Killing the Beast

1. On the censoring of *Kong*, see "King Kong."

2. *Kong*'s effects are covered by Gardner and Turner 53–64, 87–100, 127–49, 159–81; Rovin 31–44; and Shay 33–41.

3. For additional brief remarks on the racial contents of *Kong*, see Cripps 278; Geduld and Gottesman, "Introduction" 25; Hoch 48–49; Hogan 96–98; and Nesteby 121–22.

4. For studies that read *Kong* in light of Depression-era social crises, but not specifically racial crises, see Hanley; Peary, "Speculation"; and Torry.

5. Similar denials were issued by the producers of the 1976 *Kong* when they were accused of seeking to cast an "ape-like" black actor in the title role; see "Race Sensitivity."

6. On northern race riots, see Guterl 123–26; and Takaki 348–52.

7. On the rebirth of the Klan, see Maclean.

8. The association of African Americans and apes is examined by W. Jordan 28–32, 235–39, 490–97. On the image of the "black beast rapist," see Davis.

9. The statistics cited throughout this section are drawn from two 1930s sources: Patch 427–31; and Southern Commission 19–21. For a modern analysis, see Hale 199–239.

10. On the fate of the federal antilynching bill, see Sitkoff 279–97.

11. Bates's letter of 5 Jan. 1932 is reprinted in D. Carter, *Papers* n. pag. On the 1933 retrial of the "Scottsboro boys," see D. Carter, *Scottsboro* 174–242.

12. Hellenbrand goes so far as to suggest that Wright's novel is a rumination on *King Kong* and, more generally, on the representation of African Americans in the popular media of the 1930s.

13. On racial separatism and antagonism during the Depression, see Juguo 109–33. On racial discrimination in the New Deal, see C. Greenberg 65–92, 153–63; and Sitkoff 34–57. On the first stirrings of the civil rights movement during this period, see C. Greenberg 93–139, 201–7; and Sitkoff 244–67.

14. My understanding of race in the early cinema is indebted to the essays in Bernardi, *Birth*.

15. The classic study of race in the cinema is Bogle. On African Americans in 1930s film, see Bogle 35–100. Also valuable, particularly for its comments on African American participation in the cinema, is Guerrero.

16. On the tendency to divorce the racism of Griffith's film from its formal properties, see also Rocchio 29–54. For a reception-studies argument against viewing Griffith's film in terms of the binary racist/nonracist, see Staiger.

17. For the relationship between *Birth* and the rebirth of the Klan, see Simcovitch.

18. As if in tribute to its roots, *Kong* makes one brief reference to Griffith: The Long Island studio in which Darrow picked up work as an extra was, as McGurl points out, Griffith's studio (423 n. 13).

19. On the "jungle" film tradition, see Peary, "Missing"; Erb, *Tracking* 91–103; and Rony 179–80.

20. The quotation is from the Production Code's list of "Don'ts and Be Carefuls" (1927), qtd. in Vieira 214. Given my focus, I have chosen not to delve into the fascinating recent work on censorship during the Production Code years. Suffice it to say that the principal findings of such work—that censorship was less a matter of imposition by some entity ("the Hays Office") than "an instrument of social control . . . constantly and 'invisibly' exerted throughout the production process," and thus an instrument that "extended to the most delicate filiations of the text" (Lea Jacobs 99)—is consistent with my understanding of *Kong* as a film that performs the racist ideologies of its time, rather than a film whose intentions were hampered or mutilated by official interference.

21. Thus I am unconvinced by Wartenberg's claim that *Kong* cultivates the stereotype of Kong as black beast in its early movements in order to critique that stereotype later on. This strikes me as special pleading, inasmuch as Kong poses, if anything, a greater threat to white society and sexuality in Manhattan than on Skull Mountain Island.

22. Additional claims for *Kong*'s ambivalence appear in Polan; and Torry.

23. For a fuller consideration of *Kong*'s reception (and reworking) by African Americans, see Erb, *Tracking* 181–201.

24. See O'Brien. Analyses of O'Brien's life and art include Jensen 59–97; Rovin 7–51; and Shay. Unfortunately, the only book-length study of O'Brien, Archer's *Willis O'Brien*, is an uninformative compilation of plot summaries, random artifacts of personal history, and fragmentary quotes culled from film reviews.

25. Rogin's indictment of blackface minstrelsy is in part a reaction against Lott's analysis, which stresses the equivocal nature of "blacking up": "The very form of blackface acts," Lott writes, "demonstrates the permeability of the color line" (6). He goes on to say, "At every turn blackface minstrelsy has seemed a form in which transgression and containment coexisted, in which improbably threatening or startlingly sympathetic racial meanings were simultaneously produced and dissolved" (234). Lott's study would thus suggest yet another locus of ambivalence within the racial ideology of *Kong*.

26. O'Brien's initial hiring and later championing of Mexican American sculptor

Marcel Delgado, who suffered ridicule and isolation on the RKO lot due to his ethnicaty, does speak highly for the animator's character. In Delgado's first attempts at a Kong design, interestingly, the sculptor fashioned a much more human "beast" than director Cooper would allow; see Shay 25, 33.

2. The Promise of Miracles

1. On the technology of *Oz*, see Harmetz 244–61; and Scarfone and Stillman 136–61.

2. In order, the reviews quoted are from *Daily Variety* 10 Aug. 1939; *Picture Reports* 16 Aug. 1939; and *Hollywood Spectator* 2 Sept. 1939.

3. Given that Dorothy's Oz experience is treated as a dream, it is unsurprising that psychoanalytic readings of the film predominate. See, for instance, H. Greenberg, "*Wizard*"; Lindroth; and Nathanson 78–100. Some critics have hinted at *Oz*'s Depression-era significance by noting that Americans of the time longed at once for "escape" and for "home"; yet this point has generally led to claims for the movie's timelessness, as in Griswold. In the 1990s, feminist readings of *Oz* multiplied; see, for example, Friedman; and Paige. If such studies sometimes emphasize the "archetypal power of this feminine quest saga" (Rzepka 55), they nonetheless point toward a fully historicized reading of the film.

4. For an attempt to locate *Oz* within its cultural history, see Carpenter. For a novel and subtle approach to *Oz*'s cultural work, see Groch, which focuses not on the film's historical contexts per se but on the "social and cultural formations which activate and limit the possibilities of reading [it]" (88).

5. On the Bonus Force and the Hunger March, see Cowley 83–93, 123–33. On class conflict in the New Deal era, see Levine, esp. 52–57. For a reading of the Bonus Force conflict as a context for *Kong*, see Torry.

6. General studies of technological discourse in America include Marx; and Heilbroner.

7. Technological utopianism is discussed in the invaluable works by Segal, *Technological Utopianism* and "Technological Utopians." Also enlightening is Roemer. Onosko's engaging and lavishly illustrated work reveals the extent of both corporate and popular enthusiasm for technology during the Depression.

8. The 1939 World's Fair has proved fertile ground for many critics. Those who have helped me include Cusker; Franklin; and Kihlstedt. Pictorial works, particularly helpful given the fair's spectacular qualities, include Wurts; and Zim, Lerner, and Rolfes.

9. On the use of film in the World's Fair, see Bird. On the fair itself as a sci-fi movie, see Telotte, *Distant* 162–82.

10. On the Roosevelt report, see Inouye and Susskind. On Depression-era technological planning generally, see J. Jordan 207–84.

11. The Technocracy craze is covered by Akin; and Wagar.

12. For an account of Depression-era antitechnology arguments, see Beard 4–12.

13. On technophobia run rampant in 1930s pulp science fiction, see P. Carter 201–21.

14. I owe this observation to Bordwell and Thompson 81.

15. My thanks to Tom Cairns and Erica Hickenboth for alerting me to this progression.

16. On the planned communities of the Depression, see also Conkin 93–213; and Schaffer.

17. Unprompted by me, one of my students remarked that the Emerald City "looked like a factory" (Alana Cowfer, written response to *The Wizard of Oz*, 10 Nov. 2000).

18. In his comments on this book in manuscript, Rob Latham reminded me that Oz also resembles Thomas Edison, thus connecting the Wizard not only to the avuncular public persona of the inventor but to the man's behind-the-scenes efforts to monopolize

the technologies in which he trafficked—including, notably, the technology of the motion pictures.

19. The labor-management struggles of Depression-era Hollywood are detailed by Hartsough; and Ross 191–212.

20. Attempts by both business and government to advance their agendas through the cinema are covered by Thorp 279–89.

21. On the economic dominance and marketing strategies of the Big Five, see Gomery 51–75; and Huettig 54–95, 113–42.

22. Federal antitrust actions against Hollywood are discussed by Lewis Jacobs 419–32; and Whitney.

23. This is, I believe, a problem in MacDonnell's reading of the film as a fond parody of the New Deal; basing her argument on the comments of lyricist E. Y. (Yip) Harburg, MacDonnell suggests that the film "reflects" Harburg's politics.

24. My thanks to Vincent F. Rocchio and to an anonymous reader for the *Arizona Quarterly*, both of whom helped me to clarify my argument at this point.

25. That the agricultural West had itself been radically affected, for better and for worse, by advanced technology renders this message all the more suspect. On the effects of technology on agriculture during this period, see Schlebecker 244–54. On rural opposition to the industrialization of agriculture, see Danbom. Federal aid to farmers is covered by Lowitt; and Hurt, *American* 287–330. A lucid study of Dust Bowl life is Hurt, *Dust Bowl*; and Worster is valuable both for its insights and its many photographs.

26. I am not, actually, the first to bring *Oz* and *Dialectic of Enlightenment* together; Culver views the scene in which Dorothy's partners accept commodities from the humbug Wizard as a dramatization of Horkheimer and Adorno's critique of consumerism (97).

3. Monsters from the Middle East

1. See, for example, Biskind 124n; and Luciano 36–37. Hendershot does touch on Harryhausen's first independent film, though mainly as an illustrative example ("Darwin"; and *Paranoia* 77–79). Jancovich mentions *Beast* once, misspelling Harryhausen's name in the process (61). Sobchack, meanwhile, makes a brief but trenchant reference to *Beast* in the context of discussing the principles of semantic condensation and displacement in fantasy film ("Virginity" 51). The closest I have found to a scholarly treatment of Harryhausen's works is Jensen's intriguing attempt to extract the artist's personal philosophy from his films (140–53).

2. For his part, Harryhausen has insisted repeatedly that "these pictures were just entertainment. . . . If you pick them apart, you analyze them out of existence" (qtd. in Newsom, "Ray Harryhausen" 126).

3. Since the subject of my study is American attitudes and perceptions, not cultural realities, I use the phrases *Middle East* and *Arab world* interchangeably. I trust, however, that in doing so I will not be taken as ignoring the distinctions between these terms.

4. Additional studies of the Middle East in film include Fahdel; and Fuller, "Hollywood."

5. Resistance to analyzing the Sinbad films is reflected by Shaheen's comments. Though otherwise unfailingly critical of the depiction of Arab peoples in American cinema, he finds "those Arabian Nights fantasies of yesteryear" pleasant, harmless diversions (34).

6. I am particularly receptive to arguments such as MacKenzie's and McAlister's inasmuch as I have myself shown how an ahistorical approach to representations of indigenous peoples invariably reproduces what it attempts to critique; see Bellin, *Demon*, esp. 1–4.

7. On the all-seeing eye as imperialist figure, see also Pratt 58–61, 201–27; and Spurr 13–27. As McAlister notes, the connection between cinema and imperialism has a material, not merely a metaphoric, base:

> By the 1950s, international exhibition receipts often represented more than half of the ultimate film gross. Hollywood was thus part of a project of expansion in two ways: in its Orientalist mode, it was a site of representing the world abroad to U.S. audiences; as an industry, it was also deeply invested in cultivating foreign audiences for an American product. (31)

8. Writings on postwar relations between the United States and the Middle East are numerous. Studies on which I have relied include Buheiry; Fraser; Kaufman; and Spiegel.

9. These quotes are taken from letters to the editor in *Time* 10 Dec. 1973: 4 and 29 Oct. 1973: 6. On images of Arabs during this period, see also Ghareeb; and Suleiman. It is worth noting, however, that these studies may themselves be charged with negative stereotyping, inasmuch as they pin all anti-Arab sentiment on "Zionism" when, in truth, such sentiment arises from diverse sites within American culture.

10. On the fusion—and confusion—of the Middle East and the Far East in American cultural productions during the Vietnam War, see McAlister 155–97.

11. The quote is from an uncredited source—perhaps Harryhausen himself—in the liner notes to the DVD release of *The Seventh Voyage of Sinbad* (Columbia Tristar Home Video, 1999).

12. In this respect, the film's most often noted "flaw"—the virtual identity between the first Cyclops and the second—accords with its discourse on the inscrutability of power in the Middle East. Harryhausen, ever resistant to any attempt at analyzing his films, attributes the lack of a more individual design to time pressures; see Rovin 145. But whatever the reason, the sudden appearance of what seems a reanimated Cyclops causes viewers momentarily to doubt the certainty of its death, the stability of its identity, and indeed the surety of their own perceptions.

13. Though it is perhaps no more than ancillary to my purpose here, I find fascinating Shohat's argument that the use of maps in colonialist films connects the West's "'claim' over the land" to the act of "comprehending the female body" (29). This is relevant to *Golden Voyage*, in which the hero's deciphering of Margiana's tattooed body underscores his authority over a feminized Orient.

14. On the exemption of Egypt from the negative portrayals of Arabs in 1970s popular culture, see Morsy.

4. Dragon Ladies

1. Though some women had risen to positions of prominence in Hollywood during the 1990s, systemic inequalities persisted: in the scarcity of roles for women; in unequal pay for the roles they could get; and in the scant number of female directors, studio heads, and power brokers. See Abramowitz; and Sova.

2. It might be argued that the award for supporting actress should rightfully go to an up-and-coming star, not an established one. But no such motive guided the show's choice of Best Supporting Actor: old-timer Gene Hackman.

3. Notable collections on women and fantasy film include B. Grant, *Dread of Difference*; and Penley et al.

4. Additional archetypal and psychoanalytic readings of the *Alien* films include Berenstein, "Mommie"; H. Greenberg, "Reimagining"; Moore and Miles; Rushing; Scobie; Sobchack, "Virginity" 49–50; and Yunis and Ostrander.

5. For critiques of the psychoanalytic approach to monstrous-woman films, see Freeland, *Naked*, esp. 55–86; and Latham, "Phallic" 89. For readings of the *Alien* films in terms of the gender politics of their era, see Bell-Metereau; and Hermann.

6. The role of fundamentalism in family-values discourse is discussed by Hardacre.

7. For a critique of the racial arm of the family-values campaign, see D. Roberts. For a critique of antiwelfare rhetoric and legislation, see Abramovitz.

8. The duplicitous nature of profamily rhetoric is also the subject of the essay by Cohen and Katzenstein.

9. See also Quayle's book-length elaboration of his thesis, coauthored by Michael Medved's wife, Diane Medved.

10. On *Fatal Attraction*, see the essays in Babener; on the broader tradition of violent women in 1980s film, see Holmlund. Most critics find the violent-woman tradition unambiguously misogynistic; for essays that consider such films potentially empowering for women, see McCaughey and King.

11. I have yet to encounter a critical reading of *Species*. For an intriguing analysis of a comparable monstrous-woman film, *Eve of Destruction* (1991), see Fulton.

12. I incorporate elements from the DVD release into my analysis—always noting their source—both because this footage helps flesh out the film's ideology and because it is the DVD version that viewers today are most likely to encounter.

13. Given *Aliens*' equation of gunplay with infantile sexuality, it is surprising that Harvey Greenberg, typically quite sensitive to the psychoanalytic dimensions of film, considers it a celebration of Reagan-era militarism; see his amusingly titled "Fembo."

14. Rob Latham, commenting on this book in manuscript, noted that "Vasquez appears to be gay, or at least a stereotype of a butch lesbian"—a characterization that would further mark her, in family-values terms, as a grotesque mockery of a "proper" male presence.

15. For a reading of the alien queen as another of the Reagan era's racial/sexual antagonists, the Third World mother, see Berg.

16. Brief but helpful remarks on the gender politics of *Jurassic Park* include Balides 156; Freeland, "Feminist" 209–11; Mitchell 179–82; and Warner, "Monstrous" 3–5. A reading of the Michael Crichton novel that accords with my reading of the film can be found in Briggs and Kelber-Kaye.

17. See, for instance, Maertens.

18. Similar prohibitions operate in the sequel to *Jurassic Park*. On the two occasions when Sarah Harding not only looks at but touches dinosaurs—"She has to touch," Malcolm groans. "She can't not touch"—punishment swiftly ensues: Once when she is nearly killed by the adult stegosaurs whose baby she has petted, and once when her treating the infant tyrannosaur in the camper nearly leads to the death of her and her companions. Interestingly, both instances involve a woman making overtures toward babies that do not belong to her; the implication would seem to be that if she finds babies so fascinating, it is time for her to make some of her own.

5. Monstrous Minds

1. For a convincing analysis of the ways in which "slasher" films appeal to their audiences—an analysis, however, that leaves aside the question of how such films represent the mentally ill—see Clover 21–64.

2. On mental illness as metaphor, see Finzen and Hoffmann-Richter.

3. Illustrations of madness throughout Western history can be found in Gilman, *Disease* 18–49; and Gilman, *Seeing*.

4. For a scathing indictment of the American psychiatric profession, see Whitaker. A far less critical account can be found in Grob.

5. For an argument that rates of violence among the mentally ill are comparable to those among the general population, see Teplin.

6. On the stigmatization of mentally ill persons in modern America, see Farina, Fisher, and Fischer.

7. On the misrepresentation of the mentally ill in the news media, see Steadman and Cocozza; Nunnally 65–89; and Shain and Phillips. In one 1990 study, 34 percent of those polled considered news reports on the mentally ill "believable," while another 61 percent considered these reports "somewhat believable," leaving a mere 5 percent who rejected mass-media stereotypes (*Public Attitudes* 3).

8. On the criminalizing of mental illness, see Torrey et al. Torrey's admirable opposition to criminalizing the mentally ill makes it all the more unfortunate that he himself utilizes the stereotypes of violence that sustain such policies.

9. In this respect, *The Cell* continues a long-standing cinematic tradition of critiquing the psychiatric profession. See Gabbard and Gabbard 32–33, 115–31, 138–42.

10. *The Cell* thus forms somewhat of an exception to recent "psycho killer" films, which typically mount sympathy for the male villains at the expense of their female victims. On this trend, see Young, "*Silence.*"

11. One of the extra features in the DVD version of *The Cell* is an "empathy test," by which viewers can presumably measure their moral superiority to the serial killer.

12. See, for instance, Torrey, *Nowhere*; and Krauthammer.

13. For critiques of such negative representations of the homeless, see Breakey et al.; and Marin.

14. On the history of medicalizing homelessness, see Blau.

15. To question the medical model, I must make clear, is not to doubt that there are homeless persons who suffer from conditions of mental distress; it is simply to argue that individual minds cannot be lifted from the larger social network within which homelessness exists. On the social causes of homelessness, see Wright, Rubin, and Devine; Yeich; and the essays in Herman and Susser. For a moderate position, see Jencks.

16. According to Lashmet, the director was angered that the film's producer insisted on adding date-and-place subtitles to certain settings, for "Gilliam's plan was to destabilize James Cole's credibility" (60).

17. On the lack of social analysis in recent fantasy films featuring the homeless, see also Pike.

6. Seeing Things

1. On the negative reception of *Freaks*, see Larsen and Haller.

2. Throughout this chapter, I use the word *freak*, rather than more sensitive locutions such as *person with physical disabilities*, for two principal reasons. Most simply, the characters I discuss—such as the Beast from *Beauty and the Beast*—are not "disabled" by most standards, though they may be seen as "freaks." More important, I wish to recall the reprehensible manner in which those seen as physically different have historically been treated, and the term *freak* conveys this history more baldly and succinctly than any other.

3. For a discussion of metacinema, see Fredericksen; and on metacinema in fantasy film, see Stewart, "Modern." On metacinema in the films of Tod Browning, see Gaycken.

4. For a similar analysis of self-reflexivity in *Kong*, see Torry 66–68.

5. Whatever the case may be with *Kong*, Erb offers an excellent reading of Cooper and O'Brien's other giant-gorilla film, *Mighty Joe Young* (1949), as a critique of racist spectacle in *Tracking* 129–40.

6. On the ways in which special effects trouble identification and believability in fantasy film, see also Neale, "'You've.'"

7. The tendency of metacinema to deepen rather than estrange audience identification is the subject of Sconce's essay.

8. On the racial freak, see Cassuto's intriguing study, esp. 186–93.

9. On the exhibiting of freaks in the Bard's day, see Pender, "In the Bodyshop."

10. The exhibition of freaks throughout the eighteenth and nineteenth centuries is covered by Altick 34–49, 253–67. On the transition from "cabinet of curiosities" to "dime museum," see McNamara. On the circus sideshow, see Bogdan, esp. 25–68; and Thomson, *Extraordinary* 55–80.

11. Though most know Merrick as "John"—largely because Treves persisted in calling him by this name—Graham and Oehlschlaeger establish that his name was in fact "Joseph."

12. On the decline of the freak show, see Bogdan 62–67.

13. On images of freaks in the modern visual media, see also Dennett; and Hevey. For a lighthearted look at freak films, see Adrian.

14. On the ambivalence of *Freaks*, see J. Hawkins. Particularly important is Hawkins's discussion of how the transformation of Cleopatra into the chicken-woman, whatever its radical potential in regard to issues of normalcy and difference, is in keeping with the alienation of women. The disturbing power of *Freaks* has given rise to numerous studies; see Chivers; Cook; Gaycken; Markotic; Norden and Cahill; Russo 86–93; and Thomas.

15. The socially constructed nature of disability, deformity, and disease is a central tenet of the congeries of disciplines that have come to be known as "disability studies." For examples drawn from the humanities, see the collections edited by Mitchell and Snyder; and by Snyder, Brueggemann, and Thomson.

16. Along these lines, I find intriguing Adams's suggestion that the unveiling of the impossible freak Cleopatra may be an elaborate joke on a gullible film audience that takes such freaks for real (82–85).

17. Some of the more immoderate claims for the "liminal" include Beehler; J. Cohen, "Monster"; Grosz; and Uebel.

18. Most studies of *Beauty and the Beast* focus on its exploration of gender rather than of the freak. See, for example, Gray; H. Hawkins; Jeffords, "Curse"; and Warner, "Beauty."

19. Stewart concentrates on such screen-in-a-screen devices in "'Videology.'"

20. After *Beauty and the Beast*'s end credits have run, there appears a dedication to Howard Ashman, the film's lyricist, who died of complications resulting from AIDS shortly before the film's release. This tribute to a homosexual man, a member of yet another despised minority, forms a fitting conclusion to the film, yet a conclusion that makes the film's apparent return to social orthodoxy and ostracism all the more troubling.

21. One measure of *Edward*'s success in challenging narrative conventions is the frequency with which reviewers complained about its self-conscious artifice. See, for example, Kael; Klawans; and Welsh.

22. My thanks to the students in my "Monsters, Magicians, and Machines" class for this insight.

23. Ansen leads the pack in his use of "fairy tale" as a substitute for analysis; he terms Burton's film a "magical fairy tale," a "punk fairy tale," and a "fractured suburban fairy tale" in one review ("Magical" 87), and a "comic and melancholy Frankensteinian fairy

tale" in another ("Disembodied" 58). Avella calls the film a "very sweet fairy tale" (101); Maslin brands it a "bona-fide fairy tale" (C10); and James considers it a "true fairy-tale" (19). One has to wonder, if the term *fairy tale* can (or must) be modified in so many ways, what use it has at all.

24. I consider the fate of the unredeemed or irreclaimable freak more fully in an unpublished paper, "No Pity for the Freaks," which I would gladly make available to any interested reader. I can be contacted at bellinjl@laroche.edu.

25. For a reading of Edward himself as sacrificial African American victim—a reading that in my mind connects the final film I consider at length in this study, *Edward Scissorhands*, to the first, *King Kong*—see Greene 146–47.

Conclusion

1. Whatever its necessity in visualizing such a creature, the decision to cast Gollum as a computer-generated character underscores his hybridity: he is not only divided between the humanoid Sméagol and the parasitic Gollum worm that rots out its host from within but is technically a compound of the human and the inhuman. This hybridity is most memorably visualized in the creepy moment in the prologue to *The Return of the King* in which the computer-generated eyes of Gollum flicker open on the face of the human actor who plays the accursed Sméagol. The normal/freak logic of the character, however, makes him unsuitable as a cyborg in Haraway's sense.

2. For considerations of other recent sci-fi films that critique discourses of abnormality, see Cheu; and Keller.

3. Though I have not considered *Edward Scissorhands* from this angle, it too might be read as a commentary on the alienation of homosexuals in the era of AIDS: With his high-pitched voice, hairdressing aptitude, disinclination toward heterosexual contact (with either Joyce or Kim), and death-dealing touch, Edward fulfills both contemporary stereotypes and contemporary fears of the gay male. For a brief reading of *Edward* as a "sustained cinematic meditation on the figure of the monster queer," see Benshoff 266–67; quote on 266.

WORKS CITED

Abramovitz, Mimi. *Under Attack: Fighting Back: Women and Welfare in the United States.* New York: Monthly Review, 2000.

Abramowitz, Rachel. *Is That a Gun in Your Pocket? Women's Experience of Power in Hollywood.* New York: Random, 2000.

"An Act to Establish a Clear and Comprehensive Prohibition of Discrimination on the Basis of Disability." Gostin and Beyer 265–313.

Adams, Rachel. *Sideshow U.S.A.: Freaks and the American Cultural Imagination.* Chicago: U of Chicago P, 2001.

Adrian, Werner. *Freaks: Cinema of the Bizarre.* New York: Warner, 1976.

Akin, William E. *Technocracy and the American Dream: The Technocrat Movement, 1900–1941.* Berkeley: U of California P, 1977.

Alloway, Lawrence. "Monster Films." Huss and Ross 121–24.

Altick, Richard D. *The Shows of London.* Cambridge: Belknap-Harvard UP, 1978.

Ambrogio, Anthony. "Fay Wray: Horror Films' First Sex Symbol." *Eros in the Mind's Eye: Sexuality and the Fantastic in Art and Film.* Ed. Donald Palumbo. New York: Greenwood, 1986. 127–39.

American Liberty League. "Economic Planning—Mistaken but Not New." 1935. *Opposition Politics: The Anti-New Deal Tradition.* Ed. Joseph Boskin. Beverly Hills: Glencoe, 1968. 53–57.

Andriano, Joseph D. *Immortal Monster: The Mythological Evolution of the Fantastic Beast in Modern Fiction and Film.* Westport: Greenwood, 1999.

Annan, David. *Cinema of Mystery and Fantasy.* London: Lorrimer, 1984.

Ansen, David. "The Disembodied Director." *Newsweek* 21 Jan. 1991: 58–60.

———. "A Magical Mystery Tour: Tim Burton's Creation." *Newsweek* 10 Dec. 1990: 87.

"The Arabs' New Oil Squeeze: Dimouts, Slowdowns, Chills." *Time* 19 Nov. 1973: 88–95.

Archer, Steve. *Willis O'Brien: Special Effects Genius.* Jefferson: McFarland, 1993.

Association of Southern Women for the Prevention of Lynching. *Southern Women Look at Lynching.* Atlanta, 1937.

Attebery, Brian. *The Fantasy Tradition in American Literature: From Irving to Le Guin.* Bloomington: Indiana UP, 1980.

———. "The Politics (If Any) of Fantasy." *Modes of the Fantastic: Selected Essays from the Twelfth International Conference on the Fantastic in the Arts.* Ed. Robert A. Latham and Robert A. Collins. Westport: Greenwood, 1995. 1–13.

———. *Strategies of Fantasy.* Bloomington: Indiana UP, 1992.

Avella, Richard. "Sharp Edges." *Commonweal* 8 Feb. 1991: 100–101.

Babener, Liahna, ed. *Fatal Attraction* special issue, *Journal of Popular Culture* 26.3 (Winter 1992).

Bachrach, Leona L. "What We Know about Homelessness among Mentally Ill Persons: An Analytical Review and Commentary." *Treating the Homeless Mentally Ill: A Report of the Task Force on the Homeless Mentally Ill*. Ed. H. Richard Lamb, L. Bachrach, and Frederic I. Kass. Washington: American Psychiatric Assoc., 1992. 13–40.

Balides, Constance. "Jurassic Post-Fordism: Tall Tales of Encounters in the Theme Park." *Screen* 41 (2000): 139–60.

Barras, Jonetta Rose. *Whatever Happened to Daddy's Little Girl? The Impact of Fatherlessness on Black Women*. New York: Ballantine, 2000.

Baudry, Jean-Louis. "Ideological Effects of the Basic Cinematographic Apparatus." *Film Quarterly* 28.2 (Winter 1974–75): 39–47.

Bauer, Gary L. *The Family: Preserving America's Future*. Washington: GPO, 1986.

Beard, Charles A., ed. *Toward Civilization*. London: Longmans, 1930.

Beard, Charles A., and Mary R. Beard. *America in Midpassage*. New York: Macmillan, 1939.

Beehler, Michael. "Border Patrols." *Aliens: The Anthropology of Science Fiction*. Ed. George E. Slusser and Eric S. Rabkin. Carbondale: Southern Illinois UP, 1987. 26–35.

Behlmer, Rudy. Preface. Geduld and Gottesman 9–13.

Bellin, Joshua David. *The Demon of the Continent: Indians and the Shaping of American Literature*. Philadelphia: U of Pennsylvania P, 2001.

———. "No Pity for the Freaks." Unpublished manuscript, 1991.

Bell-Metereau, Rebecca. "Woman: The Other Alien in *Alien*." *Women Worldwalkers: New Dimensions of Science Fiction and Fantasy*. Ed. Jane B. Weedman. Lubbock: Texas Tech UP, 1985. 9–24.

Bennett, William J. *The Broken Hearth: Reversing the Moral Collapse of the American Family*. New York: Doubleday, 2001.

Benshoff, Harry M. *Monsters in the Closet: Homosexuality and the Horror Film*. Manchester: Manchester UP, 1997.

Berenstein, Rhona J. *Attack of the Leading Ladies: Gender, Sexuality, and Spectatorship in Classic Horror Cinema*. New York: Columbia UP, 1996.

———. "*Mommie Dearest: Aliens, Rosemary's Baby* and Mothering." *Journal of Popular Culture* 34.2 (Fall 1990): 55–73.

Berg, Charles Ramírez. "Immigrants, Aliens, and Extraterrestrials: Science Fiction's Alien 'Other' as (among *Other* Things) New Hispanic Imagery." *CineAction!* 18 (Fall 1989): 3–17.

Berger, Brigitte, and Peter L. Berger. *The War over the Family: Capturing the Middle Ground*. Garden City: Anchor, 1983.

Bernardi, Daniel Leonard, ed. *The Birth of Whiteness: Race and the Emergence of U.S. Cinema*. New Brunswick: Rutgers UP, 1996.

———. "*Star Trek*" and History: Race-ing Toward a White Future*. New Brunswick: Rutgers UP, 1998.

Bernstein, Matthew. Introduction. Bernstein and Studlar 1–18.

Bernstein, Matthew, and Gaylyn Studlar, eds. *Visions of the East: Orientalism in Film*. New Brunswick: Rutgers UP, 1997.

Bird, William. "Enterprise and Meaning: Sponsored Film, 1939–1949." *History Today* 39 (Dec. 1989): 24–30.

Biskind, Peter. *Seeing Is Believing: How Hollywood Taught Us to Stop Worrying and Love the Fifties*. New York: Pantheon, 1983.

Blankenhorn, David. *Fatherless America: Confronting Our Most Urgent Social Problem*. New York: Basic, 1995.

Blau, Joel. "On the Uses of Homelessness: A Literature Review." *Catalyst* 6.2 (1988): 5–25.

Bloom, Allan. *The Closing of the American Mind: How Higher Education Has Failed Democracy and Impoverished the Souls of Today's Students.* New York: Simon, 1987.

Bogdan, Robert. *Freak Show: Presenting Human Oddities for Amusement and Profit.* Chicago: U of Chicago P, 1988.

Bogle, Donald. *Toms, Coons, Mulattoes, Mammies, and Bucks: An Interpretive History of Blacks in American Films.* 1973. 4th ed. New York: Continuum, 2001.

Bordwell, David, and Kristin Thompson. *Film Art: An Introduction.* 5th ed. New York: McGraw, 1997.

Borsodi, Ralph. *This Ugly Civilization.* New York: Simon, 1929. Philadelphia: Porcupine, 1975.

Boskin, Joseph. *Urban Racial Violence in the Twentieth Century.* Beverly Hills: Glencoe, 1969.

Breakey, William R., et al. "Stigma and Stereotype: Homeless Mentally Ill Persons." Fink and Tasman 97–112.

Briggs, Laura, and Jodi I. Kelber-Kaye. "'There Is No Unauthorized Breeding in Jurassic Park': Gender and the Uses of Genetics." *NWSA Journal* 12.3 (2000): 92–114.

Brooks, David. "The Hardcore Homeless Should Be Arrested." Hurley 137–41. Rpt. of "Mindlessness about Homelessness." *Weekly Standard* 20 Dec. 1999.

Browder, Laura. *Slippery Characters: Ethnic Impersonators and American Identities.* Chapel Hill: U of North Carolina P, 2000.

Brown, L. Carl. "Movies and the Middle East." *Comparative Civilizations Review* 13/14 (1985–86): 17–35.

Buheiry, Marwan R. *The Formation and Perception of the Modern Arab World.* Ed. Lawrence I. Conrad. Princeton: Darwin, 1989.

Bundtzen, Lynda K. "Monstrous Mothers: Medusa, Grendel, and Now Alien." *Film Quarterly* 40.3 (Spring 1987): 11–17.

Campbell, Thomas D. "Agriculture." *Toward Civilization.* Ed. Charles A. Beard. London: Longmans, 1930. 174–84.

Carlson, Allan C. *Family Questions: Reflections on the American Social Crisis.* New Brunswick: Transaction, 1988.

Carlson, Marvin. *Performance: A Critical Introduction.* London: Routledge, 1996.

Carnacchio, C. J. "Homelessness Is Not Society's Problem." Hurley 23–27. Rpt. of "Homeless Advocates Must Face Facts." *Michigan Review* 19 Nov. 1997.

Carpenter, Lynette. "'There's No Place like Home': *The Wizard of Oz* and American Isolationism." *Film and History* 15.2 (May 1985): 37–45.

Carroll, Noel. "*King Kong*: Ape and Essence." B. Grant, *Planks of Reason* 215–44.

Carter, Dan T., ed. *Papers of the NAACP, Part 6: The Scottsboro Case, 1931–1950.* Frederick: U Publications of America, 1986.

———. *Scottsboro: A Tragedy of the American South.* Rev. ed. Baton Rouge: Louisiana State UP, 1979.

[Carter, John Franklin]. *American Messiahs, by an Unofficial Observer.* New York: Simon, 1935.

Carter, Paul A. *The Creation of Tomorrow: Fifty Years of Magazine Science Fiction.* New York: Columbia UP, 1977.

Cartmell, Deborah, et al., eds. *Alien Identities: Exploring Difference in Film and Fiction.* London: Pluto, 1999.

Cassuto, Leonard. *The Inhuman Race: The Racial Grotesque in American Literature and Culture.* New York: Columbia UP, 1997.

Chadbourne, James Harmon. *Lynching and the Law*. Chapel Hill: U of North Carolina P, 1933. New York: Johnson Reprint, 1970.

Cheney, Sheldon, and Martha Candler Cheney. *Art and the Machine: An Account of Industrial Design in 20th-Century America*. 1936. New York: Acanthus, 1992.

Cherney, James L. "Sexy Cyborgs: Disability and Erotic Politics in Cronenberg's *Crash*." Smit and Enns 165–80.

Cheu, Johnson. "De-gene-erates, Replicants and Other Aliens: (Re)defining Disability in Futuristic Film." *Disability/Postmodernity: Embodying Disability Theory*. Ed. Mairian Corker and Tom Shakespeare. London: Continuum, 2002. 198–212.

Chivers, Sally. "The Horror of Becoming 'One of Us': Tod Browning's *Freaks* and Disability." Smit and Enns 57–64.

Clover, Carol J. *Men, Women, and Chain Saws: Gender in the Modern Horror Film*. Princeton: Princeton UP, 1992.

Cofer, Lynette Friedrich, and Robin Smith Jacobvitz. "The Loss of Moral Turf: Mass Media and Family Values." *Rebuilding the Nest: A New Commitment to the American Family*. Ed. David Blankenhorn, Steven Bayme, and Jean Bethke Elshtain. Milwaukee: Family Service America, 1990. 179–204.

Cohen, Jeffrey Jerome. "Monster Culture (Seven Theses)." J. Cohen, *Monster Theory* 3–25.

——, ed. *Monster Theory: Reading Culture*. Minneapolis: U of Minnesota P, 1996.

Cohen, Susan, and Mary Fainsod Katzenstein. "The War over the Family Is Not over the Family." *Feminism, Children, and the New Families*. Ed. Sanford M. Dornbusch and Myra H. Strober. New York: Guilford, 1988. 25–46.

Conkin, Paul K. *Tomorrow a New World: The New Deal Community Program*. Ithaca: Cornell UP, 1959.

Conrad, Peter, and Joseph W. Schneider. *Deviance and Medicalization: From Badness to Sickness*. St. Louis: Mosby, 1980.

Cook, Méira. "None of Us: Ambiguity as Moral Discourse in Tod Browning's *Freaks*." Smit and Enns 47–56.

Coontz, Stephanie. *The Way We Never Were: American Families and the Nostalgia Trap*. New York: Basic, 1992.

Corn, Joseph J., ed. *Imagining Tomorrow: History, Technology, and the American Future*. Cambridge: MIT P, 1986.

Cowley, Malcolm. *The Dream of the Golden Mountains: Remembering the 1930s*. New York: Viking, 1980.

Coyle, William. "Introduction: The Nature of Fantasy." *Aspects of Fantasy: Selected Essays from the Second International Conference on the Fantastic in Literature and Film*. Ed. Coyle. Westport: Greenwood, 1986. 1–3.

Creed, Barbara. *The Monstrous-Feminine: Film, Feminism, Psychoanalysis*. London: Routledge, 1993.

Cripps, Thomas. *Slow Fade to Black: The Negro in American Film, 1900–1942*. London: Oxford UP, 1977.

Culver, Stuart. "What Manikins Want: *The Wonderful Wizard of Oz* and The Art of Decorating Dry Goods Windows." *Representations* 21 (1988): 97–116.

Cusker, Joseph P. "The World of Tomorrow: Science, Culture, and Community at the New York World's Fair." *Dawn of a New Day: The New York World's Fair, 1939/40*. Ed. Helen A. Harrison. New York: New York UP, 1980. 3–15.

Danbom, David B. *The Resisted Revolution: Urban American and the Industrialization of Agriculture, 1900–1930*. Ames: Iowa State UP, 1979.

Daniels, Cynthia R., ed. *Lost Fathers: The Politics of Fatherlessness in America*. New York: St. Martin's, 1998.

Davidson, Arnold I. "The Horror of Monsters." *The Boundaries of Humanity: Humans, Animals, Machines*. Ed. James J. Sheehan and Morton Sosna. Berkeley: U of California P, 1991. 36–67.

Davis, Angela Y. "Rape, Racism and the Myth of the Black Rapist." *Women, Race and Class*. New York: Random, 1981. 172–201.

Dennett, Andrea Stulman. "The Dime Museum Freak Show Reconfigured as Talk Show." Thomson, *Freakery* 315–26.

Dennis, Lawrence. "The Planless Roosevelt Revolution." *American Mercury* 32 (May 1934): 1–11.

Desjarlais, Robert. *Shelter Blues: Sanity and Selfhood among the Homeless*. Philadelphia: U of Pennsylvania P, 1997.

Desser, David. "Race, Space and Class: The Politics of Cityscapes in Science-Fiction Films." Kuhn, *Alien Zone II* 80–96.

Desvernine, Raoul E. *Democratic Despotism*. New York: Dodd, 1936.

Diawara, Manthia. "Black Spectatorship: Problems of Identification and Resistance." *Film Theory and Criticism: Introductory Readings*. Ed. Leo Braudy and Marshall Cohen. New York: Oxford UP, 1999. 845–53.

Douglas, Ann. *Terrible Honesty: Mongrel Manhattan in the 1920s*. New York: Farrar, 1995.

Du Bois, W. E. B. "Segregation in the North." *Writings in Periodicals Edited by W. E. B. Du Bois: Selections from "The Crisis."* Vol. 2, 1926–1934. Comp. and ed. Herbert Aptheker. Millwood: Kraus-Thomson, 1983. 745–50.

Dyer, Richard. "Entertainment and Utopia." *Genre: The Musical*. Ed. Rick Altman. London: Routledge, 1981. 175–89.

———. "White." *Screen* 29.4 (Autumn 1988): 44–64.

Erb, Cynthia. "Another World or the World of an Other? The Space of Romance in Recent Versions of 'Beauty and the Beast.'" *Cinema Journal* 34.4 (1995): 50–70.

———. *Tracking King Kong: A Hollywood Icon in World Culture*. Detroit: Wayne State UP, 1998.

Evans, Walter. "Monster Movies: A Sexual Theory." B. Grant, *Planks of Reason* 53–64.

Fahdel, Abbas. "An Orient of Myth and Mystery." *UNESCO Courier* Oct. 1989: 24–29.

Faludi, Susan. *Backlash: The Undeclared War Against American Women*. New York: Anchor, 1991.

Falwell, Jerry. *Listen, America!* Garden City: Doubleday, 1980.

Färber, Helmut. "*King Kong*: One More Interpretation, or, What Cinema Tells about Itself." *Discourse* 22.2 (Spring 2000): 104–26.

Farina, Amerigo, Jeffrey D. Fisher, and Edward H. Fischer. "Societal Factors in the Problems Faced by Deinstitutionalized Psychiatric Patients." Fink and Tasman 167–84.

Fiedler, Leslie. *Freaks: Myths and Images of the Secret Self*. New York: Simon, 1978.

Fink, Paul Jay, and Allan Tasman, eds. *Stigma and Mental Illness*. Washington: American Psychiatric, 1992.

Finzen, Asmus, and Ulrike Hoffmann-Richter. "Mental Illness as Metaphor." *The Image of Madness: The Public Facing Mental Illness and Psychiatric Treatment*. Ed. José Guimón, Werner Fischer, and Norman Sartorius. Basel: Karger, 1999. 13–19.

Fishman, Robert. *Urban Utopias in the Twentieth Century: Ebenezer Howard, Frank Lloyd Wright, and Le Corbusier*. New York: Basic, 1977.

Flake, Carol. *Redemptorama: Culture, Politics, and the New Evangelicalism*. Garden City: Anchor, 1984.

Fleming, Michael, and Roger Manvell. *Images of Madness: The Portrayal of Insanity in the Feature Film.* Rutherford: Fairleigh Dickinson UP, 1985.

Ford, Henry. "Machines as Ministers to Man." *New York Times* 5 Mar. 1939, World's Fair Section: 10, 70.

Franklin, H. Bruce. "America as Science Fiction: 1939." *Coordinates: Placing Science Fiction and Fantasy.* Ed. George E. Slusser et al. Carbondale: Southern Illinois UP, 1983. 107–21.

Fraser, T. G. *The USA and the Middle East since World War 2.* London: Macmillan, 1989.

Fredericksen, Don. "Modes of Reflexive Film." *Quarterly Review of Film Studies* 4 (1979): 299–320.

Freeland, Cynthia. "Feminist Frameworks for Horror Films." *Post-Theory: Reconstructing Film Studies.* Ed. David Bordwell and Noel Carroll. Madison: U of Wisconsin P, 1996. 195–218.

———. *The Naked and the Undead: Evil and the Appeal of Horror.* Boulder: Westview, 2000.

Freiberger, Steven Z. *Dawn over Suez: The Rise of American Power in the Middle East, 1953–1957.* Chicago: Dee, 1992.

Fricke, John, Jay Scarfone, and William Stillman. *"The Wizard of Oz": The Official 50th Anniversary Pictorial History.* New York: Warner, 1989.

Friedman, Bonnie. "Relinquishing Oz: Every Girl's Anti-Adventure Story." *Michigan Quarterly Review* 35 (1996): 9–28.

Fuller, Linda K. "From Tramps to Truth-Seekers: Images of the Homeless in the Motion Pictures." *Reading the Homeless: The Media's Image of Homeless Culture.* Ed. Eungjun Min. Westport: Praeger, 1999. 159–73.

———. "Hollywood Holding Us Hostage: Or, Why Are Terrorists in the Movies Middle Easterners?" *The U.S. Media and the Middle East: Image and Perception.* Ed. Yahya R. Kamalipour and George Gerbner. Westport: Praeger, 1995. 187–97.

Fulton, Elizabeth. "On the Eve of Destruction: Technology, Nostalgia, and the Fetishized Maternal Body." *Critical Matrix* 10.1–2 (Fall 1996): 90–105.

Gabbard, Krin, and Glen O. Gabbard. *Psychiatry and the Cinema.* Chicago: U of Chicago P, 1987.

Gardner, Orville, and George E. Turner. *The Making of "King Kong": The Story Behind a Film Classic.* New York: Barnes, 1975.

Gaycken, Oliver. "Tod Browning and the Monstrosity of Hollywood Style." Smit and Enns 73–85.

Geduld, Harry M., and Ronald Gottesman, eds. *The Girl in the Hairy Paw: King Kong as Myth, Movie, and Monster.* New York: Avon, 1976.

———. "Introduction: The Eighth Wonder of the World." Geduld and Gottesman 19–28.

Ghareeb, Edmund. *Split Vision: The Portrayal of Arabs in the American Media.* Washington: American-Arab Affairs Council, 1983.

Gilder, George. *Men and Marriage.* Gretna: Pelican, 1986.

Gilfillan, S. C. "Social Effects of Inventions." National Resources Committee 32–37.

Gilman, Sander L. *Disease and Representation: Images of Illness from Madness to AIDS.* Ithaca: Cornell UP, 1988.

———. *Picturing Health and Illness: Images of Identity and Difference.* Baltimore: Johns Hopkins UP, 1995.

———. *Seeing the Insane: A Cultural History of Madness and Art in the Western World.* New York: Wiley, 1982.

Gomery, Douglas. *The Hollywood Studio System*. London: Macmillan, 1986.

Gostin, Lawrence O., and Henry A. Beyer, eds. *Implementing the Americans with Disabilities Act: Rights and Responsibilities of All Americans*. Baltimore: Brookes, 1993.

———. Preface. Gostin and Beyer xiii–xv.

Graham, Peter W., and Fritz H. Oehlschlaeger. *Articulating the Elephant Man: Joseph Merrick and His Interpreters*. Baltimore: John Hopkins UP, 1992.

Grant, Barry Keith, ed. *The Dread of Difference: Gender and the Horror Film*. Austin: U of Texas P, 1996.

———. Introduction. B. Grant, *Dread of Difference* 1–12.

———, ed. *Planks of Reason: Essays on the Horror Film*. Lanham: Scarecrow, 1984.

———. "'Sensuous Elaboration': Reason and the Visible in the Science-Fiction Film." Kuhn, *Alien Zone II* 16–30.

Grant, Madison. "Closing the Flood-Gates." *The Alien in Our Midst: Or, Selling Our Birthright for a Mess of Pottage*. Ed. M. Grant and Charles Stewart Davison. New York: Galton, 1930. 13–24.

———. *The Passing of the Great Race: Or, the Racial Basis of European History*. New York: Scribner's, 1916.

Grant, Toni. *Being a Woman: Fulfilling Your Femininity and Finding Love*. New York: Random, 1988.

Gray, Elizabeth Dodson. "Beauty and the Beast: A Parable for Our Time." *Women Respond to the Men's Movement: A Feminist Collection*. Ed. Kay Leigh Hagan. New York: Harper, 1992. 159–68.

Greenberg, Cheryl Lynn. *"Or Does It Explode?": Black Harlem in the Great Depression*. New York: Oxford UP, 1991.

Greenberg, Harvey. "Fembo: *Aliens'* Intentions." *Journal of Popular Film and Television* 15 (1988): 165–71.

———. "*King Kong*: The Beast in the Boudoir—or, 'You Can't Marry That Girl, You're a Gorilla!'" B. Grant, *Dread of Difference* 338–51.

———. "Reimagining the Gargoyle: Psychoanalytic Notes on *Alien*." Penley et al. 83–104.

———. "*The Wizard of Oz*: Little Girl Lost—and Found." *The Movies on Your Mind*. New York: Saturday Review, 1975. 13–32.

Greene, Eric. *"Planet of the Apes" as American Myth: Race, Politics, and Popular Culture*. Middletown: Wesleyan UP, 1996.

Griswold, Jerry. "There's No Place but Home: *The Wizard of Oz*." *Antioch Review* 45 (1987): 462–75.

Grob, Gerald N. *The Mad among Us: A History of the Care of America's Mentally Ill*. New York: Free, 1994.

Groch, John R. "Corporate Reading, Corporate Writing: MGM and CBS in the Land of Oz." Diss., U of Iowa, 1996.

Grosz, Elizabeth. "Intolerable Ambiguity: Freaks as/at the Limit." Thomson, *Freakery* 55–66.

Gubar, Susan. "Spirit-Murder at the Movies: Blackface Lynchings." *Racechanges: White Skin, Black Face in American Culture*. New York: Oxford UP, 1997. 53–94.

Guerrero, Ed. *Framing Blackness: The African American Image in Film*. Philadelphia: Temple UP, 1993.

Guterl, Matthew Pratt. *The Color of Race in America, 1900–1940*. Cambridge: Harvard UP, 2001.

Hadar, Leon T. *Quagmire: America in the Middle East*. Washington: Cato, 1992.

Hale, Grace Elizabeth. *Making Whiteness: The Culture of Segregation in the South, 1890–1940.* New York: Vintage, 1999.

Hanley, Lawrence F. "Popular Culture and Crisis: King Kong Meets Edmund Wilson." *Radical Revisions: Rereading 1930s Culture.* Ed. Bill Mullen and Sherry Lee Linkon. Urbana: U of Illinois P, 1996. 242–63.

Haraway, Donna. "A Manifesto for Cyborgs: Science, Technology, and Socialist Feminism in the 1980s." *Socialist Review* 15.2 (Mar.–Apr. 1985): 65–107.

Hardacre, Helen. "The Impact of Fundamentalisms on Women, the Family, and Interpersonal Relations." *Fundamentalisms and Society: Reclaiming the Sciences, the Family, and Education.* Ed. Martin E. Marty and R. Scott Appleby. Chicago: U of Chicago P, 1993. 129–50.

Harding, Gardner. "World's Fair, 1939: A Preview." *Harper's Magazine* 176 (Jan. 1938): 129–37.

Harmetz, Aljean. *The Making of "The Wizard of Oz."* New York: Limelight, 1984.

Hartsough, Denise. "Crime Pays: The Studios' Labor Deals in the 1930s." *The Studio System.* Ed. Janet Staiger. New Brunswick: Rutgers UP, 1995. 226–48.

Harwood, Sarah. *Family Fictions: Representations of the Family in 1980s Hollywood Cinema.* New York: St. Martin's, 1997.

Hasse, Henry. "He Who Shrank." 1936. *Before the Golden Age: A Science Fiction Anthology of the 1930s.* Ed. Isaac Asimov. Garden City: Doubleday, 1974. 730–86.

Haver, Ron. "Merian C. Cooper: First King of Kong." *American Film* 2.3 (Dec.–Jan. 1977): 14–23.

Hawkins, Harriet. "Maidens and Monsters in American Popular Culture: *The Silence of the Lambs* and *Beauty and the Beast.*" *Textual Practice* 7 (1993): 258–66.

Hawkins, Joan. "'One of Us': Tod Browning's *Freaks.*" Thomson, *Freakery* 265–76.

Heath, Stephen. "The Cinematic Apparatus: Technology as Historical and Cultural Form." *Questions of Cinema.* Bloomington: Indiana UP, 1981. 221–35.

Heilbroner, Robert L. "The Impact of Technology: The Historic Debate." *Automation and Technological Change.* Ed. John T. Dunlop. Englewood Cliffs: Prentice-Hall, 1962. 7–25.

Heldreth, Leonard G. "Architecture, Duality, and Personality: Mise-en-scène and Boundaries in Tim Burton's Films." *Trajectories of the Fantastic: Selected Essays from the Fourteenth International Conference on the Fantastic in the Arts.* Ed. Michael A. Morrison. Westport: Greenwood, 1997. 141–59.

Hellenbrand, Harold. "Bigger Thomas Reconsidered: *Native Son*, Film, and *King Kong.*" *Journal of American Culture* 6.1 (1983): 84–95.

Hendershot, Cyndy. "Darwin and the Atom: Evolution/Devolution Fantasies in *The Beast from 20,000 Fathoms, Them!* and *The Incredible Shrinking Man.*" *Science Fiction Studies* 25 (1998): 319–35.

———. *I Was a Cold War Monster: Horror Films, Eroticism, and the Cold War Imagination.* Bowling Green: Bowling Green State U Popular P, 2001.

———. *Paranoia, the Bomb, and 1950s Science Fiction Films.* Bowling Green: Bowling Green State U Popular P, 1999.

Herman, Daniel B., and Ezra S. Susser, eds. *Homelessness in America.* Washington: American Public Health Assoc., 1998.

Hermann, Chad. "'Some Horrible Dream about (S)mothering': Sexuality, Gender, and Family in the *Alien* Trilogy." *Post Script* 16.3 (Summer 1997): 36–50.

Hevey, David. *The Creatures Time Forgot: Photography and Disability Imagery.* London: Routledge, 1992.

Higham, John. *Strangers in the Land: Patterns of American Nativism, 1860–1925*. 2nd ed. New Brunswick: Rutgers UP, 1988.

Hoch, Paul. *White Hero, Black Beast: Racism, Sexism and the Mask of Masculinity*. London: Pluto, 1979.

Hogan, David J. *Dark Romance: Sexuality in the Horror Film*. Jefferson: McFarland, 1986.

Holmlund, Christine. "A Decade of Deadly Dolls: Hollywood and the Woman Killer." *Moving Targets: Women, Murder, and Representation*. Ed. Helen Birch. Berkeley: U of California P, 1994. 127–51.

Horkheimer, Max, and Theodor W. Adorno. *Dialectic of Enlightenment*. 1944. Trans. John Cumming. New York: Herder, 1972.

Howard, Walter T. *Lynchings: Extralegal Violence in Florida During the 1930s*. Selinsgrove: Susquehanna UP, 1995.

Huettig, Mae D. *Economic Control of the Motion Picture Industry: A Study in Industrial Organization*. Philadelphia: U of Pennsylvania P, 1944.

Hume, Kathryn. *Fantasy and Mimesis: Responses to Reality in Western Literature*. New York: Methuen, 1984.

Hurley, Jennifer A., ed. *The Homeless: Opposing Viewpoints*. San Diego: Greenhaven, 2002.

Hurt, R. Douglas. *American Agriculture: A Brief History*. Ames: Iowa State UP, 1994.

———. *The Dust Bowl: An Agricultural and Social History*. Chicago: Nelson, 1981.

Huss, Roy, and T. J. Ross, eds. *Focus on the Horror Film*. Englewood Cliffs: Prentice, 1972.

Inouye, Arlene, and Charles Susskind. "'Technological Trends and National Policy,' 1937: The First Modern Technology Assessment." *Technology and Culture* 18 (1977): 593–621.

Irwin, W. R. *The Game of the Impossible: A Rhetoric of Fantasy*. Urbana: U of Illinois P, 1976.

Jackson, Frank. "Sinbad and the Eye of the Tiger." *Cinefantastique* 6.2 (Fall 1977): 26–27.

Jackson, Rosemary. *Fantasy: The Literature of Subversion*. London: Routledge, 2003.

Jacobs, Lea. "Industry Self-Regulation and the Problem of Textual Determination." *Controlling Hollywood: Censorship and Regulation in the Studio Era*. Ed. Matthew Bernstein. New Brunswick: Rutgers UP, 1999. 87–101.

Jacobs, Lewis. *The Rise of the American Film: A Critical History*. 1939. New York: Teachers College, 1968.

James, Caryn. "When the Script Is a Grim Fairy Tale." *New York Times* 17 Feb. 1991, sec. 2: 1, 18–19.

Jancovich, Mark. *Rational Fears: American Horror in the 1950s*. Manchester: Manchester UP, 1996.

Jefferson, Thomas. *Notes on the State of Virginia*. 1787. Ed. William Peden. New York: Norton, 1982.

Jeffords, Susan. "'The Battle of the Big Mamas': Feminism and the Alienation of Women." *Journal of American Culture* 10.3 (Fall 1987): 73–84.

———. "The Curse of Masculinity: Disney's *Beauty and the Beast*." *From Mouse to Mermaid: The Politics of Film, Gender, and Culture*. Ed. Elizabeth Bell, Lynda Haas, and Laura Sells. Bloomington: Indiana UP, 1995. 161–72.

Jencks, Christopher. *The Homeless*. Cambridge: Harvard UP, 1994.

Jensen, Paul M. *The Men Who Made the Monsters*. New York: Twayne, 1996.

Jordan, John M. *Machine-Age Ideology: Social Engineering and American Liberalism, 1911–39*. Chapel Hill: U of North Carolina P, 1994.

Jordan, Winthrop D. *White over Black: American Attitudes Toward the Negro, 1550–1812*. Chapel Hill: U of North Carolina P, 1968.

Juguo, Zhang. *W. E. B. Du Bois: The Quest for the Abolition of the Color Line*. New York: Routledge, 2001.

Kael, Pauline. "The Current Cinema: New Age Daydreams." *New Yorker* 17 Dec. 1990: 115–21.

Kaufman, Burton I. *The Arab Middle East and the United States: Inter-Arab Rivalry and Superpower Diplomacy*. New York: Twayne, 1996.

Kawin, Bruce. *How Movies Work*. Berkeley: U of California P, 1992.

Keller, James R. "'Like to a Chaos': Deformity and Depravity in Contemporary Film." *Journal of Popular Film and Television* 23 (1995): 8–14.

Kennedy, X. J. "Who Killed King Kong?" Geduld and Gottesman 122–23.

Kihlstedt, Folke T. "Utopia Realized: The World's Fairs of the 1930s." Corn 97–118.

Kim, Helen M. "Strategic Credulity: *Oz* as Mass Cultural Parable." *Cultural Critique* 33 (1996): 213–33.

"King Kong Was a Dirty Old Man." *Esquire* Sept. 1971: 146–49.

Kinnamon, Kenneth. Introduction. *New Essays on "Native Son."* Ed. Kinnamon. Cambridge: Cambridge UP, 1990. 1–33.

Kinnard, Roy. *Beasts and Behemoths: Prehistoric Creatures in the Movies*. Metuchen: Scarecrow, 1988.

Kissinger, Henry. "Statement by Secretary of State Henry Kissinger at the Opening of the Geneva Conference, December 22, 1973." *The Quest for Peace: Principal United States Public Statements and Related Documents on the Arab-Israeli Peace Process, 1967–1983*. Washington: GPO, 1984. 44–49.

Klawans, Stuart. "Holiday Celluloid Wrap-Up." *Nation* 7–14 Jan. 1991: 22–24.

Koegel, Paul, and M. Audrey Burnam. "Problems in the Assessment of Mental Illness among the Homeless: An Empirical Approach." *Homelessness: A National Perspective*. Ed. Marjorie J. Robertson and Milton Greenblatt. New York: Plenum, 1992. 77–99.

Kozol, Jonathan. "Distancing the Homeless." *Yale Review* 77 (Winter 1988): 153–67.

Krauthammer, Charles. "When Liberty Really Means Neglect." *Time* 2 Dec. 1985: 103–4.

Kroeber, Karl. *Romantic Fantasy and Science Fiction*. New Haven: Yale UP, 1988.

Kuhlman, Thomas L. *Psychology on the Streets: Mental Health Practice with Homeless Persons*. New York: Wiley, 1994.

Kuhn, Annette, ed. *Alien Zone: Cultural Theory and Contemporary Science Fiction Cinema*. London: Verso, 1990.

———, ed. *Alien Zone II: The Spaces of Science Fiction Cinema*. London: Verso, 1999.

———. Introduction. Kuhn, *Alien Zone* 1–12.

———. Introduction to Part III: "Corporeal Spaces." Kuhn, *Alien Zone II* 147–51.

Lada-Richards, Ismene. "'Foul Monster or Good Saviour'? Reflections on Ritual Monsters." *Monsters and Monstrosity in Greek and Roman Culture*. Ed. Catherine Atherton. Bari: Levante, 1998. 41–82.

Laffin, John. *The Arab Mind Considered: A Need for Understanding*. New York: Taplinger, 1975.

Landon, Brooks. "The Insistence of Fantasy in Contemporary Science Fiction Film." *The Shape of the Fantastic: Selected Essays from the Seventh International Conference on the Fantastic in the Arts*. Ed. Olena H. Saciuk. Westport: Greenwood, 1990. 249–56.

Lange, Dorothea, and Paul Schuster Taylor. *An American Exodus: A Record of Human Erosion*. New York: Reynal, 1939.

Larsen, Robin, and Beth A. Haller. "Public Reception of Real Disability: The Case of *Freaks*." *Journal of Popular Film and Television* 29 (2002): 164–72.

Lashmet, David. "'The Future Is History': *12 Monkeys* and the Origin of AIDS." *Mosaic* 33.4 (2000): 55–72.

Latham, Rob. "Phallic Mothers and Monster Queers." *Science-Fiction Studies* 25 (1998): 87–101.

———. "There's No Place like Home: Simulating Postmodern America in *The Wizard of Oz* and *Blue Velvet*." *Journal of the Fantastic in the Arts* 1.4 (1988): 49–58.

Leab, Daniel J. *From Sambo to Superspade: The Black Experience in Motion Pictures.* Boston: Houghton, 1975.

Lesch, David W. *Syria and the United States: Eisenhower's Cold War in the Middle East.* Boulder: Westview, 1992.

Levine, Rhonda F. *Class Struggle and the New Deal: Industrial Labor, Industrial Capital, and the State.* Lawrence: UP of Kansas, 1988.

Liachowitz, Claire H. *Disability as a Social Construct: Legislative Roots.* Philadelphia: U of Pennsylvania P, 1988.

Lindroth, James. "Down the Yellow Brick Road: Two Dorothys and the Journey of Initiation in Dream and Nightmare." *Literature-Film Quarterly* 18 (1990): 160–66.

Loeb, Harold. *Life in a Technocracy: What It Might Be Like.* New York: Viking, 1933.

Longmore, Paul K. "Screening Stereotypes: Images of Disabled People." *Social Policy* 16.1 (Summer 1985): 31–37.

Lott, Eric. *Love and Theft: Blackface Minstrelsy and the American Working Class.* New York: Oxford UP, 1993.

Lowitt, Richard. *The New Deal and the West.* Norman: U of Oklahoma P, 1993.

Luciano, Patrick. *Them or Us: Archetypal Interpretations of Fifties Alien Invasion Films.* Bloomington: Indiana UP, 1987.

Lutzer, Erwin. "The Myths That Could Destroy America." *The Rebirth of America.* Philadelphia: DeMoss, 1986. 80–90.

MacDonnell, Francis. "'The Emerald City Was the New Deal': E. Y. Harburg and *The Wonderful Wizard of Oz.*" *Journal of American Culture* 13.4 (Winter 1990): 71–75.

MacKenzie, John M. *Orientalism: History, Theory and the Arts.* Manchester: Manchester UP, 1995.

Maclean, Nancy. *Behind the Mask of Chivalry: The Making of the Second Ku Klux Klan.* New York: Oxford UP, 1994.

Maertens, James W. "The Dragon and the Man-Machine: Reflecting on *Jurassic Park* and *Frankenstein.*" *The Soul of Popular Culture: Looking at Contemporary Heroes, Myths, and Monsters.* Ed. Mary Lynn Kittelson. Chicago: Open Court, 1998. 181–92.

Magnet, Myron. "Homeless: Craziness, Dope and Danger." *New York Times* 26 Jan. 1990: A31.

Manchester, William. *The Glory and the Dream: A Narrative History of America, 1932–1972.* Boston: Little, 1973.

Mandell, Paul. "Of Genies and Dragons: The Career of Ray Harryhausen." *American Cinematographer* Dec. 1992: 77–81.

Manlove, C. N. *Modern Fantasy: Five Studies.* Cambridge: Cambridge UP, 1975.

Markotic, Nicole. "Disabling the Viewer: Perceptions of Disability in Tod Browning's *Freaks.*" Smit and Enns 65–72.

Marin, Peter. "Helping and Hating the Homeless: The Struggle at the Margins of America." *Harper's* Jan. 1987: 39–49.

Marx, Leo. *The Machine in the Garden: Technology and the Pastoral Ideal in America.* New York: Oxford UP, 1964.

Maslin, Janet. "And So Handy Around the Garden." *New York Times* 7 Dec. 1990: C1, C10.

Mathews, Richard. *Fantasy: The Liberation of Imagination*. New York: Twayne, 1997.

Mathieu, Arline. "The Medicalization of Homelessness and the Theater of Repression." *Medical Anthropology Quarterly* n.s. 7 (1993): 170–84.

Mayne, Judith. "'King Kong' and the Ideology of Spectacle." *Quarterly Review of Film Studies* 1 (1976): 373–87.

McAlister, Melani. *Epic Encounters: Culture, Media, and U.S. Interests in the Middle East, 1945–2000*. Berkeley: U of California P, 2001.

McCabe, Bob. *Dark Knights and Holy Fools: The Art and Films of Terry Gilliam*. New York: Universe, 1999.

McCaughey, Martha, and Neal King, eds. *Reel Knockouts: Violent Women in the Movies*. Austin: U of Texas P, 2001.

McGurl, Mark. "Making It Big: Picturing the Radio Age in *King Kong*." *Critical Inquiry* 22 (1996): 415–45.

McNamara, Brooks. "'A Congress of Wonders': The Rise and Fall of the Dime Museum." *ESQ* 20 (1974): 216–32.

Medved, Michael. *Hollywood vs. America*. New York: Harper, 1992.

Meikle, Jeffrey L. *Twentieth Century Limited: Industrial Design in America, 1925–1939*. Philadelphia: Temple UP, 1979.

Mills, Ogden L. *The Seventeen Million*. New York: Macmillan, 1937.

Mitchell, David T., and Sharon L. Snyder, eds. *The Body and Physical Difference: Discourses of Disability*. Ann Arbor: U of Michigan P, 1997.

Mitchell, W. J. T. *The Last Dinosaur Book: The Life and Times of a Cultural Icon*. Chicago: U of Chicago P, 1998.

Monahan, John. "Mental Disorder and Violent Behavior: Perceptions and Evidence." *American Psychologist* 47 (1992): 511–21.

Monleón, José B. *A Specter Is Haunting Europe: A Sociohistorical Approach to the Fantastic*. Princeton: Princeton UP, 1990.

Moore, Carol, and Geoff Miles. "Explorations, Prosthetics, and Sacrifice: Phantasies of the Maternal Body in the *Alien* Trilogy." *CineAction!* 30 (Winter 1992): 54–62.

Morsy, Soheir A. "The Bad, the Ugly, the Super-Rich, and the Exceptional Moderate: U.S. Popular Images of the Arabs." *Journal of Popular Culture* 20.3 (Winter 1986): 13–29.

Mullaney, Steven. *The Place of the Stage: License, Play, and Power in Renaissance England*. Chicago: U of Chicago P, 1988.

Mulvey, Laura. "Visual Pleasure and Narrative Cinema." *Visual and Other Pleasures*. Bloomington: Indiana UP, 1989. 14–26.

Mumford, Lewis. *Technics and Civilization*. New York: Harcourt, 1934.

Nadel, Alan. "A Whole New (Disney) World: *Aladdin*, Atomic Power, and the Muslim Middle East." Bernstein and Studlar 184–203.

Nathanson, Paul. *Over the Rainbow: "The Wizard of Oz" as a Secular Myth of America*. Albany: State U of New York P, 1991.

National Resources Committee. Subcommittee on Technology. *Technological Trends and National Policy: Including the Social Implications of New Inventions*. Washington: GPO, 1937. New York: Arno, 1972.

Neale, Steve. *Cinema and Technology: Image, Sound, Colour*. Bloomington: Indiana UP, 1985.

———. "'You've Got to Be Fucking Kidding!': Knowledge, Belief and Judgement in Science Fiction." Kuhn, *Alien Zone* 160–68.

Nesteby, James R. *Black Images in American Films, 1896–1954: The Interplay Between Civil Rights and Film Culture*. New York: UP of America, 1982.

Newby, I. A. *Jim Crow's Defense: Anti-Negro Thought in America, 1900–1930.* Baton Rouge: Louisiana State UP, 1965.

Newsom, Ted. "Ray Harryhausen: Stop-Motion Magician." *Cinefantastique* 31.1–2 (Feb. 1999): 64–81, 126.

———. "The Ray Harryhausen Story, Part One: The Early Years, 1920–1958." *Cinefantastique* 11.4 (Dec. 1981): 25–45.

Newton, Judith. "Feminism and Anxiety in *Alien.*" Kuhn, *Alien Zone* 82–87.

Nicholls, Peter. *The World of Fantasy Films: An Illustrated Survey.* New York: Dodd, 1984.

Norden, Martin F. *The Cinema of Isolation: A History of Physical Disability in the Movies.* New Brunswick: Rutgers UP, 1994.

Norden, Martin F., and Madeleine A. Cahill. "Violence, Women, and Disability in Tod Browning's *Freaks* and *The Devil Doll.*" *Journal of Popular Film and Television* 26 (1998): 86–94.

Nunnally, Jum C., Jr. *Popular Conceptions of Mental Health: Their Development and Change.* New York: Holt, 1961.

O'Brien, Willis. "Miniature Effects Shots." Geduld and Gottesman 183–84.

Onosko, Tim. *Wasn't the Future Wonderful? A View of Trends and Technology from the 1930s.* New York: Dutton, 1979.

Paige, Linda Rohrer. "Wearing the Red Shoes: Dorothy and the Power of the Female Imagination in *The Wizard of Oz.*" *Journal of Popular Film and Television* 23 (1996): 146–53.

Palumbo, Donald. "The Underground Journey and the Death and Resurrection Theme in Recent Science Fiction and Fantasy Films." *The Fantastic in World Literature and the Arts: Selected Essays from the Fifth International Conference on the Fantastic in the Arts.* Ed. Donald E. Morse. Westport: Greenwood, 1987. 211–27.

Paré, Ambroise. *On Monsters and Marvels.* 1573. Trans. Janis L. Pallister. Chicago: U of Chicago P, 1982.

Parke, Ross D., and Armin A. Brott. *Throwaway Dads: The Myths and Barriers That Keep Men from Being the Fathers They Want to Be.* Boston: Houghton, 1999.

Patai, Raphael. *The Arab Mind.* New York: Scribner's, 1973.

Patch, Buel W. *Lynching and Kidnaping.* Washington: Editorial Research Reports, 1933.

Peary, Gerald. "Missing Links: The Jungle Origins of *King Kong.*" Geduld and Gottesman 37–42.

———. "A Speculation: The Historicity of *King Kong.*" *Jump Cut* 4 (Nov.–Dec. 1974): 11–12.

Pells, Richard H. *Radical Visions and American Dreams: Culture and Social Thought in the Depression Years.* New York: Harper, 1973.

Pender, Stephen. "In the Bodyshop: Human Exhibition in Early Modern England." *"Defects": Engendering the Modern Body.* Ed. Helen Deutsch and Felicity Nussbaum. Ann Arbor: U of Michigan P, 2000. 95–126.

———. "'No Monsters at the Resurrection': Inside Some Conjoined Twins." J. Cohen, *Monster Theory* 143–67.

Penley, Constance. "Time Travel, Primal Scene, and the Critical Dystopia." Penley et al. 63–80.

Penley, Constance, et al., eds. *Close Encounters: Film, Feminism, and Science Fiction.* Minneapolis: U of Minnesota P, 1991.

Pfohl, Stephen J. *Predicting Dangerousness: The Social Construction of Psychiatric Reality.* Lexington: Heath, 1978.

Philo, Greg, ed. *Media and Mental Distress.* London: Longmans, 1996.

Pike, David L. "Urban Nightmares and Future Visions: Life Beneath New York." *Wide Angle* 20.4 (1998): 9–50.

Polan, Dana B. "Eros and Syphilization: The Contemporary Horror Film." B. Grant, *Planks of Reason* 201–12.

Potter, Russell A. "Edward Schizohands: The Postmodern Gothic Body." *Postmodern Culture* 2.3 (May 1992). http://muse.jhu.edu/journals/postmodern_culture/voo2/ 2.3potter.html (5 Feb. 2002).

Pratt, Mary Louise. *Imperial Eyes: Travel Writing and Transculturation.* London: Routledge, 1992.

Public Attitudes Toward People with Chronic Mental Illness: Executive Summary. Boston: Johnson, 1990.

Quayle, Dan, and Diane Medved. *The American Family: Discovering the Values That Make Us Strong.* New York: Harper, 1996.

Rabkin, Eric S. *The Fantastic in Literature.* Princeton: Princeton UP, 1976.

"Race Sensitivity Reactions to Quest for Ape-Like Black 'Kong.'" *Variety* 19 Nov. 1975: 7.

Raper, Arthur F. *The Tragedy of Lynching.* Chapel Hill: U of North Carolina P, 1933.

Rawlins, Jack P. "Confronting the Alien: Fantasy and Antifantasy in Science Fiction Film and Literature." *Bridges to Fantasy.* Ed. George E. Slusser, Eric S. Rabkin, and Robert Scholes. Carbondale: Southern Illinois UP, 1982. 160–74.

Roberts, Dorothy. "The Absent Black Father." Daniels 145–61.

Roberts, Robin. "Adoptive Versus Biological Mothering in *Aliens.*" *Extrapolation* 30 (1989): 353–63.

Rocchio, Vincent F. *Reel Racism: Confronting Hollywood's Construction of Afro-American Culture.* Boulder: Westview, 2000.

Roemer, Kenneth M. *The Obsolete Necessity: America in Utopian Writings, 1888–1900.* Kent: Kent State UP, 1976.

Rogin, Michael. *Blackface, White Noise: Jewish Immigrants in the Hollywood Melting Pot.* Berkeley: U of California P, 1996.

———. "'The Sword Became a Flashing Vision': D. W. Griffith's *The Birth of a Nation.*" *Representations* 9 (Winter 1985): 150–95.

Rony, Fatimah Tobing. *The Third Eye: Race, Cinema, and Ethnographic Spectacle.* Durham: Duke UP, 1996.

Rosen, David N. "*King Kong*: Race, Sex, and Rebellion." *Jump Cut* 6 (Mar.–Apr. 1975): 8–10.

Ross, Murray. *Stars and Strikes: Unionization of Hollywood.* New York: Columbia UP, 1941.

Rovin, Jeff. *From the Land Beyond Beyond: The Films of Willis O'Brien and Ray Harryhausen.* New York: Berkley, 1977.

Rubin, Barry. "America as Junior Partner: Anglo-American Relations in the Middle East, 1919–1939." *The Great Powers in the Middle East, 1919–1939.* Ed. Uriel Dann. New York: Holmes, 1988. 238–51.

Rushing, Janice Hocker. "Evolution of 'The New Frontier' in *Alien* and *Aliens*: Patriarchal Co-optation of the Feminine Archetype." *Quarterly Journal of Speech* 75 (1989): 1–24.

Russo, Mary. *The Female Grotesque: Risk, Excess and Modernity.* New York: Routledge, 1994.

Ryan, Michael, and Douglas Kellner. *Camera Politica: The Politics and Ideology of Contemporary Hollywood Film.* Bloomington: Indiana UP, 1988.

Rzepka, Charles. "'If I Can Make It There': Oz's Emerald City and the New Woman." *Studies in Popular Culture* 10 (1987): 54–66.

Said, Edward. *Orientalism*. New York: Vintage, 1979.

Salisbury, Mark, ed. *Burton on Burton*. Rev. ed. London: Faber, 2000.

Scarfone, Jay, and William Stillman. *The Wizardry of Oz: The Artistry and Magic of the 1939 M-G-M Classic*. New York: Gramercy, 1999.

Schaffer, Daniel. *Garden Cities for America: The Radburn Experience*. Philadelphia: Temple UP, 1982.

Schlebecker, John T. *Whereby We Thrive: A History of American Farming, 1607–1972*. Ames: Iowa State UP, 1975.

Schlobin, Roger C. "Introduction: Fantasy and Its Literature." *The Literature of Fantasy: A Comprehensive, Annotated Bibliography of Modern Fantasy Fiction*. Ed. Schlobin. New York: Garland, 1979. xvii–xxxv.

Schneider, Tassilo. "When the Difference Can't Be Told: The Subject in Contemporary Horror and Science Fiction Film." *Spectator* 11 (1991): 44–53.

Scobie, Stephen. "What's the Story, Mother? The Mourning of the Alien." *Science-Fiction Studies* 20 (1993): 80–93.

Sconce, Jeffrey. "Spectacles of Death: Identification, Reflexivity, and Contemporary Horror." *Film Theory Goes to the Movies*. Ed. Jim Collins, Hilary Radner, and Ava Preacher Collins. New York: Routledge, 1993. 103–19.

Searles, Baird. *Films of Science Fiction and Fantasy*. New York: AFI, 1988.

Seelye, John. "Moby-Kong." *College Literature* 17.1 (1990): 33–40.

Segal, Howard P. *Technological Utopianism in American Culture*. Chicago: U of Chicago P, 1985.

———. "The Technological Utopians." *Corn* 119–36.

Shaheen, Jack G. *Reel Bad Arabs: How Hollywood Vilifies a People*. New York: Olive Branch, 2001.

Shain, Russell E., and Julie Phillips. "The Stigma of Mental Illness: Labeling and Stereotyping in the News." *Risky Business: Communicating Issues of Science, Risk, and Public Policy*. Ed. Lee Wilkins and Philip Patterson. New York: Greenwood, 1991. 61–74.

Shakespeare, William. *The Tempest*. 1611. *The Riverside Shakespeare*. Boston: Houghton, 1974. 1606–38.

Sharman, Leslie Felperin. "New Aladdins for Old." *Sight and Sound* 3.11 (Nov. 1993): 11–15.

Shay, Don. "Willis O'Brien: Creator of the Impossible." *Cinefex* 7 (Jan. 1982): 5–70.

Shohat, Ella. "Gender and Culture of Empire: Toward a Feminist Ethnography of the Cinema." Bernstein and Studlar 19–66.

Simcovitch, Maxim. "The Impact of Griffith's *Birth of a Nation* on the Modern Ku Klux Klan." *Journal of Popular Film* 1 (1972): 45–54.

Simmon, Scott. *The Films of D. W. Griffith*. Cambridge: Cambridge UP, 1993.

Sinclair, Upton. *The Way Out: What Lies Ahead for America*. Los Angeles: Upton Sinclair, 1933.

Sitkoff, Harvard. *A New Deal for Blacks: The Emergence of Civil Rights as a National Issue*. Vol. 1, *The Depression Decade*. New York: Oxford UP, 1978.

Slusser, George, and Eric S. Rabkin. Introduction. Slusser and Rabkin vii–xvii.

———, eds. *Shadows of the Magic Lamp: Fantasy and Science Fiction in Film*. Carbondale: Southern Illinois UP, 1985.

Smit, Christopher R., and Anthony Enns, eds. *Screening Disability: Essays on Cinema and Disability*. Lanham: UP of America, 2001.

Smith, Jim, and J. Clive Mathews. *Tim Burton*. London: Virgin, 2002.

Snead, James. *White Screens, Black Images: Hollywood from the Dark Side*. Ed. Colin McCabe and Cornel West. New York: Routledge, 1994.

Snyder, Sharon L., Brenda Jo Brueggemann, and Rosemarie Garland Thomson, eds. *Disability Studies: Enabling the Humanities*. New York: MLA, 2002.

Sobchack, Vivian. "Child/Alien/Father: Patriarchal Crisis and Generic Exchange." Penley et al. 3–30.

———. "The Virginity of Astronauts: Sex and the Science Fiction Film." Slusser and Rabkin 41–57.

Sontag, Susan. *Illness as Metaphor*. New York: Farrar, 1977.

Southern Commission on the Study of Lynching. *Lynchings and What They Mean*. Atlanta: Southern Commission on the Study of Lynching, 1931.

Sova, Dawn B. *Women in Hollywood: From Vamp to Studio Head*. New York: Fromm, 1998.

Spiegel, Steven L. *The Other Arab-Israeli Conflict: Making America's Middle East Policy, from Truman to Reagan*. Chicago: U of Chicago P, 1985.

Spurr, David. *The Rhetoric of Empire: Colonial Discourse in Journalism, Travel Writing, and Imperial Administration*. Durham: Duke UP, 1993.

Stacey, Judith. "Dada-ism in the 1990s: Getting Past Baby Talk about Fatherlessness." Daniels 51–83.

Staiger, Janet. "*The Birth of a Nation*: Reconsidering Its Reception." *Interpreting Films: Studies in the Historical Reception of American Cinema*. Princeton: Princeton UP, 1992. 139–53.

Stam, Robert, and Louise Spence. "Colonialism, Racism, and Representation: An Interpretation." *Movies and Methods: An Anthology*. Ed. Bill Nichols. Vol. 2. Berkeley: U of California P, 1985. 632–49.

Steadman, Henry J., and Joseph J. Cocozza. "Selective Reporting and the Public's Misconceptions of the Criminally Insane." *Public Opinion Quarterly* 41 (1978): 523–33.

Steele, Richard. "Sadat in Israel." *Newsweek* 28 Nov. 1977: 36–46.

Stewart, Garrett. "Modern Hard Times: Chaplin and the Cinema of Self-Reflection." *Critical Inquiry* 3 (1976): 295–314.

———. "The 'Videology' of Science Fiction." Slusser and Rabkin 159–207.

Strange Newes from Scotland: Or, A Strange Relation of a Terrible and Prodigious Monster, Borne to the Amazement of All Those That Were Spectators . . . N.p.: 1647.

Streible, Dan. "Race and the Reception of Jack Johnson Fight Films." Bernardi, *Birth of Whiteness* 170–200.

Suleiman, Michael W. *The Arabs in the Mind of America*. Brattleboro: Amana, 1988.

Szasz, Thomas S. *The Manufacture of Madness: A Comparative Study of the Inquisition and the Mental Health Movement*. New York: Harper, 1970.

———. *The Myth of Mental Illness: Foundations of a Theory of Personal Conduct*. Rev. ed. New York: Harper, 1974.

Takaki, Ronald. *A Different Mirror: A History of Multicultural America*. Boston: Little, 1993.

Taubin, Amy. "Invading Bodies: *Alien 3* and the Trilogy." *Sight and Sound* n.s. 2.3 (July 1992): 8–10.

Taylor, Clyde. "The Re-Birth of the Aesthetic in Cinema." Bernardi, *Birth of Whiteness* 15–37.

Teague, Walter Dorwin. *Design This Day: The Technique of Order in the Machine Age*. New York: Harcourt, 1940.

Telotte, J. P. *A Distant Technology: Science Fiction Film and the Machine Age*. Hanover: UP of New England, 1999.

————. "The Movies as Monster: Seeing in *King Kong*." *Georgia Review* 42 (1988): 388–98.

Teplin, Linda T. "The Criminality of the Mentally Ill: A Dangerous Misconception." *American Journal of Psychiatry* 142 (1985): 593–99.

Terkel, Studs. *Hard Times: An Oral History of the Great Depression.* New York: Pantheon, 1986.

Thomas, John. "Gobble, Gobble . . . One of Us!" Huss and Ross 135–38.

Thomson, Rosemarie Garland. "The Beauty and the Freak." *Points of Contact: Disability, Art, and Culture.* Ed. Susan Crutchfield and Mary Epstein. Ann Arbor: U of Michigan P, 2000. 181–96.

————. *Extraordinary Bodies: Figuring Physical Disability in American Culture and Literature.* New York: Columbia UP, 1997.

————, ed. *Freakery: Cultural Spectacles of the Extraordinary Body.* New York: New York UP, 1996.

————. "Introduction: From Wonder to Error—A Genealogy of Freak Discourse in Modernity." Thomson, *Freakery* 1–19.

Thorp, Margaret Farrand. *America at the Movies.* New Haven: Yale UP, 1939.

Tocqueville, Alexis de. *Democracy in America.* 1835. Trans. George Lawrence. Ed. J. P. Mayer. New York: Harper, 1969.

Todorov, Tzvetan. *The Fantastic: A Structural Approach to a Literary Genre.* Trans. Richard Howard. Ithaca: Cornell UP, 1975.

Torrey, E. Fuller. *Nowhere to Go: The Tragic Odyssey of the Homeless Mentally Ill.* New York: Harper, 1988.

————. "Some of the Homeless Mentally Ill Should Be Treated Involuntarily." Hurley 150–54. Rpt. of "Stop the Madness." *Wall Street Journal* 18 July 1997.

Torrey, E. Fuller, et al. *Criminalizing the Seriously Mentally Ill: The Abuse of Jails as Mental Hospitals.* Washington: National Alliance for the Mentally Ill, 1992.

Torry, Robert. "'You Can't Look Away': Spectacle and Transgression in *King Kong*." *Arizona Quarterly* 49.4 (Winter 1993): 61–77.

Treves, Frederick. *The Elephant Man and Other Reminiscences.* London: Cassell, 1923.

Turner, Victor. "Betwixt and Between: The Liminal Period in *Rites de Passage*." *The Forest of Symbols: Aspects of Ndembu Ritual.* Ithaca: Cornell UP, 1967. 93–111.

Twelve Southerners. *I'll Take My Stand: The South and the Agrarian Tradition.* 1930. New York: Peter Smith, 1951.

Uebel, Michael. "Unthinking the Monster: Twelfth-Century Responses to Saracen Alterity." J. Cohen, *Monster Theory* 264–91.

Vasey, Ruth. *The World According to Hollywood, 1918–1939.* Madison: U of Wisconsin P, 1997.

Vieira, Mark A. *Sin in Soft Focus: Pre-Code Hollywood.* New York: Abrams, 1999.

Von Gunden, Kenneth. *Flights of Fancy: The Great Fantasy Films.* Jefferson: McFarland, 1989.

Wagar, Warren W. "The Steel-Gray Saviour: Technocracy as Utopia and Ideology." *Alternative Futures* 2.2 (Spring 1979): 38–54.

Wahl, Otto F. *Media Madness: Public Images of Mental Illness.* New Brunswick: Rutgers UP, 1995.

Warner, Marina. "Beauty and the Beasts." *Sight and Sound* 2.6 (Oct. 1992): 6–11.

————. "Monstrous Mothers: Women over the Top." *Six Myths of Our Time: Little Angels, Little Monsters, Beautiful Beasts, and More.* New York: Random, 1994. 3–23.

Wartenberg, Thomas. "Humanizing the Beast: *King Kong* and the Representation of Black Male Sexuality." *Classic Hollywood, Classic Whiteness.* Ed. Daniel Bernardi. Minneapolis: U of Minnesota P, 2001. 157–77.

Wells, H. G. "World of Tomorrow." *New York Times* 5 Mar. 1939, World's Fair Section: 4–5, 61.

Welsh, James W. "Edward Scissorhands." *Films in Review* 42.3–4 (Mar.–Apr. 1991): 110.

Wendt, Gerald. *Science for the World of Tomorrow.* New York: Norton, 1939.

West, Nathanael. *The Day of the Locust.* 1939. New York: New Classics, 1950.

Whitaker, Robert. *Mad in America: Bad Science, Bad Medicine, and the Enduring Mistreatment of the Mentally Ill.* Cambridge: Perseus, 2002.

Whitehead, John W. "Priorities and Resistance." *The Rebirth of America.* Philadelphia: DeMoss, 1986. 197–204.

Whitney, Simon N. "Antitrust Policies and the Motion Picture Industry." *The American Movie Industry: The Business of Motion Pictures.* Ed. Gorham Kindem. Carbondale: Southern Illinois UP, 1982. 161–204.

Williams, Linda. "When the Woman Looks." *Re-Vision: Essays in Feminist Film Criticism.* Ed. Mary Ann Doane, Patricia Mellencamp, and Williams. Frederick: U Publications of America, 1984. 83–99.

Wilson, Dudley. *Signs and Portents: Monstrous Births from the Middle Ages to the Enlightenment.* London: Routledge, 1993.

Wood, Robin. "The American Nightmare: Horror in the 70s." 1975. *Hollywood from Vietnam to Reagan.* New York: Columbia UP, 1986. 70–94.

Worster, Donald. *Dust Bowl: The Southern Plains in the 1930s.* New York: Oxford UP, 1979.

Wright, James D., Beth A. Rubin, and Joel A. Devine. *Beside the Golden Door: Policy, Politics, and the Homeless.* New York: De Gruyter, 1998.

Wright, Richard. *Native Son.* 1940. New York: Harper, 1993.

Wurts, Richard. *The New York World's Fair 1939/1940 in 155 Photographs.* Ed. Stanley Appelbaum. New York: Dover, 1977.

Yeich, Susan. *The Politics of Ending Homelessness.* Lanham: UP of America, 1994.

Young, Elizabeth. "Here Comes the Bride: Wedding Gender and Race in *Bride of Frankenstein.*" B. Grant, *Dread of Difference* 309–37.

———. "*The Silence of the Lambs* and the Flaying of Feminist Theory." *Camera Obscura* 27 (1991): 5–35.

Yunis, Susan, and Tammy Ostrander. "Tales Your Mother Never Told You: *Aliens* and the Horrors of Motherhood." *Journal of the Fantastic in the Arts* 14.1 (Spring 2003): 68–76.

Zangrando, Robert L. *The NAACP Crusade Against Lynching, 1909–1950.* Philadelphia: Temple UP, 1980.

Zgorzelski, Andrzej. "Is Science Fiction a Genre of Fantastic Literature?" *Science Fiction Studies* 6 (1979): 296–303.

Zim, Larry, Mel Lerner, and Herbert Rolfes. *The World of Tomorrow: The 1939 New York World's Fair.* New York: Harper, 1988.

INDEX

Joshua David Bellin is an associate professor of English at La Roche College, where he teaches courses in literature, writing, and film. He is also an amateur artist, filmmaker, and fantasist. He has published on classic fantasy film and on American literature, with a particular emphasis on the interaction of Native American and European American literatures and cultures.